WORK LIKE AN IMMIGRANT

BRTNEY, YOU ROCK.

WORK LIKE AN IMMIGRANT

9 KEYS TO UNLOCK YOUR POTENTIAL, ATTAIN TRUE FULFILLMENT, AND BUILD YOUR LEGACY TODAY

CARLOS SIQUEIRA

LIFESTYLE
ENTREPRENEURS
PRESS
LAS VEGAS, NV

ISBN: 978-1-948787-23-9

Published by
Lifestyle Entrepreneurs Press
Las Vegas, NV

If you are interested in publishing through Lifestyle Entrepreneurs Press, write to:
Publishing@LifestyleEntrepreneursPress.com

To learn more about our publications or about foreign rights acquisitions of our catalogue books, please visit: *www.LifestyleEntrepreneursPress.com*

Printed in the USA

www.WorkLikeAnImmigrant.com
www.CarlosInspire.com
www.ExpertAdvisorAlliance.net

To the most loving, humble, and hardest working person I've known, my grandma/mother Maria Lucia, who passed away in 2017 as I was finishing writing this book. Thank you, Grandma, for encouraging me when I was at my darkest times at a very young age. I will always remember you saying:

"Keep it going, Son. It may be difficult and very dark at the moment, but don't you ever stop and live in dark times, and you will come out. Sometimes the closest one to you may hurt you and won't support you. Know that I will always pray for you and support you. Don't ever allow anyone to stop you from what you believe deep inside and from fulfilling your dreams of making the world a better place."

To my loving wife, Angelica, who has always shown unconditional love and support and is the most dedicated mother I know. She almost lost her life to raise our daughter, but even in the darkest of times, she persevered and found a reason deep inside to live and awaken her lioness within.

To our amazing daughter and future lioness, Isabella, who also endured a great deal since birth and is the reason I am healthy and alive today.

And to you, reader, for being here, for taking the time to read this book and using it to become your best self, and for sharing what you learn in this book with someone in need, so that together we can raise humanity to the next level and make the world a better place.

Contents

WORK LIKE AN IMMIGRANT

Preface

I will never take you to a place I haven't been.

When I was eighteen years old, my mother and I traveled from an impoverished neighborhood in Brazil to the United States with only $800 and a few changes of clothes. We had to borrow money from my uncle to cover the flight because our savings wasn't enough. We both spoke Portuguese, and I spoke some broken English I had learned mostly from songs and movies.

Crime was rampant in my neighborhood in Brazil. Shootouts between police and criminals and among rival gangs were common. Children are taught from a very young age that when they hear gunfire, they should drop and cover their heads. Although I have always been proud and bold, I often had to fall to the ground in my youth to dodge bullets. On several occasions, I was robbed at gunpoint.

Undoubtedly, people in other countries have grown up under similar conditions and have achieved success in spite of, and perhaps partially because of, such adversity. Unfortunately, they comprise a small minority. The majority are often defeated or, in some cases, attain only a fraction of what they are truly capable of achieving.

Even more tragic, in my eyes, are those who are blessed with advantages and given ample opportunities to succeed but never reach their potential or attain fulfillment. Instead of taking control and steering their ship to the land of plenty, they drift aimlessly, letting life's currents and waves determine their destiny, even to the point of being stranded on a sandbar or crashing against the rocks.

I wrote this book to tell my story and share the lessons I learned in the process—lessons from experience and from wise souls who generously shared their knowledge and insights by mentoring me personally or through their books, videos, or audio recordings. My hope is that by reading this book, you will gain the inspiration and wisdom to dream big, make your dreams your reality, achieve a healthy work-life balance, and give generously to build thriving communities and a better world. All you need to succeed is within you, and now all you need to do is read, learn, and take action.

Introduction

We see it time and time again: a person born and raised in poverty becomes incredibly successful while another, given ample resources—a fit body, a respectable IQ, a good home, a decent education, and plenty of opportunities—struggles to pay the bills, cannot establish and maintain rewarding relationships, and is chronically unhappy and unfulfilled. We wonder: why?

We may chalk it up to differences in appearance, intelligence, talent, or even luck, all of which can play a role, but such factors do not explain everything. Even people with terrible hardships manage to achieve great things, maintain rewarding relationships, and achieve high levels of happiness and fulfillment. Some do so after a string of devastating failures. How do they do it? What makes people who succeed so different from those who feel and act defeated and deflated?

Some people attribute success to a combination of internal and external forces—usually talent, hard work, and luck, or being in the right place at the right time. I believe success takes much more than that, but I also believe that everything required to achieve success and fulfillment is within you. You can control your thoughts, which control your actions, which ultimately enable you to create your own reality. As for external forces, depending on how you look at it, either God or nature provides all the resources necessary for success, including opportunities. Yes, you will encounter adversity, and you may even fail, but with the available resources and your ability to control your own thoughts and actions, you can succeed—with persistence, of course.

When you create a vision for success, wholeheartedly believe you will achieve it, and invest the energy and effort required to make it happen, the universe responds by making the requisite resources available—people, funding, training, insight, opportunities, and whatever else you need to achieve your goal. And when I say "available," I don't mean they will be delivered to your door in a neatly wrapped package labeled "THIS IS WHAT YOU NEED." You typically must seek out the resources you need and ask for help—you must also apply for a job to get it, start a business to have one, and study and practice to develop skills, to name a few necessary actions. You must also remain vigilant, because what you need may not be exactly what you wanted or hoped for, or be in the form you expected.

So here is my story, which is more than a Horatio Alger rags-to-riches saga. As you read, keep in mind that everything I advise you to do is within you—*you* are the key component to your success. Only by taking control of your thoughts, decisions, and actions can you control your destiny.

About the Book

Work Like an Immigrant: Nine Keys to Unlock Your Potential, Attain True Fulfillment, and Build Your Legacy Today is written in three parts:

Part 1: My Story traces my journey from selling bread and dodging bullets on the streets of Brazil to earning millions selling cable TV and Internet services door to door, building and managing record-breaking sales teams, and finally to the family crisis that inspired me to become a high-performance consultant, coach, and speaker, leading others to achieve levels of happiness and fulfillment they had never imagined possible. Throughout my story, I include Life Lesson sidebars to help you learn from my experience of working like an immigrant.

Part 2: Nine Keys to Unlock Your Potential, Attain True Fulfillment, and Build Your Legacy Today reveals my nine-step program to dreaming big and achieving success by taking control of your thoughts and emotions and engaging in continuous joyful execution. Here, you find out how to harness the power of your imagination to unlock its hidden resources and overcome both internal and external limitations. You gain mastery of a variety of techniques inspired by numerous self-improvement visionaries, from Napoleon Hill and Joseph Murphy to Zig Ziglar and Tony Robbins.

Part 3: Principles and Practices presents the nine principles for achieving success, along with twenty-eight practical techniques for envisioning success, defining your mission, transforming negative thoughts to positive action, teaming up with a mentor, shifting focus from problems to solutions, and much more. If you put a small portion of the advice offered here into practice, you will immediately start to achieve amazing results.

PART 1

MY STORY

CHAPTER 1

My Journey Begins

*It's the repetition of affirmations that leads to belief.
And once that belief becomes a deep conviction,
things begin to happen.*
—Muhammad Ali

My father died in 1983 when I was only three months old. His life ended in a horrible car accident while commuting to work in heavy rain. The person driving the car my father was in made a poor decision and tried to pass another car on a two-lane highway. Unfortunately, a gas truck was traveling in the opposite direction and the two vehicles collided head-on, causing an explosion that instantly killed my father and five others.

My mother was in shock for years after that accident. She had lost the love of her life after only thirteen months of marriage, leaving her with an infant to raise on her own.

Two years before I was born, my father had planned to become a priest. Fortunately for me, my mother's alluring beauty changed his mind! He was twenty-three years old and already had his own home and a car, which is a big deal in Brazil; many people live their entire lives there without owning either one. As the manager at the local bank, and juggling courses at two colleges, I honestly don't know how he could have possibly thought he had the time to start a family. But he was driven! Not only was he highly intelligent and charismatic, he was a humble man seeking to improve the quality of life for the kids who lived on the streets of Brazil, often in hunger.

My father taught these kids how to play music. He even set up sports programs for them so that they wouldn't become criminals and end up dying at young ages like so many other impoverished Brazilians. Because of his willingness to go above and beyond to help those in need, my father was loved by many. This was most evident at his funeral, where the cars of those offering their condolences packed a quarter mile of parking spaces. People had to gather around the perimeter of my grandfather's home because they couldn't all get inside. The world had lost a great man.

Growing up, I was told numerous times that I was like my father because I always loved to help and to spend time with the less fortunate kids. Though I wanted to be just like him, I also knew that I had some huge shoes to fill.

LIFE LESSON 1: CHOOSE A ROLE MODEL

I never got to know my father, but I knew enough of him that he was my role model growing up. I never wanted to live the life he led, but I wanted to have a big, kind heart like his, to make a positive impact on the world like he did, and to earn the respect and admiration of others. Even though he was not present during my childhood to guide me, his presence was made known by all the stories my mother and others told me about him, and that served as a positive influence on my conduct and decisions.

Having a role model gives you a vision of the kind of person you want to be in each aspect of your life. You may have multiple role models—someone you admire in the business world, someone who parents better than anyone else you know, a community leader who has made a positive impact on the world, and so on. It's important to have a clear vision not only of what you want out of life, but also of the type of person you want to be. Role models can help with that.

Soon after the death of my father, my mother got a job while finishing her last year of high school. My grandma and her sisters, all of whom also had jobs, took turns caring for me while my mother worked tirelessly to keep up with the bills and her schoolwork. After graduating high school, she decided to work instead of going on to college, because she didn't have the time and money to attend college and raise me at the same time. She started selling food (empanadas, specialty breads, and sweets) to businesses and to strangers and friends, essentially feeding others to feed us and keep a roof over our heads. She did that until she met my stepfather in 1986, when I was three years old. They started dating and later moved in together.

My mother also began to sell clothing. She would travel for days on a bus to other states in Brazil to buy clothing at low prices, and then she would return home to sell it door to door to businesses and families. The clothing business didn't go so well, however, so she focused diligently on selling food and specialty breads. She also catered certain holidays for families that didn't want to cook, going to their homes to cook and serve the food. Unfortunately, that meant she had to sacrifice holidays with her own family.

My mother was relentless; she did whatever it took to keep us afloat because she didn't want to depend on my stepfather for money. He had numerous kids with other women, so he had to help support them as well. He certainly had his hands full—I remember them arguing a lot about money, and he would be gone for days leaving my mother crying at home. I suspected he was a player and was still seeing some of the other women he had kids with.

One day, when I was about six years old, a woman showed up at our home with two small children. She seemed angry, and she told me to get my stepfather. I told her to go away, that he wasn't there. I knew then that my suspicions about him were correct. I couldn't understand, even as a child, why my mother would put up with that, but I guess she loved him. (Now that I'm older, I kind of understand why people in love do crazy things!) Even when she was dealing with the chaos and emotional pain it must have caused, she continued to work tenaciously to pay the bills and keep us all fed.

On the Sundays she wasn't working, my mother contributed her time to a project my father had started. She and my grandma would help pick up kids in the streets who didn't have families and bring them to shelters where children could stay if they didn't have a home. They would also teach those kids how to cook and bake bread, sew clothing, and read, and they gave those kids a whole lot of love. My mother and grandma would make them laugh by telling them funny stories and doing whatever else they could to shift them away from violence and crime. In Brazil, that was a common pattern: kids without parents or other guardians often grew up to become violent criminals, because that was the only life they knew. My father, mother, grandmother, and others tried to show those kids that a better life was possible.

LIFE LESSON 2:
NOTHING WORTHWHILE COMES EASY
• •

My mother taught me, mostly through the example she set, that nothing worthwhile in life comes easy. If you want something, you need to go after it; nobody will do it for you.

I learned that whatever I achieve is directly proportional to the effort I exert. I learned how to save and count coins, because hard work and savings eventually enable you to buy the things you want.

I also learned that you often must sacrifice what you want in order to support your loved ones who depend on you. She sacrificed birthdays and holidays with family and gave up time with my younger brother, who was born shortly after I turned six, to make sure we had the basic necessities of food, clothing, and shelter. She taught me that when you don't have a choice, you do what is responsible first.

My mother is an incredibly strong woman, and I learned to be strong like her. Inspired by her example, I can work under stress and do whatever it takes—as long as it takes—so long as I do it with integrity. I can make tough sacrifices. I can read and learn anything I put my mind to. I can "outwork" my colleagues and competitors by inventing ways to work smarter instead of harder.

I didn't have a father figure, but I had something even better—a mother who was both. She always told me to follow my dreams regardless of how big they happened to be and regardless of the circumstances.

Life or Death?

When I was six and half years old, I made the most important decision of my life. Seeing my mother struggle so desperately to make a better life for us while my stepfather abused her was unbearable. I can remember them arguing as if it happened only yesterday; in fact, I can practically still hear my mother sobbing behind closed doors. After stirring up an emotional tempest, my stepfather would storm out of the house. My mother would try to hide her tears, but I could read her body language. Watching my mother suffer hurt me more deeply than any physical pain I had ever endured, and feeling powerless to help her made it even worse. I considered ending my life because of it, and I even had a plan: I would stab myself in the stomach with a butcher knife.

When the day came, I was holding the knife to my stomach with tears streaming down my cheeks when I heard a whisper from God: "Someone out there has it even worse than you, son. Reverse the meaning and focus on helping others. Then, watch the magic happen."

Ultimately, I chose life over death. Instead of ending it all, I decided to create a new beginning. I promised myself that I would never cry again, and that I would embrace our current struggle with such conviction that my mom and I would escape and forge a better life. Even at that young age, I realized I couldn't always change the attitudes, behaviors, or actions of others or prevent bad things from happening, but I could love myself and others—and I was in control of how I reacted. In that pivotal moment, I decided to reverse my reality and transform the negative into positive.

Every day, I thank that kid of six years and six months for pausing to reflect. Whenever adversity strikes, I remind myself, *The kid version of you has dealt with worse in life. Step up and reverse the meaning.*

After that incident, I felt the warm glow of inner joy. Every time one of my childhood friends was sad or hungry, I would make them laugh. I realized that I had the power to instantly shift not only my thoughts and feelings but also the thoughts and feelings of others using only words or gestures. Sometimes a simple smile or a hug or kiss would make a huge difference to someone in despair.

In those moments, I could envision a day that I would make millions of people happy and help them look past their suffering. Back then, I knew in my heart it would happen. I didn't know exactly how, but I did know that if I continued to focus on that vision and take steps, however small, to achieve that goal, that vision would become my reality.

LIFE LESSON 3:
PEOPLE CAN CREATE THEIR OWN REALITY
• •

Choosing between life and death and choosing to create one's own reality are something humans are uniquely capable of doing. While most animals react intuitively to external stimuli and have a survival instinct that generally prevents them from intentional self-harm, humans can imagine a better reality, analyze their situation, and invent ways to improve it. Self-consciousness and thought give people the unique ability to pause and reflect before taking action.

Think of all the ways people have created new realities— cars, airplanes, computers, print and electronic publishing, communications, robotics, governing systems, distribution systems, cities, modern medicine, mathematics, art, music, movies, and the list goes on. All of these realities are a product of the human imagination, or human thought.

Early Education

My mother and grandmother taught me a great deal when I was young. By the time I turned four, I had already learned how to read, converse with adults, and even do some basic math. My thirst for knowledge was unquenchable, so my mother decided to teach me even more by herself. (It was a much better option than having me learn on the streets.) Her valuable lessons helped me tremendously in school and in life, but even that was not enough. I would ask my teachers to push me even harder, requesting more difficult assignments because, in my mind as a kid, the quicker I learned, the sooner my mother would achieve wealth and happiness.

As I saw it, education was my ticket to a better future, and I was fortunate to have a hungry mind and easy access to experts willing to share their knowledge and life experience. When I wasn't in school or doing homework or chores, I spent much of my free time around business owners, and I soaked up knowledge at a rapid pace. I surrounded myself with people who were older than me, both successful and unsuccessful, and I asked lots of questions: "What does it take to win?" "What are your daily habits?" and to those who were struggling in business, "Why do you think your business isn't doing as well as you expected?"

I had few possessions as kid, but I was extremely happy with what I was learning. I knew deep down that if I could maintain my pace of learning, I would be able to fulfill my mother's dream of getting us out of poverty. More importantly, I was always motivated to learn more because I could apply my newly acquired knowledge and skills to everything I did to improve my life. And the more I learned, the more I realized how little I actually knew.

Out on the streets, I played soccer with a bunch of criminals, and we were not only friends, but more like family. Most criminals were inherently good; they simply made some poor decisions. I had plenty of questions for them as well, including, "Why do you do what you do?" To my surprise, I received a number of different answers. Some robbed because they needed to feed their kids and couldn't find jobs; others stole because they were humiliated and looked down on by members of the upper class; others blamed the government for not providing; and some committed crime simply because it was all they knew. Because I was young, they didn't try to recruit me. In fact, they would often tell me, "Do what I say and not what I do, kid."

I hung out with criminals because I refused to discriminate. Who was I to judge anyone? I figured that in order to continue my quest as a kid with a huge dream who was hungry for knowledge, I had to soak up information from everywhere and keep adding to my skill set. While it may sound strange that I wanted to learn from criminals, my approach was to avoid conversing about their negative actions. I more wanted to understand how they could live with so much risk. I learned that for many of them, growing up around violence—and not having a parent or other responsible adult to teach them another lifestyle—was all they knew. As a result, they felt at home with risk.

To be honest, my mother had no idea I was playing soccer with hoodlums. It didn't dawn on her until all the homes around us were robbed, while the small home we were renting was spared. It was then that she also realized I wasn't a kid anymore, that I was much more mature than my age suggested.

LIFE LESSON 4:
KEEP LEARNING AND GROWING

One of the most common and serious mistakes people make in their professional or personal lives is that they stop learning and growing as soon as they achieve a certain level of success. The problem with that approach is that although you stop changing, everything around you continues to change, leaving you unprepared to deal with your new reality. As such, I encourage you to read books, take classes, attend seminars, learn new technologies, and so forth, so you continue to acquire more knowledge and develop new skills. The pace of change is constantly accelerating. As in nature, your ability to survive and thrive is directly related to your ability to evolve.

My First Business Venture

At the age of seven, from the back of my beat-up bicycle, I started helping my mother sell bread and other goods she baked. My mother had given birth to my younger brother just months earlier, and it was a difficult time for our family. Since my stepfather's relationship with my mother was off and on, we struggled to meet our financial obligations. But my mother refused to depend on another man. I didn't want that either, because I didn't like the way he was treating her, so I felt it was my responsibility to help her.

Selling bread was my first real business venture. I decided I could sell bread on my own to help pay the bills, so I asked my mother to bake more. At first, she wasn't thrilled with the idea because of my age; in fact, we argued about it until I finally convinced her that being able to contribute made me exceptionally happy. I told my mother, "I'm going to work hard, buy you a home, and get us out of poverty. No man will ever again make you cry. I will not rest until I fulfill this promise."

LIFE LESSON 5:
LEAD A PURPOSE-DRIVEN LIFE

In his book, The Purpose Driven Life, *Rick Warren encourages readers to become more aware of the purpose for which they were placed on this planet. Regardless of whether or not you think you were born to serve a specific God-given purpose, starting anything in life with a purpose backed by a compelling reason, such as a desire to be wealthy or to find the perfect companion, gives you the focus and drive you need to overcome any obstacles in your path.*

Think about setting out on a trip to reach a certain destination—for example, Paris, France. You start your journey knowing you will reach your destination. That morning, however, your car won't start and your flight is canceled. Do you give up? Certainly not. If you are determined to get to Paris, you will. Despite any obstacles you may encounter, you will find a way.

During that time of my life, my mission was to sell all the bread and make it home without being robbed. That was no easy feat, because I sold bread all around town—and I was safe from criminals only in my neighborhood. But on one fateful day, my fears became reality when I was robbed at gunpoint.

"Kid, give me your money," the thief said, holding a gun to my head. "I see you have an empty basket tied to the back of your bicycle. That means you sold whatever was in the basket."

It wasn't much money, the equivalent of about five dollars in the U.S., and I quickly gave it to him. I was a big kid, but my grandfather had taught me that a bullet could take down anyone.

Being robbed at gunpoint was another learning experience. I discovered that I had to master my surroundings, remain vigilant at all times, and keep only a small sum of money in my pockets— enough to satisfy thieves without losing more than 25–30% of my gross sales. It turned out to be a wise decision, because I got robbed a few more times over the years. My mother didn't know that thugs had stolen from me. Had I told her, she of course would have insisted that I stay in our neighborhood from then on.

LIFE LESSON 6:
ADVERSITY DRIVES PERSONAL GROWTH

Many ministers advise their congregations to thank God for their problems. Why? As they explain, God is interested less in their comfort and more in their character. Adversity humbles us while challenging us to engage our problem-solving capacity. It not only increases our understanding of the world and our ability to empathize with others, but it makes us better people.

Nobody expects you to jump for joy when you encounter problems or experience tragedy, but when adversity strikes, try to appreciate it as a personal growth opportunity. Then, instead of focusing on pain or loss, shift your thinking to look for solutions to the problem or other ways to respond in a positive way in the given situation. For example, if you meet a person who makes your life difficult, you might ask, "Why has this person entered my life?" "What can I learn from dealing with this person?" or "How can I help this person?"

I never focused on being robbed or the other setbacks I experienced. Instead, I focused on my mission: to sell bread, make it home safely, and bring money to the table. Every time I pulled my bicycle into the driveway with an empty basket and some money, I felt like a million bucks. Mission accomplished!

When there was a *bala perdida* (Portuguese for "shootout") on the streets of Brazil, I would drop my bicycle to the ground, lie beside it, and remain there for a few minutes, assuring myself I was going to live through it and wondering what I truly wanted out of life and how it would feel when I finally had it. That vision of the future was so powerful that it blotted out any concern over the dangerous situation I was in. In that moment, my vision became my reality. As Prentice Mulford, one of the founders of the New Thought movement, and the person who coined the term "Law of Attraction" once wrote, "Thoughts are things." My thoughts became my reality.

I learned a lot of valuable lessons while selling bread on the streets, most of which centered on the importance of being emotionally fit when dealing with different types of people from varied backgrounds, and with the tremendous amount of violence. Just as today, nearly all news was bad news. Many people I knew lost their lives due to violence. The incidents I witnessed were quite extreme, violence nobody should experience, but from my perspective, everything I witnessed made me a better person. It drove me to seek the good in every bad situation, and to search for the positive in the negative. While I don't view the world through rose-colored glasses, I do look at life as panning for gold—discarding the dirt and keeping the gold nuggets.

LIFE LESSON 7:
DON'T LET FEAR RULE AND RUIN YOUR LIFE

• •

Fear is a useful emotion under certain circumstances, such as when you come face to face with a jaguar in the Amazon jungle. It triggers the fight, flight, or freeze response that can protect you from harm and death. In society, however, fear is often counterproductive. In relationships, for example, the impulse to fight or flee when confronted can shut down the dialogue necessary to clear up the misunderstanding or resolve the issue. Likewise, in our professional lives, the impulse to freeze when choosing between the familiar and the uncertainties inherent in opportunity can keep us from making positive changes, such as accepting a new job or starting a business. You may not be able to change that which you fear, but fear is an emotion you can choose (or choose not) to feel. Instead of fear, consider feeling eager anticipation.

Finding My Niche

A large part of running a successful business involves finding a niche market—an unserved or underserved consumer base—and then inventing unique ways to serve that market. Like all areas of business, choosing a niche is risky, but the niche I chose was actually dangerous, because my market covered some of the most violent neighborhoods in Brazil. In fact, part of my niche-marketing efforts targeted those areas. If any bread was left over at the end of the day, I would ride it over to the worst neighborhoods and sell it at a 25% discount. I knew my customers in these neighborhoods had little money for food due to their horrible drug habits. What I didn't realize at the start was how much respect I would earn from my attitude and actions—by playing soccer with these less fortunate people, showing compassion through discounts, and helping my mother pay the bills. When it came time for my criminal friends to rob houses, ours was always spared.

Years later, I asked some of those people why they never touched my home.

"We don't know what you're talking about," they said. "We just remember this kid with a big heart who was determined to help his mother. That kid treated everyone with respect, regardless of their status in society."

As I said before, I do not discriminate, and back then I engaged with everyone in town, from the lowest street thugs to the mayor. (Yes, I knew the mayor, and he knew me. I used to help him post flyers around town for a few extra dollars.)

LIFE LESSON 8:
NO RISK, NO GLORY

● ●

My choice to sell bread in dangerous neighborhoods carried some risk, but nearly every worthwhile pursuit does. If nothing else, the time and money you invest in pursuing an opportunity is always susceptible to potential loss. You must be willing to accept some risk in order to succeed.

Risk tolerance varies among people, and certain activities and opportunities are riskier than others, so I don't recommend that someone with a strong aversion to risk instantly engage in high-risk activities or pursuits. Nor do I recommend betting your life savings on a roll of the dice. You may simply need to wander outside your comfort zone to get what you want out of life.

My Grandparents

My grandparents, who helped raise me, were polar opposites. Grandma Maria Lucia Siqueira was humble and kind while Grandpa was a harsh authoritarian. Grandma reminded me to always be humble and respect others, and Grandpa taught me how to survive and encouraged me, in his own way, not to take the path to prison.

My grandpa had a military background and worked in the police force for many years. As a result of that, he believed in brute force. When he wasn't drunk, he taught me how to shoot and how to disarm a robber, in case one were to break into our home. When he was drunk, he would beat me until there were marks all over my body. I remember him beating me while shouting, "I'm going to beat you so that you don't disobey me again. Follow the rules! Don't skip church! Don't play on the streets with those friends of yours. They're a bad influence! And don't lie about it, saying you went to church when you were playing soccer with those criminals. I want you to really think about it! Prison is worse!"

I must admit, I did break the rules and deserved to be punished sometimes, but my grandma deserved to be treated better.

My grandpa cheated on my grandma for years, and he often refused to help her buy things for the house or school materials for my father when he went to college. Grandpa believed that after a man turned eighteen, he needed to be out of the house and be self-sufficient. That meant it was up to my grandma to work seven days a week to pay for whatever my father needed to complete his studies, or for anything else my grandpa did not approve of. Under this circumstance, she taught us to never become dependent on anyone and to work hard to buy what we wanted.

What disturbed me most, however, was the fighting. Grandpa would push Grandma against the wall, and I would step in to try to protect her. After I received a beating for intervening, I would sleep on the floor under her hammock. We would also move the furniture in front of the door so that Grandpa couldn't get inside and say or do something he would further regret.

Sure, I knew that defending Grandma would get me another beating, but I always had great respect for her and for women in general. I had seen how hard it was for a working mom to care for a house and children without any help or, even worse, with an abusive man to add to her burden. I have always hated seeing women subjected to such abuse. Perhaps this is why Grandma always told me that I had the potential to become whatever I wanted to be, because I had a warrior's mentality with a kind heart.

Just before beating me, Grandpa always asked, "You know why?"

"Because prison is worse," I always replied. Then, the beating commenced.

I suppose the beatings helped to keep me out of trouble. I never broke the law, even though I was constantly surrounded by temptation. After all, I played soccer with and sold bread to criminals, and they all told me stories of how easy it was to make money by robbing rich people. However, I was not going to rob anyone, because I lived according to certain principles—but maybe those principles were reinforced by the threat of Grandpa's belt.

LIFE LESSON 9:
TREAT EVERYONE WITH RESPECT

* *

Two valuable lessons my grandfather taught me, unfortunately by disrespecting my grandmother and me, is the importance of treating everyone with respect and not abusing whatever power you have. Everyone deserves respect, regardless of their socio-economic status, their position in the family, or the mistakes they've made. Disrespect does not benefit the other person or you; rather, it makes you an ogre and prevents you from having a productive relationship with that person. Further, it can make the other person bitter and resentful and discourage them from sharing with you what they have to offer. I always look for win-win opportunities. Disrespect is a no-win proposition.

Working Collections

When I was twelve years old, I became a collections agent. Well, actually, I was helping my uncle collect on some bad debts. One of the debtors owned a butcher shop. He had bought some meat from my uncle on credit, but he never paid. Every time I showed up at his shop asking for the money, he had an excuse. So, on my fourth attempt at collecting the money, I bought a baseball bat to take with me.

The butcher watched me closely as I walked into his business with my bat in hand. I figured, worse case, we would fight it out with bats. Wrong! The man pulled a gun on me and said, "Don't ever bring a bat to a gunfight, kid." He motioned to the door, and I made a quick exit. No shots fired. Whew!

LIFE LESSON 10:
SENDING THE WRONG MESSAGE CAN BE RISKY
• •

One of the lessons I learned was to never bring a bat to a gunfight. More importantly, I learned the importance of sending the right message. By walking into that butcher shop with bat in hand, I was sending the message that I would be willing to use violence to solve my problem. The only thing that message got me was the threat of more serious violence— violence that could have ended my life.

Be careful about the message you convey, in words or in actions. It could cost you dearly.

Challenging Bias and Discrimination

When I was a teenager, I let my hair and beard grow to challenge people's bias. I have always taken issue with people who judge others based on appearance, skin color, or even tattoos. So I studied hard to become the best student in school, practiced hard to be an exceptional athlete, worked hard to help my family financially—and avoided the barber to challenge everyone's ability to look past my appearance and see who I really was. Everyone who knew me called me the "rock 'n' roll big guy." Those who didn't know me thought I was a neighborhood thug.

At the time, I started dating a girl from a military family. Her father did not approve. The instant he saw me, he assumed I was a criminal, undeserving of his daughter. His snap judgment was based solely on my appearance. He didn't take the time or make the effort to get to know me first.

I asked her to follow her heart, and we continued dating, although we hid it from her father. Of course, he eventually discovered our secret, and he stormed to the school to find out who I was. What he learned completely blew his mind—I was only fifteen years old (he thought I was eighteen), and I was in the top ten of my class and on the dean's list. Furthermore, he learned that I was working toward an internship at a bank as part of a student program.

He apologized to me and promised to never again judge people based on their looks. Having my ex-girlfriend's father apologize was a defining moment in my life. It not only reinforced my belief that people were prone to judge others solely on their looks, but it also showed me that people's minds could be changed when challenged by facts, and that any change in behavior begins with a change in thinking.

LIFE LESSON 11:
CHALLENGE YOUR NEGATIVE THOUGHTS

All of us grow up with negative thoughts and misconceptions that were sown in our minds at a very early age. We may believe that all politicians are corrupt, that "the rich stay rich and the poor stay poor," or that you have to choose between being successful at work or at home. These misconceptions, and many others, can control you throughout your life, if you let them. I encourage you to challenge any negative thought or belief, any bias or prejudice you have. When you have such thoughts, ask yourself, "Is this really true?" and then look for evidence that challenges the belief. For example, how can it be true that the rich stay rich and the *poor stay poor if Carlos Siqueira came to the U.S. with $800 and became quite wealthy? How can it be true that "it's not what you know but who you know" that leads to success when scores of people who don't know those in high places have achieved great things?*

Although your past does not define you, thoughts you acquired from the past can hold you back. The good news is that anyone can adopt new beliefs and change their thoughts. In fact, that is the only way to begin to grow and develop into a better person, and it is the only way a society can evolve.

Early Days as a Coach

By the time I was fourteen, I had a lot of people coming to me for advice on numerous topics. I had developed a new niche—helping people with fear, depression, or anxiety shift their mindset. With my guidance, people mired in negativity could transform their thinking. They could find the positive in the negative, leave their past behind, and start to envision and work toward a better future. Because I had a good mind, asked questions, listened to the advice of my elders, and already had considerable life experience as a young teen, I could offer valuable guidance on a wide range of topics.

My friends who also sold goods on the street started coming to me for advice on marketing toward speed to profit. They had noticed the amount of product I was selling (sweet breads, empanadas, and so on) and how fast I was able to sell it, and they wanted to know how I did it. They also told their parents about me, and their parents came to me for advice. I told them that you have to be different and create new ways of advertising whatever you're selling. To stay on top as the best at what you do in your marketplace, you have to be constantly innovating and creating better, faster, and newer conversations. For example, I wasn't merely selling bread; I was selling an experience that filled my customers with joy. I would sing, dance, wave a flag, make funny sounds, and do any other crazy thing I could think of to draw attention and make people laugh. I would constantly seek new ways to create excitement so my customers would have a great time while they ate.

I had come up with this technique through my own experience, observation, and experimentation. When I wanted to eat filet mignon, which we could never afford, I would imagine that whatever I was eating was filet mignon, and I would also sing out loud, which seemed to make the food taste even better. I figured that if I could re-create that experience for my customers, they would buy from me instead of from one of my competitors. It worked!

Long before earning any certification, I had become the coach and consultant in the family simply because I had experienced so many situations, dealt with so much adversity, and succeeded when everything seemed to go against me in my personal and business life. I did the same for everyone who came to me for advice. I loved seeing people who didn't believe in themselves succeed beyond anything they had imagined possible. I always told them, "everything we need is within us, never forget that."

Every time adversity struck, which was a regular occurrence in my life, I sought solutions and got creative. I fell back on my tried-and-true method of asking questions, such as, "What are some possible solutions to this problem?" and "Have I considered different perspectives?"

In difficult situations, I strove to extend the pause between my initial impulse to act and the action itself. I would visualize myself stepping outside my body and observing the situation from a more objective standpoint. In doing so, I started seeing the world through a different set of lenses, and I magnified my presence a hundredfold and analyzed the way I made decisions during emotional or unexpected situations.

By taking myself outside the situation, at least in my mind, I could more effectively analyze it and make logical and well-informed decisions. It took the emotion out of the equation and enabled me to be more rational and less reactive. If I couldn't figure out how to handle a situation, I researched and sought advice from experts in relevant fields of business to get different perspectives. (You might be surprised by how much free, high-quality advice you can get from others simply by asking!) Successful people love to share what they've learned from their experiences. Because I didn't have access to the Internet until I was thirteen, asking experts for advice directly was my only option, and it is still often the best approach.

When I was young, I also hung around bars and listened to entrepreneurs share their stories of failure and success. (Some entrepreneurs open up more after they've had a couple drinks!) I might start by asking what they did for a living and whether they owned their own business. Then I would follow up with more targeted questions, such as, "Based on your experience, what does it take to succeed in business?" and "If you could start all over again, what would you do differently?" I would also ask personal questions, such as, "Are you married?" If the answer was yes, I followed up with more pointed questions, such as, "What do you think is the secret to a good marriage?" or "If you were to give advice to a newly married couple, what would you say?" I also asked, "How do you find the perfect balance between work and family?"

As I gathered knowledge and insight through these conversations, I continued to develop a genuine interest in people. My caring attitude combined with my knowledge and problem-solving skills enabled me to help others overcome challenges and achieve their objectives.

(Nowadays, I get out of my office and work a few days a week at a local coffee shop as part of my continuing love to help other entrepreneurs in need. I will approach someone, then engage them in conversation; if they tell me about their problems, I offer solutions and strategies and I challenge them to go apply it. The training never stops!)

LIFE LESSON 12:
IT'S ABOUT THE MISSION, NOT THE COMMISSION

As a mentor, my goal is to make my clients successful in ways that are exciting and different from anything they've ever experienced. For example, a husband's goal should be to make his wife successful; a parent's goal should be to make his or her children successful; a company's goal should be to make its employees and customers successful; a government's goal should be to make its citizens successful. When everyone around you is successful and they know you contributed to their success, they will contribute to yours, and they will have much more to contribute. Whenever I conduct a sales training session for a company, or speak with a chief executive officer (CEO), I always tell the salespeople and CEO, "It's about the mission, not the commission." Focus on the mission, on serving your clients' needs, and your reward will follow.

One day, some friends of mine who had a small garage rock band asked me for help. They were scheduled to play at two house parties in two nearby college towns and needed a van or SUV for transportation. The car they planned to use had broken down, and they had run out of options. With the house parties only two days away, they were desperate.

I knew a politician in the area who might be willing and able to help, so I visited his office, explained the situation, and presented a proposal: If he would provide a suitable vehicle for the band, I would distribute his campaign flyers around those towns and post them in schools, businesses, and so on. Worse case, he would say no, which I was mentally prepared for; after all, if he said no, I would be no worse off than before I asked. Having that mindset going in, along with the knowledge that my offer was a win-win, I could pitch my proposal with confidence. When I did, not only did he say yes, but he also provided us a school bus, a driver, and money for food!

My problem-solving abilities amazed my friends. For whatever reason, regardless of the complexity of the problem and the time constraints, I have always been able to come up with creative solutions. Of course, knowing a lot of people helped. Even now, by knowing people and what they do, what they have, and what they need, I can solve problems simply by matching needs to resources.

Drug Daze

In my youth, many of my friends, customers, and acquaintances did drugs, but my exposure to the drug scene increased when I became a teenager. Always a huge rock 'n' roll fan, I loved heavy metal, hard rock, and reggae, and I would go to concerts and hang out at house parties where my friends were playing. As you might imagine, those parties weren't only about the music; the band members would sit down beside me and do drugs. Eventually, they started prodding me to try them, and I did.

Over time, the drugs started to cloud my thinking. I was hanging out with all the wrong people and doing stupid stuff, such as jumping the fence at concerts to avoid paying. Because I knew a lot of cops in town, and because I wasn't thinking straight, I felt impervious to the risk. That thinking began to change when I started seeing my friends get into trouble because of their drug use. One of my friends had hopped the fence at an event and was running from the security guards when he bumped into the wrong people. He was so jacked up on drugs and adrenaline that he got into a fight and was shot. Another friend almost died from a drive-by shooting at a local bar where we often hung out on Sundays.

I would like to say that these incidents convinced me to give up drugs and stop hanging out with that crowd, but it was actually divine intervention that saved me. I would soon be turning eighteen, traveling to the United States, and leaving that life behind.

LIFE LESSON 13:
DON'T ABUSE DRUGS OR ALCOHOL
• •

Many people use various legal and illegal substances to cope with their problems and frustrations or to give themselves a boost when they feel exhausted or depressed. Although these substances may make you feel better for a while, you will ultimately pay a price in the form of poor health, lost motivation, reduced cognitive abilities, emotional instability, legal issues, and perhaps even addiction or death.

Instead of going the route of chemical dependence, explore healthier means—enjoyable activities that are not only calming or stimulating but that also improve your body and brain. Go for a power walk; throw some jabs and hooks like Rocky Balboa, and keep reminding yourself that as long as you continue to pursue your dreams, you will succeed. Command your subconscious mind to embrace the struggle with joy instead of hiding behind drugs. Remind yourself that negative news and gossip are always around us and abundantly available, but so too are goodness and awesomeness. You have the power to choose what to focus on. What you think, do, and practice is what you become.

A Growing Desire

Throughout my youth, I had a growing desire to leave Brazil and seek my fortune in the U.S., the land of opportunity. It's not that I didn't love my homeland. I did and still do, but it was not the best place to start a family and raise children. Government corruption was rampant, opportunities were scarce, and the streets were dangerous. It wasn't only the small-time crooks that made life difficult; organized crime was big business, and they targeted the most successful people—the business owners who were trying to make a better life for themselves and their families.

In Brazil, the gangsters knew everything about you. They knew where your kids went to school, where your wife got her hair done, and when you left home in the morning. They knew the exact time you opened the safe at your business and when you were heading to the bank to make a deposit—and they would not hesitate to pay for such information. For example, it was not uncommon for them to pay a bank employee to find out which of the bank's customers had the most money. As soon as you became financially successful, you became a target. They would threaten you, your spouse, your children, and even your housekeeper and your security guards and their families to get what they wanted. What's more, the gangsters would share information with one another.

Some of my uncles in Brazil would often get robbed and have guns pulled on their kids. I can't imagine how horrible it would be to have someone pointing a gun at my daughter's head.

I once asked one of my uncles, "How can you guys tolerate all of that violence? Why put up with that vicious cycle of robberies, where thugs take all the money you work so hard for? Why not move overseas and start over in a safer environment for you and your kids?"

He replied, "We are already used to it."

I, on the other hand, was not about to become "used to it."

LIFE LESSON 14:
REFUSE TO ACCEPT THE UNACCEPTABLE

Great people, great families, great communities, and great countries are not built on complacency. They do not accept the unacceptable. When the British monarchy became too oppressive for its American colonies, the colonies revolted and broke away. Of course, declaring independence came at a price—the wages of war, along with the loss of British protection and support. However, the first Americans were willing to pay that price to secure their rights to life, liberty, and the pursuit of happiness.

If you are complacent in any area of your life that you feel, or should feel, is unacceptable—health and fitness, career, relationships, finance, and so on—I encourage you to snap out of it. Don't settle for less. Reach for more.

My Last Day in Brazil

A few months before our last day in Brazil, my mother told me that our paperwork was approved, and we received our passports to fly to the United States of America. I was undeniably excited and eager to leave Brazil and seek a better future in the USA.

I cut my long hair and sold it for money to take driving classes. I spent the rest of the money on Johnnie Walker Black, a few grams of marijuana, and a bus ticket to my favorite Amazonian island. Brazil is home to numerous beach paradises, but Algodoal has always been my favorite. It is located on the northern coast of Brazil with the Atlantic Ocean to the north, the Marapanim River to the west, the Maracana River to the east, and a narrow channel to the south that separates the island from the mainland. There are no cars, everything runs on generators, and the air is always pure.

The locals are amazingly humble, loving people. They called me *chefe aparte* (chief warrior of peace) because I would always take their side when the big-city boys made fun of them or treated them like lesser beings. The locals are small, and even at age eighteen I was bigger and stronger than most of those city boys. I would point out to them, "You wouldn't be so disrespectful if they were my size." They rarely said anything back.

On one occasion, I used my skills in martial arts to immobilize a drunken city boy to keep him from hurting one of the villagers. I hate violence, because it attracts more violence, but I believe in defending oneself or someone else from being bullied by stopping the fight and immobilizing the aggressor. Through my love and respect for the natives, and my commitment to what is right, I earned their respect in stepping forward on their behalf.

LIFE LESSON 15:
TAKE THE TWO-HUNDRED-YEAR PERSPECTIVE
• •

Two hundred years from now, none of us is going to be here. This fact is significant for two reasons: First, any mistakes you make now won't matter two hundred years from now, so don't be overly concerned about taking risks or failing. Second, we are all born into this world completely dependent upon others for our survival, and we leave with nothing. That makes us all equal, so we need to treat each other accordingly. Having more money, more possessions, a more advanced college degree or certification, a higher position in a company, or some other conventional measure of success does not make one person better than another. Treat others with respect, and you will receive respect in return.

On that last day in Algodoal, my friends and I had so much fun that I passed out on the beach. Nowadays, I rarely drink, and when I do, I always control how much I imbibe and never get drunk. But that day, we had a blast. It was my last day in Brazil, and I wanted to spend it on my favorite island with my local friends.

Later, I learned that the locals had kept an eye on me so that no one would try to rob me while I was passed out. When I woke up, I realized that I had to get moving; my plane was supposed to leave for the United States that night, and I was out on an island. Poor people didn't have cell phones back then, so the closest phone was thirty minutes away—after taking a boat back to the city.

My mother thought I had died, because I had forgotten to tell her I was going to Algodoal. Fortunately, I made it on time, but we had to leave for the airport without saying goodbye to anyone except my grandparents and younger brother. At the time, I was too emotional to say goodbye to everyone—and there were hundreds of people to say goodbye to! (I have a very large extended family: my grandparents had twelve children, including my mother, and they also have a few dozen grandchildren.) It was a tough and tearful goodbye not only because we are all very close, but because we knew it might be the last time we would see each other.

The plan was that my mother and I would go to America, wait for our visas to expire, and then stay until God showed us the path to take. I made a promise to God when I boarded the airplane that I would do whatever it took to succeed, to be honest, and to work hard. I was committed to outwork all my competitors, and I wasn't going to fail. If I did fail, I would come back a hundred times stronger and ever more present and focused on the end result. I was committed to never returning to Brazil unless I had something to my name, because I swore my mother and I would never again feel the humiliation of abject poverty.

The trip seemed endless—twenty-one hours with connecting flights and layovers—but we finally landed in Miami. We had reached our destination, but our journey had just begun.

LIFE LESSON 16:
APPROACH THE UNCERTAIN WITH TOTAL CERTAINTY

• •

When I stepped off the airplane and onto American soil, I had two options: I could be overwhelmed by the challenges we faced, or I could embrace the uncertainty with certainty. Because I was brimming with eager anticipation, like David in the story of David and Goliath, I knew with utmost certainty that I would succeed. Holding tight to this assurance, I was actually free of doubt and fear.

Imagine how you would feel facing a challenge with the conviction and certainty that you would emerge victorious? Your confidence would soar. You would feel no stress. You would act without hesitation. You would have no reason to find excuses or blame others. With this mindset, what do you think the outcome would be? How would the outcome differ if you thought you might fail?

Conviction and certainty are fully in your grasp. You simply need to nurture those thoughts and feelings while ignoring any self-defeating thoughts. It's all about conditioning yourself to adopt a new mindset.

CHAPTER 2

Early Days in the United States

Fortune favors the bold.
—Virgil

July, 2001. When we landed in Miami, I told my mother to let me do the talking because I knew so many English words. If you have ever tried to converse in a foreign language, however, you know the problem with that line of thinking: sure, you can understand a few words and phrases and can ask simple questions, but as soon as the other person starts talking, you realize you have no idea what they are saying. I had memorized one statement in particular, and I was determined to use it that day: "We are tourists who are here to stay for thirty days on vacation."

We had already cleared the first and most difficult hurdle, we had our passports and visas, which was no easy task, even back then. We now faced our second hurdle, passing through the many lines of immigration and customs.

A Brazilian guy I had talked to on the airplane called me over to his line because it was shorter. I followed his advice, and my mother followed me. Unfortunately, a few minutes later, a guard came over, took that man out of line, and sent him to a private room. Illegal immigration was common at the time, and the guards were taught to scrutinize travelers with nonimmigrant visas more closely. They were worried about people who claimed to be staying temporarily but planned to stay permanently.

I didn't know all that at the time, but I sensed that talking to someone who was just sent to a separate room did not bode well for my mother and me. I noticed the guards talking and looking in our direction, so I decided to pretend I didn't know any English. Then, they started walking toward me and speaking to me. I didn't understand what they were saying, but I figured they were probably instructing us to step out of line and go to a room like the other guy. I imagined they thought that guy was helping us move to the U.S., which is big business. I kept saying, "No English at all, very bad English, can't understand." I repeated multiple times, "I am here with my mother on vacation." Thank God none of them spoke Portuguese or Spanish. They probably didn't understand what I had said in English, either, because my accent was so thick.

Eventually, they walked away and let us go. I thanked God, because if they had sent us to that room and decided we were working with that other guy to get into the U.S. under false pretenses, we probably would have been deported and had little hope of ever returning to the U.S. Once deported from this country, you are done; gaining reentry or citizenship is highly difficult. In addition, we probably couldn't afford a second trip, because all we had for this trip was my mother's savings and some money we had borrowed from my uncle.

Once we finally reached the guard at the checkpoint, he asked for my passport and I handed it to him. He looked it over and asked why I was in the United States, so I told him we were tourists on vacation for thirty days. He stamped my passport and handed it back to me. He did the same for my mother. Finally, we were able to breathe a sigh of relief.

Tears of happiness filled my eyes as my mother and I passed through the checkpoint carrying our luggage. In that moment, I knew my life would change forever. We shouted, "Thank you, God!" out of sheer happiness. We still had another flight to catch, but the hardest part was over. I decided right then that I would never return to Brazil unless I had something to my name and was a permanent resident or a U.S. citizen as I am now.

LIFE LESSON 17:
YOU MAY BE JUDGED BY
THE COMPANY YOU KEEP

I have never been careful about the company I keep, because I believe that everyone has something to offer and something I can learn. However, you do need to choose your associates carefully for two reasons:

1) *People may judge you by the company you keep. If you associate with people who hold beliefs or engage in activities that harm or offend others, most people will assume you share their values.*

2) *People who are negative can drag you down with them, turning your positive thoughts in a negative direction. Sometimes, avoiding these people is better than trying to help someone who is determined to remain self-destructive.*

From Boston to Framingham to Marlborough

The final leg of our flight placed us in Boston, but then we needed to travel to Framingham, where one of our cousins, Jonathan, lived as an immigrant. Upon our arrival in Boston, I tried calling him, but he didn't answer. At the time, I didn't know why he didn't answer, which made me a little nervous. However, I saw it as merely another problem we needed to solve. We knew the name of the town, so it was only a matter of getting there. One nice thing about big cities like Boston is that transportation is readily available. Although my English wasn't the best, we had the good fortune of meeting a seventy-year-old gentleman who understood Spanish, which is very similar to Portuguese. From him, we learned that there was a bus from the airport to Framingham. He directed us to the bus terminal, and from there all we had to do was buy the tickets and get on board.

My mother was panicking most of the time, but I managed to calm her down by making silly sounds, such as Donald Duck or a Brazilian reporter who speaks funny in the midst of total chaos. After a few hours, we boarded the bus and headed to Framingham. Being in America was amazing. Boston was even more wondrous seeing it from the bus than it was in the numerous movies I had watched growing up. I truly felt I was living a dream. Even though we had only $800 to our names, I was confident that we would find a way to succeed. We didn't have social security numbers, state driver's licenses, or jobs, but we did have desire, certainty, and the determination to do whatever we had to in order to succeed, short of breaking the law or harming others.

LIFE LESSON 18:
BREAK THE TENSION

If you're working with someone to solve a problem or complete a mission and that person starts to panic, find a way to break the tension. Don't get swept up in the emotion or erupt in anger or frustration, because it only adds fuel to the fire. Disengage. Break the pattern. If you have a good sense of humor, use it to defuse the situation. If not, simply remain calm and rational and speak softly. The other person will follow your lead.

When we arrived in Framingham, I called my cousin again from a pay phone. No answer. So I kept calling until he finally picked up two hours later. Those two hours were agonizing for my mother, but I remained calm. From my perspective, at least we were in the town where he lived, and, worst-case, we could sleep in chairs in the station and pretend we were waiting for a bus.

Bottom line: whenever I'm in an unpleasant situation outside my control, I try to think of the worst-case scenario and I ask myself what else does this mean? Usually, the worst-case isn't so bad.

LIFE LESSON 19:
IMAGINE THE WORST-CASE SCENARIO

When you notice yourself overwhelmed by worry, ask yourself, "What's the worst that can happen?" Chances are good that the worst that can happen does not justify the level of worry your mind is inflicting on you. Thinking of the worst-case scenario places the situation in the proper perspective.

I always advise people to think positively, so you may think I am contradicting myself when I tell you to imagine the worst-case scenario. However, worry often exceeds what we worry about. For example, we act as though our lives will end if we lose our jobs or our homes, but such worst-case scenarios are rarely so devastating, even if they do occur, and they often build character and reveal new opportunities.

Thinking "What's the worst that can happen?" often makes us realize that even if the worst happens, we will be okay, and okay is a good place to start.

Later, we learned that Jonathan had put his phone on mute while he was at work. We felt a sense of relief when he finally answered, and even more relief when he arrived at the bus station to pick us up. His home was already full, so he contacted his friend Palao, who graciously agreed to let us stay at his place in a town called Marlborough, about thirty minutes from Framingham. Palao lived in a nice two-bedroom apartment, where he provided a place to stay for a number of other Brazilian immigrants. We slept in the living room—my mother on the sofa, and me on the floor.

Sharing living space is not out of the ordinary for immigrants, and it's not because they are cheap. Most of them dream of owning their own home or at least having their own apartment. However, immigrants often arrive with little money and few belongings, and those who have a place to live know how challenging it is to find a job; find a place to eat, shower, and sleep; and find their way around.

First Full Day in the USA

My mother and I woke up earlier than anyone else, and she prepared an amazing breakfast for everyone (seven of us) with toast, baked potatoes, and scrambled eggs with tomatoes and onions. Crowded into the dining area, we enjoyed eating and talking and laughing, bonding instantly through the shared experience of immigrating to the U.S. and the sharing of food and living quarters. After breakfast, nobody had to drag themselves to work. All were happy and eager to start the day.

Everyone contributed to the household, some with money, others with groceries or transportation. My mother and I did our share by cleaning and cooking with whatever food was available. I had no employment yet, so I gave myself two jobs: 1) learn English and 2) become familiar with the area.

LIFE LESSON 20:
INDEPENDENCE IS HIGHLY OVERRATED

Most people don't want to have to rely on others. We strive to be independent. However, while the drive to become independent is natural and noble, it is highly overrated. We can accomplish so much more by becoming interdependent. More importantly, perhaps, is that life is much richer and more vibrant when we expand our circles to include more people from diverse backgrounds.

Look at independence as a stage between dependence and interdependence—a phase you must pass through to achieve a higher level of being. When you achieve interdependence in your relationships, your business, or your community, you begin to develop a greater respect for others and an increased willingness to work with others in pursuit of ever greater achievements.

Learning English

If I was to have any chance of succeeding in the United States, I needed to learn English—fast. Fortunately, I already knew a lot of English words and phrases from the rock songs I had listened to in my youth. I knew the basics: the alphabet; how to count; the names of animals, fruits, and vegetables; and numerous other common words. I even knew some everyday phrases and could form simple sentences, such as, "How are you? My name is Carlos." Of course, I sounded like a robot, but Americans seemed to love my accent. They would "roll with it" and help me.

I knew I needed to learn faster so I could get a job. To become more proficient, I bought a Portuguese/English dictionary and picked up a bunch of free newspapers and magazines in the nearby supermarkets and pharmacies. For the first week, I spent most of my time in the apartment reading, watching television, and talking to myself—in English. I also spent time reading books at the local library, translating them to build my vocabulary. My dictionary was with me at all times.

I watched the news a lot too, and I would watch the same movies over and over, pausing frequently to look up words I didn't know. In the evenings, when we all watched movies together, I annoyed my housemates by asking them what certain words meant. Yes, I was *that* guy—the guy who talked during the movie. I can appreciate their frustration; after working all day, nobody wanted to sit through a two-hour film that's interrupted with a continuous stream of questions. My housemates had big hearts, though, and were very accommodating.

LIFE LESSON 21:
IMMERSE YOURSELF IN WHATEVER YOU CHOOSE TO DO
• •

When you engage in any activity, immerse yourself in it to the point of greatness. As Martin Luther King, Jr. once said,

"If a man is called to be a street sweeper, he should sweep streets even as Michelangelo painted or Beethoven composed music or Shakespeare wrote poetry. He should sweep streets so well that all the hosts of heaven and earth will pause to say, 'Here lived a great street sweeper who did his job well.'"

Whenever you study, work, exercise, cook, clean, or do anything at all, focus on the moment, allowing everything else to fade into the background. This approach not only enables you to raise the quality of whatever it is you're doing, but it is also a great way to strengthen your ability to focus on the positive.

Finding My Way Around

After breakfast each day, I took a long walk around the neighborhood to become familiar with the area and to talk to people. One of those people was a Brazilian man named Vava, and another, an American named Jake.

Vava and Jake shared some tips on finding work. One was to apply at local supermarkets and restaurants within walking or bicycling distance from where I was staying. I knew that the $800 my mother and I had would quickly run out, so I needed to make something happen soon. I applied to as many places as possible, and, as I waited to hear from employers, I continued to work on mastering English.

On one of my walks, I passed city hall, which was a few miles from the apartment, and discovered that anyone who needed it could get free potatoes, bread, and a few cans of food. This became a frequent stop on my future walks. Walking several miles did not bother me, because that's what most people do to get around in Brazil—walk or ride their bicycles.

LIFE LESSON 22:
THE LAW OF ATTRACTION REQUIRES ACTION
• •

When I was at Palao's and had no job, I could have easily stayed in the apartment and simply waited to hear from employers. Instead, I studied English, explored the area, applied for more jobs, and talked with people. Imagining success, by itself, would not make me successful. I had to get out and do something.

As soon as I started to take action, good things started to come my way. I established valuable contacts, gathered new ideas on how to find employment, and even scored some free food. None of this would have happened if I had stayed shut up in Palao's apartment.

My First Car

The two women who lived in Palao's apartment worked at an ice-cream factory, so my mother and I applied for jobs there. Within a few weeks, they called my mother. A month later, they called me. I was elated because we were down to $500, and we really needed those jobs. Unfortunately, we also needed a car to get there.

One of my new friends informed me that I could buy an older model car and make payments. To Americans, that seems obvious, but in Brazil, more than half the population can't afford a car. Most people have to work diligently just to put roofs over their heads and pay the bills, because too few jobs are available, and those that are pay a small fraction of what even immigrants get paid in the U.S. People living outside Brazil see the beautiful beaches in Rio de Janeiro, the awesome soccer stadiums, and our world-famous carnival parades, but they don't see the pervasive government corruption and widespread poverty. In my days growing up in Brazil, only the rich owned cars; everybody else took busses or bicycles or walked. A large majority had no hope of ever owning a car.

So with my friend's advice, I went to a small car lot owned by a nice Latin man. Having only $500 to my name, I didn't expect to be driving home. To make matters worse, I didn't have a social security number or a U.S. driver's license—all I had was a passport and an international driving permit. I described my situation to the car salesman, and, to my surprise, he told me that thousands of people were in the same situation. He sold me a car, my very first—a light blue 1989 Honda Accord!

I cried from sheer joy while driving off the lot. The United States is an amazing country. In the span of eight weeks, my mother and I had jobs, and I had a car. My mornings always began with this prayer of gratitude: "God bless the United States of America."

LIFE LESSON 23:
LASER-FOCUSED ENERGY DRIVES PROGRESS

The reason my mother and I were able to get jobs and a car in so little time is that we were on a mission. Our goal was to secure a better life in the U.S. Our immediate objective was to obtain jobs, and I also had the objective to learn English. Every day, those objectives were our focus. Each objective had a clearly defined outcome, and everything I did each day aligned with those objectives. Although other people certainly helped us, we had to take the initiative and make it happen.

Take that same approach in everything you do, and you will be successful:

1) *Define your goal.*
2) *Think of your goal as a necessity, not an option, and believe that it will happen.*
3) *List the objectives you must meet to achieve that goal. (Make sure each objective has a clearly defined outcome.)*
4) *Align your daily activities with your objectives.*
5) *Drop all expectations and embrace the obstacles and uncertainties that lie in your path. The only certainty that matters is that you will meet your objectives and achieve your goal.*
6) *Persist until you succeed. Focus on your goal, pursue it relentlessly and with the certainty of getting it, and the universe will respond generously.*

Setbacks and Success

Soon after I bought my first car, I ran out of gas in the middle of town, right in the middle of the road. I started to panic but then paused to restore my focus. I asked myself, "What is good about this situation?" and the answers came to me immediately: I hadn't crashed the car, I was going slightly downhill, I weigh 250 pounds, and I have money to buy gas. I got out of the car and started pushing it, praying to God that the police didn't stop me and ask for identification. Since I didn't have a state driver's license, I probably would have been deported had they found out that I wasn't a U.S. citizen. I was able to push the car about a quarter mile to a gas station without getting stopped, and I filled the tank. To this day, I never let the gas get below a quarter tank before stopping to fill up.

LIFE LESSON 24:
WE ARE THE SOURCE OF MUCH OF
OUR OWN STRESS

• •

Stress may not be entirely avoidable, but we can reduce it significantly by taking steps to avoid stressful situations. In this instance, the anxiety I felt was the product of my own carelessness and procrastination. Had I watched the gas gauge and filled up when I should have, I would not have been in that stressful predicament. The same is true when we rush out the door in the morning and head to work, worrying the entire time that we will be late. Waking up a little earlier is a simple solution, but many of us continue to behave in ways that stress us out.

I encourage you to make a list of all stressors in your life. These can be people, places, situations, or even your own behaviors. After identifying your stressors, try to think of one or two ways you can eliminate each of them from your life. For example, if you worry about your car breaking down on your way to work, two possible solutions would be to buy a more reliable vehicle or take your current vehicle to a mechanic for inspection and maintenance. If you constantly stress about being late, setting your clocks ten or fifteen minutes fast may be enough to give you the confidence that you will always be on time.

The day before I was scheduled to start my job at the ice cream company, I made sure my car had enough gas. I woke up early so I could get there in plenty of time, hopped in the car, and turned the key. I heard some clicks and whirrs, but the engine would not start. I tried again and again as I felt a wave of panic washing over me. Concerned about being late, I called a cab to take me to work.

Yes, I ended up being late to my first day of work at my first job in the U.S., a job that took me about two months to get. I tried explaining to the manager that I had car problems and had to take a cab to work, but my English still wasn't quite good enough for him to understand. In fact, the more I tried explaining the situation, the angrier he became. Instead of firing me on the spot, he decided to make my first day a living hell. He criticized everything I did, glared at me, and talked in my ear the whole time. After four hours, he fired me. Was I worried? Yes. However, I had applied for so many jobs that I was confident I would find another. The next day, as my friends and I were talking, I told them my story about the shortest job I ever had, and we all shared a laugh.

That same afternoon, I got a call from Boston Market; they wanted me to start the day after next. I knew I would get another job, but I had no idea it would happen so soon. It's truly amazing how the doors of opportunity fly open when you start to knock, and I had knocked on a lot of doors.

I made absolutely sure my car was in great shape to get me to my new job on time. My buddy Jake knew about cars, so I had him take a look at it a couple days before as well as the day before. He said that everything was fine; it simply needed a new battery.

LIFE LESSON 25:
LEARN, LAUGH, LEAVE

• •

Learn from your failures, laugh at them, and then leave them behind as you pursue future success. Even though I really needed that job at the ice cream company, I knew that being depressed or beating myself up over getting fired would only add negative energy to that disappointing event. It would have made me miserable in the present and put my future prospects in jeopardy. After all, who wants to hire someone who is depressed and down on himself? Besides, I was certain I would get another job.

Two great ways to learn from your mistakes are to journal each experience and tell someone else about it. In fact, I encourage you to journal about all your adversities, how you responded to them, and what you could have done differently or better. By documenting your actions and thinking about other approaches, you can create your own personal manual for dealing with adversity. Such a manual will equip you and your family with effective tools and strategies in case a similar adversity strikes again.

The fact that my car did not start cost me my first job. That was something I refused to let happen again; in fact, after landing the job at Boston Market, I woke up several times throughout the night to make sure my car would start. I could not afford to lose another job. I had bills to pay and a mission to accomplish.

The next morning, I made it to work at Boston Market on time. They were happy with the amount of energy and enthusiasm I brought;

it was at a bustling location and most workers seemed stressed from working under pressure. I worked hard, was good under pressure, and always kept a huge smile on my face. Once, my manager, Stacy, even asked me, "Do you ever get mad, worry, or feel anxious?"

"Yes," I replied. "But I try not to." I attempted to explain in my broken English that I strove to live in the present, appreciating everything so that my mind wouldn't trick me into believing I was suffering. I told her that I knew a lot of people who had it good suffered because their minds tricked them, that my life was great compared to the lives of children around the world who suffered each day from starvation, war, and other terrible hardships. I told her about my life in Brazil and how I would shift my thinking when bad things happened to maintain a positive attitude.

After I told Stacy my story, she said, "I wish a lot of people around here and other people I know had the same mentality you do."

LIFE LESSON 26:
HAVE AN ATTITUDE OF GRATITUDE

Motivational guru Zig Ziglar coined the phrase "attitude of gratitude." According to Ziglar, "The more you recognize and express gratitude for the things you have, the more things you will have to express gratitude for."

I have found this to be true. I appreciate every little thing that happens in my life, especially when I have the opportunity to help someone or make them feel better. It could be something as simple as making a person smile in a difficult situation. I often impersonate celebrities or Disney characters to make people laugh and interrupt their pattern of negative thinking.

Stacy liked me so much that after two weeks, she gave me a raise of fifty cents an hour. One of my coworkers was jealous because he had worked there for ten years, and it had taken him much longer to get his first raise. But I continued getting raises because of my work ethic, ability to work under pressure, and over-delivering. I not only worked tenaciously to prove myself and make the customers happy, but I never complained about my schedule or the amount of work. I felt fortunate to be alive, living in the U.S., and having a job. And because I was full of joy and energy, I was able to perform at a higher level and make that Boston Market location a much more enjoyable place for customers and my fellow employees.

A Second Job

The bakery to which I applied next was adjacent to the Boston Market where I worked. During the initial interview, I was a bit nervous because I couldn't understand some of the questions the manager asked; he spoke very fast like me and had a thick European accent. Despite my typical high level of confidence, I was not assured enough in my English at that time to converse with someone who spoke that fast with an accent. When he asked the first question, "How old are you?" I actually answered, "Good, sir. And you?"

My English was so bad and his accent so thick that he had to repeat the question three times before I understood. When I finally did, I replied in very broken English, "How old am I? I am eighteen years old, sir."

Even though my English was horrible, my energy and personality seemed to win him over. The interview continued and went well, I presumed, because he laughed. Later, I *knew* it went well because he offered me a job.

For this job, all I had to do was carry things from a refrigerator at the back of the bakery to the employees at the front and help them with whatever they needed. Even better, the five other people who worked there were enthusiastic and smiling all the time. Life is so much better when you are surrounded by happy people. They were incredibly nice and helped me with my English, which inspired me to love the American culture even more!

LIFE LESSON 27:
YOU HAVE THE POWER TO CONTROL YOUR OWN EMOTIONS AND INFLUENCE THOSE OF OTHERS

Some psychologists believe that people are hardwired with a so-called mirror neuron to feel what others experience. For example, if you see someone slip and fall, you may recoil in sympathy. Seeing someone cry is likely to make you sad. Hearing someone laugh will lift your spirits. Certainly, each of us is responsible for his or her own emotions, but be aware of how your emotions may be affecting others and how their emotions may be affecting you.

Your ability to control your emotions and influence those of others can be a powerful tool in getting what you want. Even though my interview for the bakery job did not appear to be going very well, my confidence and inner joy showed through and not only made the interviewer happier, but confident enough to hire me.

I Want a *Faca*

On my first day at the bakery, I needed a knife to cut some boxes. I had forgotten the English word "knife," so I used "*faca*," which is Portuguese for "knife." But when I asked a female coworker for a *faca*, she gave me the strangest look. Her eyes widened in shock, but because I had no idea why, I said again, "I want a *faca*."

She said, "Hold on" and walked to the front of the bakery. She returned with the manager, who asked me to repeat the question.

"I want a *faca*," I repeated seriously, making a cutting motion with my arm. Of course, that same motion could have been taken to mean something else.

I kept telling them ever so seriously, "I just want a *faca*."

It took them both a few minutes before it dawned on them what I was saying, and as soon as they did, they started laughing. When they explained their confusion, I started laughing too. We became great friends after that.

**LIFE LESSON 28:
CONFLICT CAN OFTEN BE RESOLVED
WITH CLARIFICATION**

• •

Obviously, I learned something from this incident that I will never again forget—the English word "knife." However, I also learned that miscommunication can lead to conflict, which can often be resolved through clarification. Far too often, we have a knee-jerk reaction to something someone said or did when we don't fully understand that person, and that reaction often deepens the conflict.

The next time you feel upset or angry with someone over something they said or did, or were supposed to say or do but didn't, pause and think about that person's motivation or what they possibly could have meant. Better yet, ask them about it and continue asking questions until you fully understand. Chances are good that you were becoming upset or angry over something your mind concocted in the absence of sufficient detail instead of over what the person actually intended.

A Third Job

Now I had two jobs, but I needed more money to achieve another objective—getting our own place. So I got a third job doing landscaping work. That money allowed us to rent a small studio apartment—a large one-room basement unit with three beds—with a friend of mine. Having a bed for each person was definitely a step up from sharing a two-bedroom apartment with multiple people, with my mother sleeping on the sofa and me on the floor.

Working three jobs was extremely difficult; I slept only three to four hours a day. It was only a month before I quit my bakery job and spent more time landscaping, which paid more. But it was still not enough to be in the position I wanted to be in.

Deciding I was not going to settle for less than my goal, I constantly focused on finding a better job, continuing to grow, and working smarter. I always knew inside that I was meant to do something big that would help countless people, so I made that my focus from there on out.

LIFE LESSON 29:
CHANGE YOUR FOCUS, CHANGE YOUR LIFE

Many of my friends noticed how much progress I had made in such a short period of time, and they asked me how I did it. I would tell them, "Change your focus, change your life. If you focus on the fear of being deported or not making enough money to pay your bills, that's exactly what you will get." I advised them to focus instead on acquiring what they wanted—whether it was a job, a car, an apartment, or something else—and taking positive steps toward obtaining it, such as learning a skill or getting a job.

Pulled Over by the Police

One day while driving, I was pulled over by a police officer who asked for my driver's license. Now, most immigrants in that situation would probably feel nervous and act suspicious, but I had no reason to feel that way. I felt as though I was already a U.S. citizen, and I knew I had done nothing wrong, so I was confident and polite. The officer checked my international driving permit (from Brazil) and let me go. Only after I was on my way did I get a little nervous, because I didn't know how much longer I could use my permit without getting into trouble.

LIFE LESSON 30:
ACT "AS IF"

While many mentors, including me, encourage you to change the way you think in order to be the person you want to be, nineteenth-century philosopher and psychologist William

James turned that thinking on its head. According to James, to change the way you think and feel, you must change the way you act. In James's own words, "You do not run from a bear because you are afraid of it, but rather become afraid of the bear because you run from it." Thus, smiling makes you feel happy. Frowning makes you feel sad. Acting like a superstar will make you a superstar. Acting wealthy will make you wealthy.

I think it is not a matter of either/or, but both. To achieve success in any endeavor, the best approach is to think and act the part. When I was stopped by the police, I was confident, because I believed and acted as though I were a U.S. citizen. Had I any doubt in my mind, that doubt would have shown through in my actions or demeanor, which may have drawn suspicion—and that suspicion could have resulted in deportation, in which case I probably never would have attained citizenship. In other words, had I feared deportation, that fear would have increased my chances of being deported.

Committed to My Mission

Despite the challenges I faced and setbacks I experienced, I remained committed to my mission—changing people's lives for the better. My focus on that mission placed challenges and setbacks in my peripheral vision, relegating them to the level of annoyances rather obstacles.

I knew I had what it would take to achieve my mission—the ability to make people laugh and show them how to transform negative emotions into positives ones. I simply needed a way to earn more money working fewer hours so I could spend more time on skill-building and self-development.

LIFE LESSON 31:
ALIGN YOUR GOALS AND OBJECTIVES
• •

To get where you want to be in life, first choose a destination—a dream-big goal or, as James Collins and Jerry Porras describe in their book, Built to Last: Successful Habits of Visionary Companies, *a Big Hairy Audacious Goal (BHAG). Then, map your route by identifying objectives (smaller goals) that you must accomplish in order to achieve your BHAG. Think of each objective as a vector (a force applied in a specific direction) that propels you closer to your goal. By aligning your objectives with your goal, you maximize the energy that drives progress in the desired direction.*

My BHAG is to educate children in third-world countries to dream big and achieve happiness, wealth, and fulfillment through self-mastery. I want to help them escape lives of poverty, crime, and abuse and show them how to become true leaders and make a positive impact. The goal is highly ambitious, but by setting the following objectives, I made my goal less overwhelming:

1) Learn English.

2) Travel to the United States.

3) Get a job, a car, and a place to live.

4) Master emotional intelligence and the art of self-fulfillment.

5) *Become a mentor of mentors by mentoring others worldwide about business strategies and how to master emotional intelligence and the art of self-fulfillment.*

6) *Become wealthy so I can contribute even more to kids around the world who are hungry like I was as a kid in need. Life is about contribution, not acquisition.*

7) *Use my wealth, knowledge, skills, connections, and other resources to lead by example, and to inspire other leaders to find ways to contribute even more to children living in poverty worldwide and make the world a better place along the way.*

Throughout my early years in the U.S., I discovered that fortune truly does favor the bold. To achieve success, you must know what you want, focus on getting it, and pursue it boldly and with unquestioning faith that you will get it. When you do, any obstacles or hardships become little more than distractions whose power to undermine your efforts is only as great as the amount of attention you give them.

CHAPTER 3

Door to Door Sales

Sales are contingent upon the attitude of the salesman—not the attitude of the prospect.
—W. Clement Stone

One Friday in early December, 2001, I was taking a break behind the Boston Market when I noticed several men talking in the parking lot. They had nice cars, were all smiling, and seemed confident. For several weeks, I had been wondering how I could work smarter instead of harder, and I felt the urge to walk over there to find out what they did for a living. I followed my instincts and approached the group. One guy in particular was bigger than the others, and when he talked the others listened.

When I was a child, my grandfather always told me that if I ever wanted to know something about business, I should approach the owner or manager of the business, because that person had valuable wisdom and advice to share. He also told me how to spot the leader in a group—to look for the person everyone else was listening and talking to. I practiced this technique when growing up in Brazil, and I found it worked splendidly.

So I approached the guys in the parking lot, and in broken English, I said, "Hi. How are you guys doing? My name is Carlos. What do you guys do?" Imagine my voice, robotic with a Portuguese accent. They started to laugh. I don't know whether they were laughing at my accent or because I was so brash, but I was glad to see them laughing. Whatever I had said or done that was so funny broke the ice. (I later learned that they liked my accent and respected my courage to strike up a conversation.)

LIFE LESSON 32:
FOLLOW YOUR GUT

• •

In his book, The Power of Your Subconscious Mind, *Joseph Murphy explains that the mind functions consciously and subconsciously and that any idea the conscious mind impresses upon the subconscious mind, the subconscious mind will find a way to make happen.*

To understand this further, the subconscious mind functions behind the scenes. It is what keeps your heart beating and keeps you breathing. It is what connects us all to one another and to the universal creative force that flows through all things. It is also the source of intuition, and it directs us, through instincts and urges (not thought), to take action.

People can choose to act as their intuition or urge directs them or consciously ignore such directives. This is good, because some urges and instincts can be destructive, such as the urge to prejudge others. However, too often, due to fear or consciously overthinking a situation, we ignore urges that we really should act on.

In this instance, my mind had impressed upon my subconscious the idea of working smarter instead of harder, and my subconscious mind found a way to make it happen. I believe my subconscious mind, in connection with the universal creative force, drew those men to that parking lot and urged me to approach them. I could have consciously convinced myself to stay where I was, but had I done that, I would have missed out on a golden opportunity.

When the men stopped laughing, they told me all about their jobs. They said they sold cable television door to door for a few hours a day and earned a couple of hundred dollars a day doing it. What they said was so inconceivable to me I was certain I had heard them wrong. After all, I was working a hundred hours *a week* to make a little over five hundred dollars. So I asked the leader of the group, Luke, to repeat it, and he did. I hadn't heard them wrong; they were telling me that each of them was earning a couple hundred dollars a day selling cable television *part-time*!

I wanted in.

"I would like to do what you do. Please give me a chance," I said. "I won't disappoint you guys."

Luke told me to meet him in Boston on Monday morning, and he wrote down his phone number and the address of his office. I was so excited I couldn't sleep that entire weekend.

I had been praying to God to put people in my path who would help me earn more money without having to work longer hours. I knew this was the answer to that prayer.

LIFE LESSON 33:
ASK AND YOU SHALL RECEIVE

Many people struggle in business or their careers and even in their personal lives simply because they don't ask for what they want. They feel shy or awkward approaching another person and having a conversation, requesting a job, asking whether the person could use their services, or even inviting someone to lunch.

You need to get over that. Think about it: what do you have to lose? The worst that can happen is that the person ignores you or says no, in which case you haven't lost anything. You stand to lose much more by not approaching the other person and missing the opportunity to form a relationship, a true friendship, or the business you've been dreaming of for so long.

If you are a shy person or don't feel comfortable approaching someone for personal or business reasons, I want you to try this: Stand up and feel the energy coming from the ground transforming you into a samurai warrior. Then, in your best samurai warrior voice, tell yourself, "Embrace this fear of yours with the highest level of certainty you've ever had. You have nothing to lose." If the person you approach ignores you or acts rude, simply say to yourself, "Next! Millions of other doors will open."

I'm on Fire: My First Day

It was a monumental day in my life, so I remember it vividly. It was my first day at this new job, and because my motivation was at its highest, I decided to wear my T-shirt that read, "I am on fire, and nothing will put this fire out." (I dressed like the guys I had met outside Boston Market, but I had forgotten that they were not working when I met them.)

It was Monday morning, so the traffic in Boston was heavy. I had never been in Boston on my own, and if you've ever been there, you know how confusing the streets can be. The area is not a simple grid; it is very hilly, and many streets angle and curve. Adding to my confusion is the fact that Boston drivers are quite aggressive. Long story short, I got lost and was late again for my first day on the job.

When I arrived, Fred (Frederico), the owner of the company, approached me. He looked like one of those Italian Mafia bosses from the movies. I expected to be scolded about being late, but the first words out of his mouth had nothing to do with my tardiness. He looked at my shirt and asked, "Do you seriously think you can sell to someone if you show up at their door wearing that shirt?" He wore his gruffness like a badge of honor.

"Yes, sir!" I said. "It's not the shirt. It's the person wearing it. Let me follow your best guy around for a few hours and prove myself."

He gave me the opportunity (and a uniform T-shirt). As soon as I put the shirt on, I felt like a member of the team and it was great!

What didn't feel so great was walking into my first training session late, with the entire team in attendance. After the first few hours of the session, the trainers started handing out our assignments—the locations we needed to visit in an attempt to sell the cable TV service. Prior to that meeting, I had no idea what the job would entail. However, I did remember one of the guys I met outside Boston Market telling me that he had fun selling cable television to people. (I later learned he was the boss's son.) Talking and having fun with people was my thing, so I knew I could do it. I prayed to God that the customers would understand me.

Our mission was to sell cable television, giving away the first three months for free. The idea was to introduce the new technology to customers—more channels, better reception, and a remote control, so the customer could change channels without getting off the couch. It was late 2001, so cable TV had been around for quite a while, but a lot of people in Boston were still tuning in to aerial broadcasts and watching on old TVs without remote controls. I still remember my sales pitch, "Wouldn't it be nice to have this remote control that will change the channel for you when you come home tired from work?"

LIFE LESSON 34:
USE NAYSAYERS AS MOTIVATION

You are likely to encounter people who will tell you that you can't or won't be able to get or achieve what you want in life. Even worse are those who won't say it, but through subtle gestures and comments, they'll try to make you feel as though you have set your goals and expectations too high. I encourage you to ignore them. Better yet, use them as motivation. My mantra as a kid was, "Prove them all wrong. I can do it, I will do it. My positive energy will wash over and engulf their negative energy like a tsunami."

When Fred called attention to my T-shirt, I shifted both his and my focus from the shirt to the person wearing the shirt—the person who was going to be his best salesperson.

My first day in the field was that same Monday afternoon. I followed the company's best salesman, Eddie, who was making around seven sales per day. He got seven sales in only three hours, so I asked him how much money he made. "Three hundred fifty dollars," he replied.

"Are you serious?" I said. It was hard to believe, but it was completely true. I saw the targets for this market as people who only needed some television to watch when they came home from work. Because everyone needs some form of entertainment, I saw my job as providing that entertainment. The target market simply needed someone like me to knock on doors and describe the service. It almost sold itself.

After watching Eddie for several hours, I told him I didn't want to follow him anymore, that I wanted to do it myself. He was fine with that; in fact, I think he was actually relieved not to have me following him around. So he took me back to his car where he retrieved a metal folder with blank work orders and a list of addresses to visit.

It was already 5:00 p.m. when I started working.

When the homeowner of the first house I visited opened the door, the first thing she saw was this enormous Brazilian guy. If you imagine the experience from her perspective, this is what she encountered on her doorstep:

With a funny accent, the Brazilian guy said, "How are you today? My name is Carlos. I am here to give you a trial for free cable TV for three months. You won't even have to walk to the television anymore. You can change channels by remote control. That way, you can get some additional entertainment into your life without leaving your home. It's totally free for three months, with absolutely no catch."

I'm not sure whether it was my accent, my sales pitch, my smile and energy, or the service itself, but she signed up for the package, and I earned my first sales commission—$50! I almost cried. In that moment, I knew this was the job I had dreamt about for so long. On my first day, I worked hard into the night and finished with ten sales in the span of only four hours, earning $500 for a half day's work!

LIFE LESSON 35:
LEARN FROM THE BEST

• •

I have always paid close attention to what the most successful people around me were doing to be successful and put what I learned into practice. Then, I used their methods myself and put in twice the effort. I would also develop other ways to achieve higher levels of success.

For example, I appreciated that Fred had assigned his best salesperson to train me, and after only a couple hours of watching Eddie sell, I had picked up his technique.

Eddie wasn't just selling cable TV; he was bringing fun and joy to every household he visited. He separated himself from the transaction and made every prospective customer feel good every time, regardless of whether or not they signed up for the service. He also made a TV remote seem like the greatest invention since the light bulb. If people had children, he sold the family on having more channels to entertain the kids and give everyone in the family a way to kick back and relax. After a few hours with Eddie, I was ready to start selling with even greater drive.

I related to his approach because it was very similar to the one I used to sell bakery goods on the streets of Brazil. I was always happy and striving to bring joy to everyone, even if they didn't buy what I was selling. Because I separated myself from the outcomes, I was happy to merely make another contact and meet someone new every day.

I couldn't wait to show my boss how many sales I had made. I called Fred and asked to meet with him, so he gave me his hotel address. I found him sitting next to a table in the lobby, and I walked over and dropped the ten work orders on the table. He laughed a little while counting them. After he was finished, I reminded him of what I had said earlier—that the guy wearing the "fire T-shirt" was unique and had the confidence to become the best. I also reminded him that I beat his best guy on my first day.

On that day, Fred and I became friends. As I drove home that night, I realized I had found a way to make all of my dreams a reality. Something very special had happened that day, and I couldn't wait to share my day with my mother. As I told her the story, we were both filled with joy. We had been working so hard just to keep up with our bills, and now we could see that our dreams of a better life in America were becoming our reality.

Reaching Higher

Brimming with confidence and ambition, I loved my new job, in part because my pay consisted solely of commissions. That meant that I controlled how successful I would be; the more I sold, the more I earned, and there was no limit. While my big goal remained the same—to change people's lives for the better—I raised my objectives and defined them for more clarity. I now wanted to earn even more money, not only to support my mother and me, but my family in Brazil as well. I also wanted to help even more kids out of hunger.

At that point, I knew I needed to continue to improve myself and strengthen my mindset—if I could help more people bring fun into everything they did, I couldn't lose. I knew from my brief experience in sales that if you do something fun and get paid to do it, you can attain a lifestyle of sustainable joy by being in the present (by living in the "now"). My self-improvement would be the key to being able to help others condition their mindsets to focus on what is right versus what is wrong, to find ways to have more fun in what they do, and to pace themselves for future success by setting goals and objectives and following up with strategic hard work to bring certainty to uncertain times.

I set my daily sales goals as if I owned the company and needed those sales to stay in business; I would not stop for the day until I made at least seven sales, no matter what. Every time I got a yes, I would get fifty dollars. When I got a no, I lost nothing. It only meant I needed to knock on more doors. I could get twenty no's in a row, and that would not stop me.

I made a decision to face uncertainty with certainty no matter what was happening, because I knew that allowing negative thoughts into my mind would lead to negative beliefs that would control my actions. For example, if I let myself think, *It's hard to get a client*, or *Sales are down*, or *The weather is bad*, or *It's the holidays and nobody is buying*, or *It's hard*, or *It's getting dark*, or *It's cold outside*, then those lies would become so vivid I would start to believe them, even though they were imaginary. I simply had to keep going until I found the next customer, and I had to prevent any thought standing between me and my goals from entering my mind, because I knew they were not going to serve me or my potential clients. I reminded myself that there was always someone else in the world facing a bigger challenge, and I was grateful for what I had.

When you make this adjustment in your mindset, it's a game changer, especially when you're in sales. Some people were extremely rude; others got angry with me. Some would stay hidden behind their locked doors, threatening to call the police because they thought I was running a scam: they didn't believe my company was actually *giving away* three months of free cable TV because it was a completely new concept. But nothing people said or did discouraged me. I was so focused on the end result that nothing could prevent me from getting my seven sales a day.

After knocking on a lot of doors, I again started to look for ways to work smarter rather than harder. I realized that if more people said yes, I would not have to knock on so many doors. Because I figured some people might be reluctant to come to the door simply because of my size, I decided to take a softer approach. I put myself in a fun and peaceful state before every interaction by singing and or making a silly physical gesture. I rang the doorbell or knocked on the door while making fun sounds, then stepped back to appear less intimidating since I am so tall. I also toned down my voice and talked more slowly due to my accent. My sales pitch was all about them and bringing value and convenience to their lives, and I separated myself from the transaction every time.

These adjustments and others paid off, increasing my productivity in the field. After they bought from me, my clients always mentioned that they loved my style and attitude, and they never felt that I was being pushy, unlike other salespeople who knocked on their door in the past.

LIFE LESSON 36:
THE ONLY ONE STANDING IN THE WAY OF YOUR SUCCESS IS YOU

When you have a purpose and a vision of becoming the best, then you are the only person who can stop yourself. Don't get caught up in any negative self-talk. Think positive at all times. If you begin to get discouraged or notice yourself thinking negatively, start repeating affirmations to crowd out those thoughts. Tell yourself that the situation will improve, opportunity is near, you are on fire, you can do it, you will do it.

Work smarter and harder than your colleagues and others in your field. Set more ambitious goals. Read books, take classes and seminars (online and off), and attend conferences. Engage in continual self-improvement. Whenever you will be involved in a deal or negotiation, do your homework, read any agreements closely, and ask questions until you fully understand what you stand to gain and lose (if anything). Make sure everything you do furthers your objectives and that your objectives align with your goal.

Once you achieve your goal, raise the bar. Maintaining success can be even more difficult than achieving it, so you must always give yourself something to strive for.

Second Chances

As I continued selling cable services door to door, I was promoted to team leader, which allowed me to recruit and coach others. It didn't take long for me to notice that many of those applying for these positions had criminal backgrounds. No one else would hire them because they believed that criminals would always be criminals, that "a leopard can't change his spots." That may be true to a certain degree, but people are not leopards. I have always loved people and believed that everyone has the potential for greatness, that a person who decides to break harmful and self-destructive patterns, shift their mindset, and set higher standards can do anything they set out to do.

I took a lot of people under my wing and showed them how much potential they had beyond doing drugs, stealing, selling drugs or guns, or engaging in other activities that got them into trouble.

I even showed them how they could sleep at night without having to feel paranoid about people breaking into their homes and killing them due to gang-related turf wars. In sharing how I grew up under extreme violence and turned it around by shifting my focus and establishing daily outcomes that aligned with my dreams, I modeled that it did not take a miracle, but rather relentless conditioning, self-development, and hard work.

I had seen and heard about terrible things on the streets of Brazil—robberies, shootings, racism, intimidation, beatings, stabbings, and so on. I told the people I mentored, "If I could deal with that as a seven-year-old child and rise above it, so can you. It's all about strengthening your resolve, leaving the past behind, and not making excuses. Whatever happened to you when you were a child, whatever social injustices you suffered or think you suffered, whatever mistakes you made no longer matter. You can choose to detach yourself from all that and from other people's opinions and the negative things they say to you and about you. Believe in yourself. At this point, I believe in you more than you do. I want you to believe in yourself far more than that."

LIFE LESSON 37:
LACK OF TIME IS A POOR EXCUSE

Many people try to use the excuse that they don't have enough time to spend on self-improvement or looking for a better job, but that is almost always nonsense. The average American watches thirty-five hours of television per week— that's nearly a full-time job! Cut that time in half and you free up over seventeen hours every week. That's a little over two hours a day that Americans could dedicate to self-improvement. When I made the switch years ago, I used that time to read self-help books, exercise more, spend more time with my family, and mentor and coach anyone in need of my guidance.

If everyone slashed their TV time in half and devoted that time to improving themselves, their relationships, and their community, we would drastically improve the quality of our lives and others. We would not only be healthier, happier, and achieve a much greater sense of fulfillment, we would have stronger families and thriving communities.

Serving as a supervisor and mentor helped me to fulfill my goal of helping people to improve their lives. It also brought me closer to achieving one of my key objectives—to become a life coach and someone who now mentors leaders. I began empowering addicts to stop using drugs and live healthier lives with meaning and purpose. Although they tried throwing excuses at me all the time—they had nothing to eat, they didn't have the right clothes, they couldn't afford to take classes, they had criminal records so nobody would hire them—for every excuse, every problem they cited as an obstacle to their success, I had a solution. If they didn't have anything to eat, they could pick up free food at city hall as I had done. If they needed clothes, they could go to the Salvation Army or Goodwill. They could get an education by reading books at the local public library or by signing up for free classes offered around the city. If they had a criminal background preventing them from getting a regular job, they could try to find a job through subcontractors, who don't check backgrounds so carefully. I reminded those who came to me complaining that they weren't making enough money that almost 70% of the world's workforce lives on two dollars a day.

LIFE LESSON 38:
THERE ARE ALWAYS OPTIONS, BUT MAKING EXCUSES IS NOT ONE OF THEM

* *

Forces beyond your control can block your path to wealth, happiness, and self-fulfillment only if you let them. Social injustice, bigotry, poverty, and temptation have been in existence since the beginning of humanity and will not be going away anytime soon. You may have a criminal record that will follow you your entire life. Some things you simply can't change. However, you can change what you do in response to those challenges, and every problem has a solution. Stop wasting focus and energy on excuses. Divert it to finding solutions. As Richard Bach writes in his book Illusions: The Adventures of a Reluctant Messiah, *"Argue for your limitations and sure enough they're yours."*

Hope for the Hopeless

What I loved most about recruiting and coaching was that it gave me the opportunity to instill hope in the hopeless, especially in people with criminal backgrounds who had lost the hope of ever having a regular job or a fulfilling life. I gave them hope by giving them a second chance, pumping them up, challenging their self-defeating thoughts, sharing my stories, leading by example, and having them follow me door to door to see how I did it. In doing this, they began to envision how *they* could do it. And if they could not bring themselves to be passionate about door to door sales, I encouraged them to work even harder, go back to school, and save their money to pay for school or a professional course that would enable them to pursue a career doing what they were passionate about.

Best of all, for me, I was doing something daily that aligned with my values and my goal of helping others be their best selves and attain wealth, happiness, and fulfillment. My primary questions to myself were, *How can I find amazing people to inspire today—people with a sleeping giant that just needs to wake up? How can I transform them from a life of crime to one of personal fulfillment through the process of selling cable TV door to door?*

The 'hood had its fair share of individuals with leadership qualities, but they were foundering simply because no one had ever shown them a better way. Given the right mentorship and opportunities, they could achieve success beyond their wildest dreams. My job was to find those people, give them an opportunity, and teach them how to use the opportunity as a stepping stone on their path to greatness, however they envisioned it.

When I found out the company I worked for needed more salespeople to expand sales to other cities across the country, I saw it as an opportunity to recruit more people to spread my message that anyone can succeed regardless of their past. I discovered I could meet both objectives by hiring skilled salespeople with criminal pasts, so I focused my efforts on individuals with sales experience in low-income areas who were known to sell drugs, guns, and other illicit goods. I figured they already had sales skills and experience; all I needed to do was redirect their energy and expertise into selling cable TV.

My idea was a great success. Once I convinced ex-cons to switch from illegal to legal sales, our team sales soared past those of any other contracting teams in the cable industry. More importantly, we gave hope to scores of people who had lost it.

LIFE LESSON 39:
SOCIAL PROBLEMS CAN BE SIGNIFICANTLY REDUCED BY INSTILLING SELF-MOTIVATION AND SELF-DEVELOPMENT IN OUR YOUTH

● ●

Education often falls short by focusing exclusively on academics at the expense of self-motivation and self-development. We need to not only encourage our youth to dream, but teach them how to envision themselves as successfully pursuing their dreams, so they have the motivation and hunger for academics as well as a clear appreciation of why learning is essential to helping them achieve their dreams. We need to teach them how to use affirmations to pump themselves up and believe they can achieve their goals regardless of challenges, setbacks, hardships, and the pervasive negativity in the world. We need to show them how to find opportunities and create their own.

Children get very little training like this in school, so if you're a parent, establish a daily family ritual of reading a minimum of fifteen minutes daily on different topics in motivation, personal development, relationships, and faith. Have each family member teach someone what they learned—a friend, a neighbor, someone on social media. Teaching reinforces the learning and makes it more a part of who you are, so you're better equipped to apply what you learned at an opportune time. Sharing your knowledge is also one of the most valuable gifts you can give someone; you're likely to find that those who receive your gift of knowledge or insight receive it at a point in their life when they need it most.

I believe my approach worked for two reasons. First, I never treated people like second-class citizens, regardless of their appearance or past misdeeds. Second, I told people what they needed to do; I didn't do it for them.

Here's the approach I took step by step:

1. I planted seeds in their minds and shared strategies and techniques I had found helpful. I encouraged them to set goals and establish objectives, and I continually reminded them that they were capable and deserving of success.

2. I asked if they had access to food. If they said no, I showed them how to get food at local churches, certain city halls, or food banks. I was never turned down.

3. Once they had access to food, I encouraged them to start improving themselves by spending time in the library. Every library I have ever visited has a great collection of motivational and personal development books, videos, and audio recordings.

4. I urged them to learn how to use a computer and search the Internet for additional valuable information and resources. Specifically, I introduced them to YouTube as a great place for learning how to conduct themselves during job interviews.

5. Once they had studied and prepared for a couple of weeks, I told them to visit the Salvation Army or Goodwill to buy some nice clothing for little money.

LIFE LESSON 40:
SUCCESS HAS A LOW ENTRY FEE

• •

Regardless of your situation, you can always improve yourself and start taking steps to achieve greater levels of happiness and self-fulfillment. Even if you have lost everything, all you need is the courage to start again. You can always find the resources you need, but you must get out there and look for them. If you are in a dire financial situation, start by asking family members or friends, or visit a church or community center. You can find organizations that will help you with food, clothing, job training, financial issues (such as credit repair), and other challenges, but you must take the initiative.

In numerous neighborhoods where I worked, I noticed a familiar pattern of drug use and abusive behavior. As I talked to the people on the streets, I asked myself one question: *How can I maximize the chances of helping these people out of poverty?* I wanted to provide street hustlers with the tools they needed to turn their lives around, because I knew it was possible. After all, I had changed my life, and if I could do it, then so could anyone else.

Because I wanted them to believe they could change their current circumstances if they truly wanted to, I decided that the best way to help them was to show them that applying small changes to their daily habits would lead to greater wealth, happiness, and fulfillment. To show them how they could also change their environment by choosing a different way to make money, I would choose a candidate and have him follow me around for three to five hours to watch me sell. After that, I would stand back and let him try a few door to door sales on his own and coach him through it.

Some of the young hustlers I met on the street would tell me that they didn't have a chance of getting a decent job with good pay because they were competing against candidates who came from rich families and had better educations. Therefore, they chose to sell drugs or perform other illegal activities to support themselves and their families. Most of them grew up with the false limiting belief that people born in their neighborhood would die there—that there was no way out.

Countless families had become content accepting food stamps and other government assistance, but these programs simply aren't enough to fix this problem. Instead of working toward helping people become independent, they make people dependent on the government. As such, I believe that in addition to these programs, the government should also offer personal development and job training to enable them to improve the quality of their lives.

Sometimes, I wish that when I was younger, I had the knowledge I possess now. I could have helped a lot more people who suffered in poverty and died too young. I can't go back in time, though, so I continue to do whatever possible to help as many people as I can, and I ask you to do the same. Here are a few ways you can help:

- Coach or mentor someone in need. Teach the person what you know and share your insight. Give them self-improvement assignments and check on them once a month to make sure they did as instructed. In the meantime, provide additional guidance, support, and encouragement.

- Post blog content and videos promoting personal development. Share what you've learned from reading and from experience.

- Share your rags-to-riches stories or any story of how you overcame a hardship or setback. We need more of these types of stories online so people know it's possible to escape poverty and overcome adversity.

LIFE LESSON 41:
HELPING OTHERS MAKES YOU HAPPY

People who are depressed, anxious, or neurotic are often that way because they are caught up in a vortex of their own negative thought processes and focused on whatever they have chosen to be miserable about. If you are in that trap, one way out is to shift your focus to something outside yourself— an interest, a cause, or someone else. When you're focused on something outside yourself, a mission for example, you begin to engage in productive thought and activity, which lifts your mood and improves your attitude. Being active and engaged feels much better than wallowing in despair. Helping someone else feels even better and can help you shed any feelings of isolation.

If you're feeling down, I encourage you to shift your center from yourself to someone or something else. Surely you know a friend, a family member, or a coworker who could use help, guidance, or just someone to listen. If you can't think of anyone, then explore volunteer opportunities in your community by searching online at places like VolunteerMatch. org. Volunteering is also a great way to network and learn new skills.

When you reach out to help someone, however, be careful. You don't want to be dragged down by people who are comfortable only when they're miserable, and you don't want to be taken advantage of. Look for ways to give the person a hand up, not a handout. Yes, sometimes people will need food, shelter, and clothing, but don't make them dependent on you. Show them where to go to get what they need to climb out of their hole, but stop short of trying to do it for them. Sometimes, all they need is a job lead or to be shown the path to a better life, but ultimately, they are responsible for their own success or failure.

CHAPTER 4

A Downward Spiral

*Success is to be measured not so much
by the position that one has reached
in life as by the obstacles he overcomes.*
—Booker T. Washington

In 2002, the company I worked for was expanding, so the owner asked me if I would move to Hartford, Connecticut, an hour-and-forty-minute drive from Boston, where I was living with my mother. I would not have minded the daily commute since I was accustomed to driving all over the east coast, but my mentor wanted me to be closer to the local team and not waste three to four hours a day commuting. The only reservation I had was that I didn't want my mother to have to live alone with our roommate. My concern, however, was unmerited; my mother had already been thinking about returning to Brazil to take care of my grandparents. They needed her help, so she encouraged me to follow my dreams.

With nothing keeping me from moving to Connecticut, I once again left my friends behind to pursue a new opportunity. This time was harder, though, because my mother would not be joining me. Other than a distant cousin who lived a few hundred miles away, I had no family members in the U.S. Even so, I was eager to make the move. Opportunity had knocked, and I was going to answer.

After arriving in Connecticut, I continued selling cable TV and Internet service door to door and recruiting and training others, as I had back in Boston. One day, I hired a great salesman who happened to have an extra room for rent in his home. It worked out great for both of us for me to become his roommate—he needed the money to support his family; he also needed a ride to work every day, and I had a car. He quickly became my right-hand man. We even converted a spare room in his home into an office, and sometime later I hired his brother. We formed a great team.

LIFE LESSON 42:
OPPORTUNITY KNOCKS ONLY
A FEW TIMES IN YOUR LIFE
• •

Opportunities abound, but certain opportunities knock only a few times in your life, and you must answer. If you don't, you will never know where that doorway leads, and you will never grow. Personal and professional growth is often painful, requiring you to let go of what may be a comfortable life to reach for something higher but uncertain. The fear of loss and failure discourages far too many people from achieving their full potential. When opportunity knocks, I encourage you to take a leap of faith.

Poor Choices

In 2002, I quit smoking. More accurately, I replaced smoking tobacco with smoking marijuana. Prior to moving to Connecticut, I would smoke pot only on weekends, but after the move, it became a daily habit. I had planned to quit both nicotine and marijuana, but I succumbed to the temptation of smoking pot. At the time, I found all sorts of reasons to justify my habit: smoking weed kept me from smoking cigarettes, my roommates were smoking it seven days a week, and I needed something to dull the emotional pain of being separated from my friends and family. The truth is that I was hanging out with the wrong people, focusing on the wrong things, and making bad decisions. The choices were entirely mine, and I made poor ones.

It turned out that my roommates were deep into drugs, and the guy I was renting from was continuously arguing with his wife, creating an environment of constant stress. I had seen similar relationships when I was growing up in Brazil, and even back then I knew I did not want to be around all that stress and negativity. I should have left, but I was comfortable in my misery, a self-destructive comfort that the marijuana no doubt contributed to.

LIFE LESSON 43:
CHOOSE YOUR FRIENDS WISELY

My grandfather Raimundo Siqueira used to say, "Tell me who you hang with, and I will tell you who you are." American entrepreneur, author, and motivational speaker Jim Rohn echoed that statement when he claimed that you become the average of the five people you spend the most time with. Both spoke the truth. By hanging with the wrong crowd, I began to adopt their lifestyle and habits. Had I continued to do so, I would not have enjoyed the level of success I do today.

Over time, I grew anxious and would more easily lose my patience in frustrating or stressful situations. I started missing my family and friends even more—and it was worse on Sundays. When I wasn't working, my mind would take me back to the fun times of barbecuing, playing soccer, and cracking jokes with family and friends. Those joyous times were in stark contrast to the loneliness, chaos, and stress that engulfed me in my current situation. With no dreams and ambitions to crowd them out, doubts and negative thinking seeped into my mind, and I wasn't able to break my own pattern of negative thinking as I had done so many times in the past.

As Tony Robbins says, "Where your focus goes, energy flows," and in my current living situation, all I focused on was conflict, stress, and my own misery: the constant yelling and screaming, drug abuse, out-of-control kids, missing my family, and so on. Somehow, I managed to convince myself that smoking more marijuana was the solution to my problem. Because I was so focused on the chaos around me, my energy flowed into self-destructive habits.

LIFE LESSON 44:
WHEN YOU'RE IN YOUR HEAD, YOU'RE DEAD

The mind is a powerful creative force, but it can be just as destructive if you plant the wrong seeds. As negative thinking escalates, the mind turns inward, so you no longer notice all the positive that surrounds you or the things that can challenge your negative thoughts and pull you out of your own head. This is why you need to be careful to filter out negativity, especially in a world in which the media sifts out most of the positive news to focus our minds on negative events.

It Gets Worse

One day, while selling door to door, I saw three young guys and asked if they knew where I could buy some marijuana. They said they did, and that they would drive me there. So I got into the backseat and started sharing what I did for a living. As I explained how they could also make a lot of money by selling cable services door to door, they asked questions about the job, as if they were genuinely interested and considering the prospect.

When we finally stopped, it was in a remote location near a cemetery with a lot of abandoned homes. It seemed strange, but I figured that the marijuana was hidden in one of the ramshackle houses. Suddenly, I heard a click and knew instantly that a gun was pointed at my head. "Cell phone and wallet, now," one of the guys said.

I had learned martial arts back in Brazil as a form of self-defense, so I tried something stupid, something I never recommend doing. I moved away from the guy holding the gun and tried to disarm him, but my timing was off completely. He pulled the trigger. When nothing happened, I hit him so hard I knocked him out.

But I still had two guys to deal with. One of them was armed with a baseball bat, and I got hit a couple times before I finally managed to rip the bat out of his hands. I fought both of them and landed a few solid punches. Though I didn't knock them out, they quickly lost interest in fighting me and drove off. I then walked a few blocks to a liquor store and called a friend to pick me up. Fortunately, I got out of it with only a few bruises. To this day, I believe God prevented that gun from going off and ending my life.

In utter shock, all I could think about was that if I had died, my family back in Brazil would suffer even more because I wouldn't be there to help them. Soon after that incident, and for the first time in my life, I fell victim to depression.

LIFE LESSON 45:
TRUST YOUR INSTINCTS

• •

As we approached that remote location with the abandoned homes, I felt that something wasn't right. I should have jumped out of the car as soon as I had that feeling—instincts are your subconscious mind sending you signals to act. Unfortunately, the signals aren't always clear, but when you're sensitive to what your instincts are telling you, you'll find that they're almost always right.

Depression Closes In

Even after that traumatic incident, I continued to smoke pot and ask myself the wrong questions. Instead of asking, "What will I accomplish today to further my goal of helping others?" I would ask questions like, "What if I had died that day?" and "What if I had gotten injured and could no longer do my job?" Negative thoughts kept streaming in from all directions, and my focus shifted to all of the bad things that would happen to my family if I were to die.

To fight the depression, I used drugs, but that only deepened and prolonged my suffering. Though I completely support the use of medical marijuana, when it's used recreationally, certain strains smoked in excess can impair thought processes and intensify complacency. For me, it gave me the ability to tolerate the intolerable, discouraging me from taking action to improve my situation. At one point, I stayed high for a whole week with my roommate just so I wouldn't have to bear the agony of depression. It didn't work, however. Nor did I stop smoking marijuana. And it got even worse when I learned that one of my good friends back in Brazil had hanged himself. Within a week, I had been robbed at gunpoint, nearly shot, and lost a close friend to suicide. My response? Try smoking crack.

LIFE LESSON 46:
THE MIND IS VERY IMPRESSIONABLE

The human mind is like a sponge—it tends to accept as true the information, opinions, and images most often presented to it. A skeptical mind can certainly question and filter content, but if it is constantly exposed to misinformation and unfounded beliefs, that content will eventually seep in, especially if it's generally accepted. The mind is even more impressionable in the midst of heightened emotion, when reason takes a backseat and is unable to challenge what's presented.

Carefully and continuously choose what you feed your mind. If you feed it doubt, anxiety, scarcity, or fear, that is exactly what it will start to believe and act upon, even if it's not true. Question and challenge any beliefs before accepting them as fact, especially when you're in a highly emotional state. An emotionally charged thought makes a deep impression.

Smoking Crack Cocaine

I knew for some time that the guy I had hired and was rooming with was a crack addict. One day, prior to my period of depression, I had caught him with a glass pipe and confronted him about it. He admitted to the addiction but asked me not to tell his wife. I honored his request.

Sometime later, when I started my downward spiral into depression, I mentioned to him that marijuana wasn't doing the trick anymore. When he saw me completely distressed in my darkest hours, he asked if I wanted to try crack. Even though I knew how destructive crack was, I conceded. All I cared about was alleviating the mental anguish. I had created weakness in myself by choosing to focus on thoughts of death and disappointment, which made me more vulnerable to temptation.

Most addicts lie to themselves or others in an attempt to justify their use of drugs or alcohol, and to a certain extent, I did the same. I had convinced myself that crack would pull me out of my depression and give me a boost. But I won't lie about it: I tried crack, and I liked it. In a matter of only a few days, I was addicted. Unfortunately, even though it gave me some temporary relief, my dark thoughts persisted.

LIFE LESSON 47:
SUCCESS CAN BE CHALLENGING TOO

Funny how I could escape poverty in Brazil, arrive in the U.S. with only $800, become highly successful, and then bottom out. I always wondered how people who apparently had such a great life could simply throw it away. Now I knew. I had taken my eye off the ball, so to speak. I had stopped focusing on my goal, stopped reaching for something more, and stopped doing what I had done to become successful.

Over time I realized that maintaining success can be just as difficult as achieving it. It's an uphill climb, and when you stop climbing, you may slip and fall.

Redemption

As I write this, I can vividly remember the mental anguish I felt. It was the darkest period of my life. I had lost control of my own mind, I was alone, and I kept feeding drugs into my body to numb the pain. This cycle had me trapped until one fateful day when I came upon a woman with her two children living on the street. She had obviously not showered in days and was dressed in threadbare clothing. Her two children looked dejected and were probably hungry and feeling hopeless. The image shocked me.

I had only forty dollars to my name, and there I was, planning to use that money to buy crack. I realized at that moment that I had a choice: I could purchase more crack to feed my addiction or help this woman feed her kids. I chose the latter. It was a powerful, life-changing choice, and I made it by pausing and analyzing what I was doing in my life and what I could do right in that moment to alleviate the suffering for this mother and her children.

The encounter triggered a flood of associations in my mind—images, thoughts, and feelings of past and present. I thought about my mother, my brother, and me struggling to make a living in Brazil. I thought about being given the opportunity to travel to the U.S. and the chance to make a lot of money simply by selling cable TV and Internet door to door. I asked myself why I had come to the U.S. and left my entire family behind. My goal had always been to inspire and lead by example, and I wasn't doing it. In fact, I was no longer even trying. I replayed these hurtful images in my mind until it was so painful that I decided to make a change.

Raise your standard, I told myself. I had done it before. I had started from nothing and succeeded by taking small steps daily and applying strategies to achieve my goal and objectives. What had happened to me? I knew deep down that I was not being my best self, and I reminded myself that I was destined for more than my current reality. My mantra became: "*As long as I have a goal and set objectives that align with that goal, and I continue to learn and make the right choices, persevere, and surround myself with the right people, I will win.*"

From that day forward, I started asking myself better questions—questions that forced me to analyze my current situation and that sparked more positive and creative thoughts, such as the following:

- Am I living my truth now?
- What is my purpose in life?
- Who depends on my support?
- Are my actions aligned with my goals and objectives?
- What can I do today to help meet my objectives?
- What thoughts or dreams do I want to impress on my subconscious?
- What should I feed my conscious mind now to reinforce those impressions?
- Whom can I call or surround myself with who has similar goals and values?

Asking better questions, along with exercising, helped me to stop feeding my mind-limiting beliefs and to change my life for the better. I replaced doing drugs with going on power walks, acting like I was Rocky Balboa, saying over and over out loud, "All I need is within me now!" I also played basketball to clear my mind. Doing these activities motivated me to work harder than ever by aligning myself with my mission and purpose and focusing on my more immediate objectives.

Once again, I had to start from zero. All my money had been going to bills and drugs, so I had to make something happen fast. Because I had been working just enough hours to fund my addiction and stay afloat, and because I worked on commission, I had to kick myself back into high gear. Thank God I still had my car, because I would soon be on the move again.

LIFE LESSON 48:
ASK THE RIGHT QUESTIONS
• •

Ask negative, demoralizing questions, and you'll get negative, demoralizing answers. Ask positive, motivating questions, and you'll get positive answers that energize you. Here are a few negative questions you need to stop asking yourself:

Why me?
What if I'm not good enough?
Why didn't I . . . ?

Instead of asking questions like these whose answers will drag you down, ask the following questions to challenge your negative thoughts and build yourself up:

Is this true or only my opinion?
Is there any evidence to support my thinking?
What am I holding on to that I need to let go of?
What's the right thing to do?
What am I really great at?

Soon after my "aha moment," I contacted Fred and told him I needed to move back to Boston immediately, because I couldn't afford to surround myself with the people in my environment. He agreed to relocate me to Baltimore, Maryland, where the company was planning to expand its market, and he helped me get an apartment. I felt blessed that I would still be in charge of hiring and training others to sell cable TV and Internet door to door. It also warmed my heart that I was given the second chance I had been able to give so many others. Best of all, I was off the crack and back on track—the right track.

CHAPTER 5

A New Beginning

*Let's forget the baggages of the past
and make a new beginning.*
—Shehbaz Sharif

Moving to Baltimore in the second half of 2002 was a high point in my life. I have always loved traveling to new places to work; the feeling of uncertainty is always thrilling. In this case, it was a fresh, new city in which I could make new friends, and it helped me transform from a drug addict into a man who had revitalized his dreams.

The moment I set foot in Baltimore, it was love at first sight. Every door I knocked on in the 'hood was always fun. I had never seen so many people who were happy with what they had. They reminded me of people I knew while growing up in Brazil—always pleased with the little things, such as eating rice and beans or even getting cheap meat in cans. We could always pretend we were eating at the most expensive restaurant in town by closing our eyes and imagining it.

The powerful imagination I had developed in my youth ultimately became my salvation. Soon after I arrived in Baltimore, news broke of the Beltway sniper attacks (also known as the D.C. sniper attacks). Over the span of three weeks, from October 2nd to October 24th, ten people in two states (Maryland and Virginia) and in Washington D.C. were randomly gunned down while going about their daily business—mowing the lawn, pumping gas, shopping, reading a book. Three were critically injured. Understandably, people in the area were frightened.

Imagine what was going through my head at the time. Because everyone on my sales team was working on commission, we had no choice but to be out and about. So we continued selling door to door on a rotating cycle between Baltimore and Washington, D.C. finishing our routes in one and then driving to the other. Though no one knew where the next shooting would occur, we had no choice but to work in the D.C. metropolitan area where most of the shootings were happening. It seemed as though everyone was freaking out, but I managed to remain calm, the way I had in my youth when danger surrounded us. Part of my job as a leader was to lead by example, and I knew that any fear I showed would be mirrored and magnified by other members of my team.

I told them I would never expect them to do something I wasn't willing to do myself, and I modeled that by being the first one to knock on a door and the last one to leave the field for the day after knocking on the last door.

I also taught my team the same two lessons I had learned in Brazil: 1) When you hear gunshots, drop to the ground and wait for the situation to calm down; and 2) never focus on the negative news, because doing so will hinder your ability to complete your mission. I told them that when I was a kid, my mission was to sell all of my bread and make it home safely, which was no small feat in that dangerous environment. I also told them that violence is always happening somewhere and that people die, but they shouldn't worry about it to the point of not being able to do their jobs and enjoy their lives. Yes, we worked under threat of danger, but I was able to help my team shift their focus away from that. In short, my philosophy was that if you're not living fully, you are partially dead already.

LIFE LESSON 49:
UNLEASH THE POWER OF YOUR IMAGINATION
• •

Imagination is a powerful tool, especially when you use it to envision the life you desire. Condition your mind by engaging your imagination daily. Take a break to imagine the perfect vacation, or your ideal job or business. Imagine the perfect weekend with friends and family. Imagine yourself doing a good deed for someone. As your imaginative faculty strengthens, you will notice that the struggles and obstacles in life become easier to face, especially during tragedy and extremely difficult situations.

I am not suggesting that you use your imagination solely as a means to escape reality (although it's really good for that too). I am suggesting that you use your imagination to stamp positive impressions on your subconscious mind, so that it can begin to work on transforming your reality into what you want it to be.

During this tumultuous period, I kept my eyes on the prize. I knew the importance of maintaining my confidence and poise, especially during tragic and uncertain times. And it worked—my team mirrored my confidence. As we met the uncertainty with conviction, we embraced the notion that the dark times would pass. We also knew, from observing other sales teams, that fear and uncertainty sap energy and enthusiasm, so while other teams were slowing down, we accelerated our sales.

LIFE LESSON 50:
YOU CAN CAPITALIZE ON BAD TIMES
• •

During economic tough times, only a handful of entrepreneurs and salespeople excel, and those who do can make a tremendous amount of money as others in the field struggle. They excel by refusing to feed the beasts of fear and doubt. Instead, they feed their higher selves thoughts of opportunity and prosperity, and they ramp up their efforts.

That's what I want you to do for yourself, your company, and your team. Go all in on whatever you do. Keep your foot on the accelerator when others are pressing the brake. Let everyone know in your office and on your team that you won't accept any doubts, limiting beliefs, or anything negative to be spread around the office. Kill the monster of doubt and limitation before it has a chance to take control.

Next Stop: Harrisburg

After completing a project in the Baltimore area, I teamed up with the son of the company's owner to do a special project in Harrisburg, Pennsylvania, and we moved there temporarily. The special project still involved selling cable and Internet service door to door, and one day, I knocked on the wrong door.

I heard chaos break out inside the apartment as people started yelling and running. When it quieted down, a man answered the door and looked up at me in my uniformed shirt.

"What do you want?" he said gruffly.

I explained that I was selling cable TV and Internet service.

"So you're not a cop?" he asked.

"No," I replied.

Not certain I was telling the truth, he said, "Then you won't mind if I check to see if you're wired or carrying a gun?"

"No," I said, and he proceeded to pat me down. Satisfied, he let me into the apartment to talk, and after listening to me, he signed up for the service.

It wasn't uncommon for people to see a big, tall guy at their door in a neatly tucked company shirt and automatically assume I was with law enforcement. I suppose I should have been more cautious at the time; after all, I could have knocked on a door where people shoot first and ask questions later. However, it didn't bother me. I thought it was funny—and I got a sale!

LIFE LESSON 51:
A GOOD SENSE OF HUMOR IS PRICELESS

Although I am certainly saddened by tragedy and hardship, I have been able to retain my sense of humor even in the most stressful situations, and sometimes especially in the most stressful situations, many of which are ridiculous when you think about it.

Perhaps what's best about a good sense of humor is that it gets you completely out of your head and can often neutralize a highly toxic situation. That's why so many stand-up comedians joke about controversial topics and taboo subjects, such as prejudice, cancer, terrorism, and sex. The tension is there, and the laughter breaks the tension.

I find that a good sense of humor also makes me more confident and comfortable. If I can laugh at a situation I'm in, such as getting frisked by prospective customers, my demeanor is such that people are more likely to buy what I'm selling.

A Challenging Mentee

While I was in Harrisburg, I roomed with one of the sales executives I had trained in another state. He and I had shared a room before, and I knew when I hired him that he did drugs, but I didn't know to what extent.

When he first started, he was doing exceedingly well, but then I noticed that his sales started to slip, and I wondered what was going on. When I asked him about it, he told me he was dealing with some personal matters so I didn't pry. Later, I found out that he was far deeper into drugs than I had suspected.

Like me, his family lived far away, and he was pretty much on his own, except for the few people on our team. Unfortunately, he wasn't much of a talker, so he kept his feelings inside, which is the worst thing to do when you're struggling. The less he talked, the more negative he became, and our customers could sense it.

One day, I noticed that he had no sales for a few days, which was strange for someone who had been performing well. Over time, his performance continued to drop. So one night after work, when we were all driving back to our apartment, I gave my troubled roommate some advice about a new technique he could use to shift his focus from anything negative happening in his personal life and, as a result, boost his sales. I knew the owner would let him go soon if his sales didn't improve, and I knew from my own experience that he was in a vicious cycle that would be challenging to break. I had already witnessed that the more he stressed over his personal problems, the more negative he became. The more negative he became, the deeper his sales slump, which added to his growing collection of problems—giving him even more to be stressed out about. In an attempt to break the cycle, he did drugs, which temporarily relieved the stress but added to his problems, both in number and severity. I knew that the only solution was to shift his thinking.

As his mentor, I shared one of my techniques—that once you stop a negative thought, you must replace it with a positive thought, and you must do this on a consistent basis until it becomes an unconscious habit. I also told him to slow down on the drugs because they slow down the brain's ability to control our thoughts in the long term, and because the drugs he was doing were extremely destructive and dangerous, and I didn't want him overdosing. I had met his mother when we roomed together in the past, and even she had reached out to me with concern. I told him I had promised his mother I was going to help him turn his life around—that if I could turn mine around when I was deep into drugs, so could he.

That's when things took a turn for the worse.

He started arguing with me and then pulled out a knife. He was sitting behind me and wrapped his arm around the seat, pressing the knife to my throat.

"I don't care," he shouted. "I'll take you out right now and then kill myself too!"

My heart began to pound, but it's in these moments that emotional fitness comes in handy. The wrong word or movement could have cost me my life, but I didn't focus on the fear of death. Instead, I stayed calm and asked myself two powerful questions: *What outcome do I want for this bad situation?* and *What else could this mean?*

The answer to the first question was that I wanted both of us to be safe and calm, and for my mentee to shift his thinking to more positive thoughts. For whatever reason, I also felt confident that the outcome would be positive and that we were going to be okay. The answer to the second question was that the greater meaning revolved around the fact that my mentee was hurting deeply.

I took a deep breath and said, "You don't want to do this, because that's not who you are at your core. You have a heart full of love, joy, and passion underneath any thoughts you may be thinking right now. Before it got to this point, it was good. The dark will pass, and you know it. You've succeeded before, and you can do it again. Your mother and sister, and my mother, brother, and grandma, depend on us to earn money to help them. You and I both have people who depend on us for their survival. Killing us both won't solve the problem. It will just burden our families, and I know that's the last thing you want to do."

Slowly, he put down the knife and retreated.

LIFE LESSON 52:
TREAD CAREFULLY AROUND UNSTABLE PEOPLE

When I offered advice to my mentee, I made at least three mistakes. I wish I knew what I know now, but my nineteen-year-old self was a rookie.

First, I should have realized the state he was in; he was hurting, frustrated, and fearful—all feelings that can quickly turn to anger. Second, I should not have advised him in the car in front of our other roommate, because it probably hurt his pride—another factor that can fuel anger. Finally, I should have been very careful in choosing my words, so they would more likely be perceived as advice rather than criticism, although in the state he was in, he probably would have perceived any advice as criticism.

I am not trying to excuse my mentee's actions or blame the victim (me) here. I only provide this advice to help you avoid situations that can blow up on you. When people are unstable, remaining calm and asking better questions to deeply understand their world and where they come from is much more effective than confrontation.

I was fortunate that I was able to talk my mentee down calmly and avert yet another attempt on my life. But it was at that moment that I realized I couldn't help everyone, as much as I wanted to. Sometimes people like where they are; they're comfortable and don't want to change. They may adopt a few new practices for a while, but if they have one bad week or month and let the negative, limiting beliefs of scarcity creep in, they fall right back into their old patterns.

In sales, when all of that negativity swirls around in a person's brain, they become unable to connect with their clients. The old adage that "people buy from people they like" is true, and when a salesperson stops liking himself, he becomes joyless, and few people (if any) will buy from someone with a negative attitude.

LIFE LESSON 53:
YOU MUST BELIEVE IT TO SEE IT

* *

The old saying, "I'll believe it when I see it" should be reversed to: "I'll see it when I believe it." Whether you are trying to defuse a bad situation or create something good, you must have faith and conviction in the desired outcome.

I was able to remain calm and confident while my mentee was holding a knife to my throat because I had no doubt that everything was going to turn out okay. Had I been afraid or doubtful, chances are pretty good I would have done or said something that would have amplified my mentee's hurt, fear, and frustration and stirred up more anger.

When it comes to faith, I always tell people that you don't need more faith when you experience a hardship; you simply need to exercise the faith you have. The key lesson here is that I was confident in the outcome and calm the entire time my mentee had snapped. I wasn't merely hoping it would be okay. I knew.

Heading South

After having the knife held to my throat, the owner of the company decided to move six of his veterans, including me, to Florida. The decision to move was not difficult; I loved Florida, and as I've mentioned before, I always find new opportunities thrilling.

Florida was paradise for me. It felt like I was back in Brazil, but much safer. I believed I could start a family there without having to worry about my future wife and kids being kidnapped or threatened in an extortion scheme—an all too common occurrence in Brazil. Florida is also the state in which the most Brazilians live because the climate is similar, so I was able to find plenty of stores selling Brazilian goodies and numerous restaurants that served traditional Brazilian cuisine.

My colleagues and I rented a home in Hollywood, Florida, about forty-five minutes from Miami. Yes, we worked hard, but it was also our party house!

LIFE LESSON 54:
ALL WORK AND NO PLAY WILL FRY YOUR BRAIN

Becoming successful requires hard work, but it also requires some time to relax and recharge your batteries. Set aside some time for fun. If you don't, mental fatigue will creep in, and your mind will have trouble making even the most basic decisions.

Working and having an awesome time, my colleagues and I made more than enough money to pay our bills and cover our other financial responsibilities. We had mastered the door to door, telemarketing, and marketing sales game and knew exactly how to sell our products faster, working fewer hours in the field and training others to do the same.

Perils of Success

As soon as sales took off and we had plenty of money coming in, we fell into the all too familiar pattern of working during the week and partying like crazy on the weekends. I quickly became like everyone around me—content to pay the bills, support my family, and live paycheck to paycheck. Even worse, I succumbed to spending money I didn't even have. I had embraced the concept of play now pay later, which is how so many people become prisoners of debt.

Worse yet, I ceased doing what I had been doing to achieve this level of success. I stopped reading, asking questions, seeking direction from my mentor, and spending time to refocus on my goal and objectives and evaluate my progress. And because I stopped learning, I became stagnant. Although I continued to perform very well in sales, I was setting myself up for future failure by not engaging in continuous self-development.

I knew at the time that I had become a reflection of my peer group; they earned a lot of money and then blew it on parties, and I did the same. But in becoming content with this way of life, I made the worst mistake anyone can make. You can't be content and stop growing. Not in this fast paced environment. It's crucial to consistently seek guidance, ways to grow, and mentorship from others who have been living the lifestyle you dream of having. So, at a certain point, I decided to cut back on my partying and refocus on personal development and reaching out more often to my mentor. As a result, I returned my attention to the things that truly mattered: accelerating my growth in sales, recruiting, helping others in need, and saving money.

Tragedy Strikes Again

In August of 2003, after regaining my mojo, I was doing great. Then, I received some devastating news. My mother called me from Brazil to tell me that my stepfather had been murdered. He had loaned some money to a friend who owned a small farm. That same friend called my stepfather one day long after borrowing the money and told him to come get the money he was owed. When the two met, that man pulled out a gun and shot my stepfather.

It was the second time my mother had lost the man she loved, but she managed to remain strong. She has an incredible ability to shift her thinking, and she has always been a master at handling bad situations and turning things around. As we were growing up, my brother and I were the beneficiaries of her talents. On countless occasions, when we were experiencing hard times, she shifted our thinking and made sure that neither of us had time to wallow in negativity.

LIFE LESSON 55:
DON'T GIVE YOURSELF TIME TO BE MISERABLE. INSTEAD, CELEBRATE EVERYTHING AND REMIND YOURSELF THAT YOU ARE ENOUGH

Idle hands are the devil's workshop in more ways than one. When idle, a person is more prone to getting into trouble but is also prone to becoming miserable as the mind begins to overanalyze.

A key secret to a happy life is to stay busy. If you schedule a sixteen-hour day in time blocks to remain in a "must fun mode" as I call it, you'll be happier and more productive. What's more, you won't have time to waste on limiting beliefs.

Each day, be sure you have something fun and productive to do, or something you love to do (or can make fun to do). Take your kids to the park or some other fun place, read a book, take a five-minute break to meditate or pray, drop your kids off at daycare for a little quiet time for yourself, take some type of martial arts classes, go to the dry cleaner, go shopping. All these activities are productive uses of your time blocks, and you can make them all fun—even the most mundane ones—by celebrating them.

Most people who come to my company for help—from CEOs to entrepreneurs to stay-at-home moms and dads who want become a coach, consultant, or speaker—are struggling to enjoy life to the fullest, because they're completely absorbed in helping everyone else. This subjects them to an incredible burden of stress that results in burnout and gets them stuck in a rut. As such, I advise them to function in "must fun mode" and bring joy to everything they do.

Although we grieved for my stepfather, his death introduced a greater mental and emotional challenge: he had been murdered, and in Brazil, that meant somebody had to avenge his death—a tradition that served only to create more misery and chaos.

My brothers, uncles, and thirteen-year-old brother wanted to kill the man, which would have destroyed my brother's life. As everyone seemed to be in reaction mode, and being protective of my little brother, I felt responsible for helping to prevent him from doing something stupid. So I packed my bags and was ready to fly to Brazil when my mother called and told me not to risk it. I, too, had strong reservations about returning to Brazil—I was afraid I would never be allowed back into the U.S. I still had immigrant status and didn't have legal papers at that time. But I was even more afraid of what would happen if my brother killed that farmer. Luckily, the killer became a fugitive, so my presence would have done no good. My mother reminded me that my family would suffer more if I returned and lost my career. So in place of flying to South America, I talked to my brother over the phone, urging him to consider how his father would have responded, which would have been something along the lines of, "Calm your ass down! One of your uncles is probably going to handle it anyway."

After we spoke, however, I remained worried that my brother would set out to look for the fugitive, and I felt powerless to stop him. Fortunately, my mother called again to give me some good news: the fugitive had fled the state. Since there was no longer a risk of my brother going to look for him, I decided to stay put.

Months later, that fugitive was caught and thrown in prison. My decision to remain in the U.S. had been the right one, and I was able to regain my focus and start working again at peak efficiency.

LIFE LESSON 56:
IT'S BETTER TO LAUGH THAN TO CRY

A few months after my stepfather's funeral, my cousins started referring to my mother as the "black widow," because she had two husbands who had died. Of course, everyone knows that's inappropriate, but when my mother heard it, she laughed. In fact, our family motto is, "It's better to laugh than to cry." I told my younger brother not to allow the rude nickname to get to him or to feel anger or sadness about it. "If someone jokes about our mother," I said, "we will lead by example."

Yes, crying is okay for a little while, because we're only human, but eventually, you need to let go of whatever it is you're sad about or address the issue or situation that's making you sad. Although the old saying "Crying doesn't help" isn't entirely true, it mostly is, especially if your sadness is preventing you from living a life of happiness and fulfillment.

Every time you feel particularly sad, try doing this: Close your eyes and think about one of the best, most memorable moments in your life, a time when you laughed uncontrollably or an accomplishment you felt sincerely proud of. Make that feeling as vivid as though you're experiencing it all over again right now. With your eyes still closed, imagine taking four photos of that moment from four different angles and printing them. Now imagine having a magic stick that you wave to make the photos the size of a movie theater screen, then make the images brighter and even more beautiful. Picture storing those images and the feelings they evoke in your watch or a piece of jewelry, so you carry them with you at all times.

If you perform this exercise each time you feel sad, you can learn to break the pattern of thought that created the sadness and switch to an empowering belief.

CHAPTER 6

Leaps of Faith

*Only those who will risk going too far
can possibly find out how far one can go.*
—T. S. Eliot

After all the madness of my stepfather's murder had passed, the owner of the company I worked for came to Florida and asked me if I wanted to move to California. He wanted to start another system for hiring and training new people to sell and install our packages, and I was a top candidate. I told him no at first, because I loved Florida, but my inner voice kept pushing me to make the move. That voice reminded me of my commitment to keep growing and taking on new challenges.

My boss told me that I had nothing to lose and everything to gain, but that wasn't entirely true. I would lose my entire network of clients to whom I had already sold, and I wouldn't be allowed to place orders in Florida any longer. I didn't agree with that rule because I thought it was bad for me and bad for business. It also caused a lot of turnover. In fact, when people were transferred to another state, they would often quit because moving meant leaving their hometown and starting over.

The prospect of moving from the East Coast to the West Coast was scary, because I was comfortable in Florida and had no idea of what to expect in California. I was young, earning good money, and living near the beach; it doesn't get much better than that. However, I had reached a plateau, and I knew from past experience that plateaus could be dangerous for me. Because comfort tends to seduce me into a mindset of complacency that stunts growth, I've found that when I start to feel too comfortable, it's time to mix things up a bit. So I asked myself questions about my current situation: *Is this the best I can do?* and *Will this get me where I want to be?* The answer to both was no, so I started leaning toward saying yes to the question of whether to move to California.

Then my boss sweetened the pot. He offered to pay for my hotel—which was only a half mile from the corporate office in El Segundo, a Los Angeles suburb—for six months. My job would be the same as it had been everywhere else—selling cable television, Internet, and home phone service to new customers and recruiting and training others. I was great at sales, but my boss was even better at selling me this offer. I said yes, and that turned out to be the best decision I had ever made (up to that point in time).

LIFE LESSON 57:
GIVE MORE WEIGHT TO THE PROS
THAN TO THE CONS
• •

With every choice comes a certain degree of uncertainty, which can generate fear that triggers the fight, flight, or freeze response. When you feel relatively comfortable and opportunity knocks, often what happens is that concerns about what you have to lose eclipse the hopes of what you can potentially gain. Two fears kick in—the fear of loss and the fear of the unknown. To overcome that double dose of fear, give more weight to the potential benefits than you do to

the possible drawbacks. Otherwise, you may miss out on the
best thing that could ever happen to you.

A New Challenge: Gangs

Back in 2004, high-tech navigation wasn't as good or as available as it is today, so I went old school, using traditional maps to plot my routes, which helped me learn back roads and shortcuts to beat traffic. In Los Angeles, my team worked in the El Segundo, Long Beach, Santa Monica, Compton, East Los Angeles, and downtown areas, and one of the biggest problems we faced was harassment from gang members in certain areas.

After receiving regular calls from my guys complaining about being stopped and questioned by gangs, I was determined to teach my team how to sell more effectively in these neighborhoods. After all, I'd had plenty of experience with this. So I told them to keep an eye out for gang members and anyone who looked like a drug dealer (nice car, lots of jewelry), and that they were easy to spot because they usually hung out on the streets checking out everyone else.

Then I took it a step further.

I told my salespeople to approach the gangsters and say, "Hey, guys, I'm the cable guy, my name is so and so, and I'll be in the area for the next couple days hooking everybody up with cable and offering special deals. Even if you guys have a balance with your current provider, we have specials to legally wipe out that balance and hook you up with new services, so you can have some entertainment for your family. As a bonus, I'll throw in HBO and Playboy. Please let everyone you know I'll be in the area so they don't confuse me with someone from a gang from another area, okay? I can easily take care of everyone who wants our service installed."

But my team wouldn't do it.

Being stared down by intimidating gang members, they would go blank and show weakness, which is understandable. But if you do that on the streets of L.A., they will eat you alive and rob you, or at least give you a really hard time.

With my experience dealing with thugs, I knew that the first thing to do was learn which gangs ran each area and try to spot the person who looked like he ran the show on each block. After identifying each gang's turf, I approached their leaders to explain exactly what we were doing—bringing better TV and communication services to their neighborhoods. My Brazilian accent and my smile were enough for them not to shoot me on sight. They actually told me I had a lot of courage for approaching them. It was not actually courage, though; it was reason and respect. I knew we needed the gangs' approval if we were to sell successfully in those neighborhoods, and all they really wanted was recognition of that fact and assurance that we posed no risk to whatever activities they were engaged in.

What Americans call "ghetto" in the United States is middle-class in Brazil. Because I was used to violence way worse than any that happens here, I knew you couldn't show fear. Fear makes you look vulnerable, and thugs harass and rob vulnerable people.

LIFE LESSON 58:
FEAR IS A PRODUCT OF THE MIND THAT INFLUENCES DECISIONS AND BEHAVIOR

* *

Fear is solely in the mind, but it finds expression through your demeanor and behavior. You can amplify it by focusing on it, or diminish it by ignoring it. If you begin to feel afraid, don't focus on the fear or what is triggering that fear. Shift your focus from what's out of your control to what's in your control. For example, if you're walking down the street and you feel afraid of a group of people walking toward you, focus on your destination. If you're changing a flat tire in a bad neighborhood, focus on changing the tire. If you start thinking of all the possible threats, you will be thinking about and looking for trouble, and you'll be more likely to find it, or it will be more likely to find you.

Follow this same philosophy when starting a new job or a business. Don't let fear of failure or the unknown cripple you. Accept that you will feel uncomfortable at times, but you must continue to move forward with full certainty that you already won, independent of how uncertain it feels. You must bring all you have—full presence and your most courageous self—to every situation. Your confidence affects your energy and what you project to the world. There's no other way to succeed.

Another tactic we used when selling in certain neighborhoods was to blend in. Our sales team embraced diversity, so we had team members who were Latin, African American, Asian, and so on, and we assigned team members to neighborhoods accordingly. As a result, my team became significantly more productive. In fact, our sales tripled—from one hundred sales per week to three hundred! Corporate managers were so impressed that they gave me access to special promotions not available to the masses, along with a technical team to help with installations if we got too many orders.

LIFE LESSON 59:
BEHIND EVERY PROBLEM IS AN OPPORTUNITY
● ●

Whenever my sales team encountered a problem, we shifted our focus to solutions and we found opportunities. We knew that achieving the highest level of success required innovation, so we embraced that and tried different approaches to making sales. What's interesting is that most of the methods that boosted our sales most significantly were free. All we needed to do was to focus on our objectives and think of ways to achieve them.

Sometimes all you need to do to improve performance is to go back to the basics and analyze your life, career, or business structure. Find any areas in which you can improve. Ask: Am I investing too much in one area at the expense of another? Is one area weaker than the others? What obstacles are standing in my way? What are the possible solutions for overcoming those obstacles?

Conquering Fresno, Merced, and Modesto

In using the same innovative philosophy when I sold cable in other states, the corporate leaders at Comcast fell in love with my team and me as well as the subcontracting company I was working for. Because we were earning a lot of money for Comcast, its higher-ups asked us to work through the entire state. After just six months in Los Angeles, we moved about two hundred miles northwest to Fresno to start another system.

Though I continued to improve my skills and was the top salesperson in the company, I was aware of the risks inherent in staying on that plateau—complacency had been deadly in the past, so I needed to continue to improve. As a result, I set my sights on breaking records, which I love to do, always striving to surpass my personal best. I see myself, not others, as my competition, so I constantly look for ways to outcompete myself. To do this, I imagine being a competing company trying to put myself out of business, determined not to lose. With this approach, I tend to break my records. And even when I don't, simply striving to do so always produces remarkable results.

LIFE LESSON 60:
COMPETE WITH YOURSELF

* *

A secret to staying at the top of your game is to compete with yourself. Imagine you have a twin who is outperforming you, living the life you dreamed of, while you and your family struggle to make ends meet. What would you do? Would you just let it happen, or would you try to learn from your sibling and do better for yourself and your family? There's nothing wrong with a little healthy competition—it has kept me at the top of my game for years.

So go for it and try to take yourself out of business. Challenge yourself daily to ask better questions and foster new conversations in your marketplace that your competitors aren't. Raise the necessity and watch the magic happen.

In Fresno, I had to build another team by recruiting and training people to work on commission. I chose people without much formal education—many with criminal backgrounds and in whom no one else believed—and gave them opportunities to make more money than college graduates, assuming they followed my guidance from A to Z. In helping them realize that they didn't have to sell drugs or hustle in order to become successful, I taught them how to become what I call "executive hustlers"—individuals who start from nothing and work at their crafts until they become successful.

After we did so well in Fresno, the company moved us to Merced and Modesto to start new systems. As always, our team produced amazing results. Just like before, we were able to adapt instantly to each new area by connecting with the population of that area and consistently delivering above and beyond customer expectations. It didn't matter where we worked. We made it happen.

Of course, it didn't hurt that we loved the products we sold. We were bringing quality entertainment, speedy Internet, and more affordable phone service into every home we sold to, and we were offering a generous free-trial period. We couldn't believe that anyone in their right mind would say no, and that made a huge difference. Clients can tell when you're enthusiastic and passionate about a product or service; after all, if *you're* not excited about it, why would they buy it? This is especially true when you're selling to people face to face. The clients can't help but feel your excitement—or not.

One of the things my team was skilled at was making a great first impression, which can make or break a sale. Most people know that if you're not confident in your organization, your product, or yourself, your clients will sense it, and your chances of closing deals with them will dwindle. As such, we always showed up confident, professional, friendly, knowledgeable, and eager to please. We also knew our competition. We studied their products, services, offers, and the changes they were making, so we knew what we were up against at all times. As a result, we could anticipate any new client's objections to our products and why they might choose a competing product over ours.

LIFE LESSON 61:
FIND A JOB THAT DOESN'T FEEL LIKE WORK

I have always had a job I loved. When I sold cable TV, Internet, and phone services, I loved my work so much that I couldn't believe I could earn so much money doing it! I didn't mind working long hours six or seven days a week to support my family, my causes, and myself.

Most people end up at a job they don't like, working forty hours a week their entire lives. Why not work extra long hours for a few years doing something you truly enjoy to achieve the life you want? Yes, you may have to accept some positions along the way that are not exactly what you have always dreamed of doing. If that's the case, then put in forty hours a week and enjoy what you're doing, because it is providing you with the money to support yourself and your family and finance your dream. When you're not working that job, devote another twenty to thirty hours a week in pursuit of the career or business you've always wanted. As long as you have a dream, the time and effort you exert to achieve it won't feel so much like work.

Changing Teams

As independent contractors selling for Comcast, we were the best in the business, outselling independent contractors who were selling DISH Network and other competing products. To remain competitive, the owner of the DISH Network contract began recruiting members of my sales team, and more than half left to work for their company as independent contractors. DISH offered higher compensation and more attractive promotions, and eventually, the contract owner reached out to me, offering a bigger override for me to lead my old team. (An override is a commission paid to a manager on the sales of the people working under him.) It was a sweet deal, so I accepted. Only later would I discover that I had made a mistake.

Comcast had made some changes to their system, including requiring full credit checks and upfront collection on all sales, which made it harder to sell, because a large number of our clients were immigrants. Selling for DISH on the other hand was easy; they offered a three-month trial period and didn't require social security numbers, credit checks, or upfront credit card payments. Two months after my team started selling for DISH, however, they changed their policy. Because we were acquiring so many clients, they also began requiring that customers provide social security numbers. Unfortunately, the Latin immigrant customers—who had no social security numbers—were out of luck, and so were we. Whether my team was tricked or simply a victim of a policy change did not matter; our sales dropped, and we struggled.

LIFE LESSON 62:
BE VERY CAREFUL WHEN THE COMPETITION MAKES AN OFFER THAT SEEMS TOO GOOD TO BE TRUE

• •

If you love the company you work for and the job you're doing, be very careful when a competing company recruits you and dangles sweet offers. They may be less interested in you and more interested in destroying the competitor you're working for. As a result, you may be better off staying put or at least letting your current employer know what's going on and giving them a chance to match the recruiter's offer.

Our decision to move to the DISH contractor was a huge mistake. Even if we wanted to return to Comcast, it was too late. The Comcast contract owner we had been working for lost his contract because his sales dropped. To make matters worse, my teammates and I were renting an apartment from him, and he gave us only ten days to move out. With no job, no prospects, and no place to live, we were in a bad spot for sure. I had to act fast since I was going to be homeless in less than ten days. I was able to find a sofa to sleep on at a friend's home that wanted to hire me for door to door satellite TV sales.

My team members were all being overly negative and turning to drugs instead of facing the crisis, but I had seen worse, and that gave me the mindset to persevere. It would have taken a lot more than what had just transpired to darken my mood. When I found myself starting to have negative thoughts, I used my sixty-second rule: I closed my eyes for sixty seconds and imagined myself in a much happier situation. When I opened my eyes, I was in a better place in both mind and spirit.

Finding the Love of My Life

There is no such thing as coincidence when it comes to finding the love of your life. What might seem like a coincidence is actually destiny, and I met my destiny, Angie, on a Saturday night.

It was after a long day at work, and I was tired. My business partner wanted to go out clubbing, and I told him no. My buddies loved it when I went out with them because once I had regained my signature positive attitude, I was good at lifting everyone's mood and pumped energy into every outing. With some prodding, they ended up convincing me to go out with them.

Angie almost didn't go out that night because her mother always worried and was very protective. But despite the guilt her mother laid on her, Angie went out anyway. She had just gotten out of a nine-year relationship a month earlier, so she wanted to have a good time. Thank God she defied her mother's wishes that night!

I saw her from across the room, and we locked eyes as if we were in a movie. It may sound trite, but it was love at first sight, and the little voice in my head encouraged me to go talk to her. She agreed to dance with me, but when I leaned in to sniff the fragrance near her neck and then kissed it, she pulled away. My "vampire kiss" was moving too fast for her. She even gave me a wrong number when I asked for her phone number. But before leaving the club, something prompted her to give me the right number, and we went out again a couple of days later, thus starting our incredible journey together.

Angie and I had at least one thing in common: we had both come to the U.S. at a very young age. In fact, Angie's mother had come to America from Mexico when she was pregnant, so Angie was born in California. Angie's mother had also lost her husband at a young age the way my mother had. Left with six kids to raise on her own, she came to America to build a better life for herself and her children. As a single mother, she was understandably overprotective, especially in situations involving women and children (particularly her own).

On Angie's and my second date, we went to a movie. When her mother, sister, and brother showed up at the same theater, I thought it was a setup to spy on us. It turned out to be merely an odd coincidence—when I met her family, they were all humble and gracious, and I loved them instantly.

Everything was going wonderfully in our relationship, but my career was still on the skids. With no job or money coming in, I had to make something happen soon. Having made some bad investments in Brazil, I had also lost all my savings I'd worked so hard to build up over the years. Starting over was nothing new to me, however, so I refused to lose confidence.

LIFE LESSON 63:
THERE ARE ALWAYS OPTIONS

• •

Starting from scratch doesn't mean that all is lost. There are always options. As I've said before, you can get cheap clothing from the Salvation Army and free food from government programs and local food pantries. Survival isn't that difficult, especially in the U.S. The real trick is to visualize yourself during a time of hardship as having accomplished your objectives and achieved your goal. You must ask yourself, "What do I bring to the table that is unique and different than everybody else?" "What made me effective in the past?" For me, I knew it was sales, marketing, mentoring, coaching, and beating my sales quota by raising the necessity and simply getting things done. So I knew the number-one thing was to not focus on the negative, regardless of how difficult my situation might be. To put myself in a more positive frame of mind, I would tell myself, "I've seen worse, and others are worse off. I'll figure this out again."

Not long after I lost my job at DISH Network, another cable and communications company contacted me about an opportunity to work in the San Francisco Bay area, but it was a hundred miles from where Angie lived. I had been out of a job for a few weeks and didn't have a choice. Afraid that Angie might not agree to a long-distance relationship, I took the gamble nonetheless and she agreed to it. Despite the fact that remote relationships rarely work—at least that's what typically happens—she knew I had to make a living and that this was one of those opportunities I shouldn't pass up. So I accepted the position and was back selling cable TV door to door, which I loved. Even better, I believed I had found my soul mate!

One year later, Angie and I were married in a courthouse. Seven months afterward, we had a big wedding in Brazil. Though I had promised myself I wouldn't return to Brazil until I was financially stable, this situation was special—I was about to formally marry the love of my life. I went all out for Angie, reserving a beautiful basilica where only rich people get married. (In fact, that same weekend, Ms. Brazil got married in the same church.) I was filled with joy and gratitude, and I was proud of being able to hold our wedding in such a beautiful and sacred place. Getting married there was a wonderful dream come true.

Best of all, I was marrying the most beautiful woman in the world to me—both inside and out. I knew I couldn't have been luckier to have her as my best friend and future mother of my kids.

After we returned from Brazil, we moved into a cozy and humble studio apartment, and a new journey began.

LIFE LESSON 64:
INNER BEAUTY IS MORE IMPORTANT

My wife is beautiful inside and out, but of the two, her inner beauty is more important and lasting. Those who focus solely on appearance usually end up alone or unhappy. The choice of whom to spend the rest of your life with is the most important choice you will ever make. Choose carefully.

CHAPTER 7

Struggling to Achieve My Work-Life Balance

> *Success without fulfillment is the ultimate failure.*
> —Tony Robbins

In April, 2007, just a few months after Angie and I were married, I was offered a salary plus commission job at Comcast. The corporate office had noticed that I was working diligently as a contractor and racking up some crazy sales numbers—fifty to seventy-five per week when everyone else was averaging fifteen to thirty. So one day, during a meeting at the contracting company I was working for, a guy by the name of Robert came in from corporate to conduct training and we connected right away.

I asked him a number of questions about how we could improve customer service and get the service installed faster for our customers. He loved my attitude and the questions I asked, and we exchanged phone numbers. Long story short, he advised me to apply for a job as a direct sales representative. The application process was elaborate; it was as though I was applying for a job with the National Security Agency (NSA). I had to fill out forms, go through a series of interviews, and endure long waiting periods. What's more, I had to compete against people with far more advanced degrees than the one I had (a high school diploma from Brazil). But I had something they didn't: my tenacity and certainty to acquire the position. Full of energy and determined not to lose, I embraced my hunger to win, my drive to put our competitors out of business, and my constant motivation to out-compete myself—all things that no university could teach.

I envisioned myself doing the job, complete with a 30-, 60-, and 90-day plan with detailed steps on what we needed to do to succeed. I was already visualizing and suggesting ways to implement ideas for offering greater customer value and improving services, and I went into every interview confident that the job was mine.

When, after multiple interviews, they offered me the job, I was thrilled that I would be working directly for the company and no longer for a contractor. I accepted the offer, and it was one of the best decisions I ever made, second only to my decision to marry Angie.

When I started working for Comcast, I followed every lead, and I refused to pass by any door without knocking, which was an enthusiastic outlook my bosses loved. Though I had learned long ago how to work smarter, not harder, I nonetheless knocked on every door myself for three years in my area before I shifted to boosting sales in a more productive way. In order to maximize my sales, I realized I needed to grow my network and start making warm calls instead of cold calls. After all, I could knock on only so many doors a day—it was better to knock on doors where people were more likely to say yes.

So I began harvesting leads from my existing customers, asking if they knew people who had recently moved or were about to move, as well as people they knew who used a competitor's services. With basic information on the referral in hand, I would call the prospective customer. In addition, I started networking with all the leasing and real estate agents in my area to help with their move-ins and technical matters, teaching them about the most exciting features of our products and how we differentiated from our competitors. I also went around to all of the restaurants in town and asked them to set out my business cards for their customers. It was all about mutually beneficial networking—and positioning ourselves a step above anything the competition had to offer.

I networked everywhere I could. For example, standing in line at the pharmacy, I would hand someone my card and say, "If you ever move or need to get a new service, call me, because I treat my clients like family." I had different pitches depending on where I was, but one thing was constant: I did treat my clients like family. If they had a billing error or if a technician showed up late, they would call me because I was so committed to delivering an exceptional customer experience beyond what they had ever encountered, they knew I'd take care of it.

But my dedication did pay off. After only a few weeks of selling cable services, I was making two to three times as many sales as anyone else. The small things I did made all the difference—answering the phone after hours, returning phone calls, following up, and anything else that exceeded my customers' expectations.

LIFE LESSON 65:
TAKE CARE OF THE PEOPLE WHO TAKE CARE OF YOU
• •

Few people achieve success on their own; they require other people to accomplish their goals. With this in mind, be sure you take care of these other people. For example, if you're in sales, reward the people in your referral network. In my case, I knew all of my leasing agents and treated them like family. While my competitors would give entire VIP suites in stadiums as gifts to those same leasing agents, I would surprise them by bringing them coffee or pizza. Though that may seem like small potatoes compared to box seats, getting to know the leasing agents personally proved to be more effective.

Likewise, if you have clients who provide you with work projects, get to know them and their families. Take a genuine interest in their lives, and try to help them in any way you can. If you have affiliates who sell your products, sponsor promotions to help drive their sales. If you have employees, be generous; provide them with incentives to improve their performance and reward and recognize their accomplishments. If you are a coach or consultant, offer a free two- to four-session beta program for business owners or anyone in need and help them achieve positive results. Whether you help them reach a breakthrough that saves their marriage, information that can help a relative who's struggling, or advice on how to improve their business, they will appreciate the gift. And when it comes time for them to hire a coach or consultant, guess who they'll call? You! Remember, it's about contribution, not acquisition. It's about the mission, not the commission. Take care of people, and they'll hire you and recommend you to everyone they know.

I love winning, but what I love even more is to see my clients and team winning, because that creates impact beyond my business. With that motivation in mind, I took the initiative to teach my system to several of the company's new managers so that they could duplicate it for the rest of the organization, making it a win for everyone. I also brought to their attention the fact that they were having too many meetings and that the meetings were too long, both of which were preventing the sales teams from achieving their quotas. Instead, I suggested training underperforming employees in the field to analyze and address their specific areas of weakness, and the company agreed it would be more productive.

My plan was to work strategically harder for three to five years and pretend that Comcast was *my* business—that I was the owner. As such, I surrounded myself with mentors and high-performance employees to continue upgrading my skill set to grow my business and consistently produce outstanding results.

I was earning some crazy commissions—around $500 to $800 a day six days a week—so work was going wonderfully. And that was not even counting my stock options or the entire package plus salary. But I was a newlywed, and I wanted to spend more time with my wife. The problem was that I had hardwired myself to work long hours. Despite having a wife I adored, I was so focused on work that over time I began to neglect Angie and my responsibilities at home. It's not uncommon that as we focus on one aspect of our lives, we neglect others. But we must be cognizant that if we focus on work and making money, and we forget to take care of ourselves and our loved ones, we neglect the very reason we work so hard in the first place.

So as you work toward achieving your dreams, keep your *why* in front of you and remind yourself what's important. If you consistently ask yourself, *What is that one thing worth fighting for at the end of the day?*, you'll be much more likely to prioritize the things that matter most.

LIFE LESSON 66:
WORK TO LIVE, DON'T LIVE TO WORK

• •

Be careful with the amount of time you focus on your job. If you feel as though you spend too much time at work and are often thinking about work when you get home, you probably have an imbalance. Most of us, especially the overachievers among us, spend far more time thinking about work than about anything else.

I encourage you to establish a daily routine or ritual to create separation between work and home. For example, whenever my workday ends, I say to myself, I love my family, and I'm grateful for the happiness we share. The time I'm about to spend with them is precious. I can't wait! When I do this, my mind instantly shifts from work to home and family.

You also want to disconnect from any chaos and bring your best self by asking, "How can I be the best spouse/parent/ son/daughter I can be?" You don't have to use the same wording specifically, but you should have some question or internal statement that creates a clear break between your work life and your home life.

You can take this same approach when you're heading to work too. Say something out loud like, "I love my job and the work I do. The time I spend at work is productive and rewarding. I can't wait to get started." Then ask yourself, "How can I be the best at what I'm doing at work today?"

When I started with Comcast, one of my goals was to train its entire workforce. But because I was earning so much money as a sales executive, I was reluctant to quit the sales position and devote my time to training. I kept delaying the pursuit of my goal, waiting for the right time to make my move, and that right time never came. Because of Comcast's model, I could make more money in sales than in management or training, and I was so money-driven at the time, I lost sight of my goal. In continuing to work in the same position for years, I let promotions pass me by.

LIFE LESSON 67:
CONTENTMENT IS A LULLABY

• •

I contend that contentment is a lullaby; it will put you to sleep. In other words, when you start to feel too comfortable, you're probably not following your dreams, and you need to make a change. I had already mastered door to door sales and training, so I wasn't growing by staying in that sales position. I would have been better off taking a pay cut, moving up, and challenging myself to learn a new position.

Family Illness

The birth of our daughter in October 2011 was an awesome experience for me, and an exhausting and painful (and joyous) one for Angie, who had to endure twenty-four hours of labor due to complications. I could tell that Angie's pain was intense. Sweating profusely and breathing hard, she was giving it all she had. Fortunately, we had a veteran nurse to coach us, recommending several things we could do to help ensure a normal delivery without the need for surgery. (Angie mentioned later that her nurse, being six feet tall with a thick Russian accent and deep voice, was a little scary, but she knew what she was doing!) One of the nurse's suggestions was to tie a blanket in knots to facilitate pushing through the contractions. It was quite a sight with me holding one end while Angie pulled the other, our Amazonian nurse urging us on.

As the hours passed, we realized that Angie was giving birth to a real fighter. When our priceless Isabella finally entered the world, I was grateful she wasn't as big as I was when I was born—a baby T-rex at fourteen pounds! Isabella was the greatest gift I could ever imagine or hope for. Not wanting to miss a single moment, for the first time in my life since I'd left Brazil sixteen years earlier, I took three months off and worked on and off for three more months to help my Angie.

When I returned to work full-time, our newborn gave me an added incentive to perform at my very best. But it wasn't long before Isabella started having problems sleeping at night. She was not only tossing and turning and crying a lot, but she would randomly wake up screaming in the middle of the night, and she didn't sleep for any longer than a couple minutes at a time. I thought it was normal, because babies are notorious for keeping their parents up all night, but Angie knew something was wrong. Deeply concerned, we took Isabella to see several different doctors to find out what was going on.

The doctors ran tests and told us that everything was okay, that it was merely a stage she would grow out of when she turned a year old, but Angie wasn't convinced. She kept changing doctors because she believed there was something they weren't finding. Though I wasn't as committed as Angie was to finding the truth—like many people, I was trained to listen to the doctors and follow their advice—I accompanied her to as many appointments as I could. But because I had a lot of catching up to do at work, my focus was more there than at home. You know the saying, "Wherever your focus goes, your energy flows." Well, my energy was flowing mostly into work, hoping that Isabella's sleeping problem was indeed a stage that would pass soon. After dealing with the first five doctors, I actually began to think that Angie was overreacting.

However, after Isabella turned one, the madness continued. In fact, Isabella didn't sleep through the night for years. The burden of our daughter tossing, turning, crying, and screaming every few minutes fell mostly on Angie so that I could rest for work each day, but that meant Angie wasn't able to get the sleep she needed. Only on weekends was I able to help, and that simply wasn't enough.

The medical bills made matters worse. Though I had to work harder to pay the bills, however, I figured the more money I made, the more I could afford to take off work when I needed to in order to help Angie and Isabella. But the harder I worked, the more stressed out I became, and the more stressed and anxious Angie became because she was the one losing sleep nearly 24/7. The doctors continued telling us nothing was wrong, unable to explain why Isabella had so much trouble sleeping.

Ten different doctors later, we still had no answer.

It was clear this wasn't normal and that time wouldn't solve it.

For three long years, Angie conducted her own research and consulted with numerous doctors and other people she knew in an attempt to find out what was going on.

Finally, Angie had a breakthrough. After gathering so much information and advice that didn't work, she decided to follow her mother instinct: she asked that Isabella have an X-ray of her throat and nose. Doctors had ordered blood work and X-rays of her organs, but never of her throat and nose. With her frustration turned to exasperation, Angie demanded not only an X-ray but a nasal endoscopy (an examination of the nasal passages using a special camera). The doctor finally consented and instantly found something wrong: Isabella's tonsils and adenoids were obstructing her breathing at night—something we were grateful to learn that surgery could rectify.

While we were relieved to finally know what was causing the problem and to know it could be fixed, we were about to experience another setback. Isabella was fine when they wheeled her off to surgery, but something went wrong during the procedure and she lost a lot of blood. Thankfully, the surgical team was able to turn things around and she recovered. Immediately after the surgery, she stopped waking up screaming in the middle of the night.

But our nightmare wasn't completely over. Though Isabella wasn't waking up every few minutes, she continued to toss and turn and wake up every thirty minutes, crying or in terror. It was incredibly disappointing and frustrating, especially for Angie, because we expected the operation to put the ordeal to rest.

Despite our worry and angst over Isabella, Angie became pregnant again. But in the span of two months, she had a miscarriage—and I learned that my position would be eliminated.

LIFE LESSON 68:
TAKE CONTROL OF YOUR HEALTH

Doctors don't know everything, and they won't tell you everything you need to know. Some doctors are so busy, and the information so plentiful, that they cannot possibly keep up on all the latest research, and they rarely have the time to educate patients. Therefore, it's up to you to do your research, ask questions, and draw your own conclusions about what is best for your health and the health of your family. The Internet makes it easier than ever—but do make sure you're getting your information from reliable medical sources. And one more thing: if you have any reason to doubt a doctor's recommendation, get a second or third opinion; it never hurts to have the benefit of another person's perspective. In our case, we had over ten "second" opinions with no answers, which is why it's vital to never give up searching for answers on your own.

Another Blow

I had joked (and ended up sabotaging myself) by saying that Comcast could never afford for me to train the entire company, and sure enough, in January of 2015, I received some bad news: my position in the company was being eliminated. After making the company tens of millions of dollars, and being number one in sales and a consistent role model across the country, I thought my position was always going to be protected. I was wrong.

As I was reeling in the fact that no job is secure these days, I was given two options: 1) I could walk away with a $100,000 severance package for almost a decade of work; or 2) I could apply for an executive management position, making one third of what I had been making. Neither option was attractive, not only because of the money but also because I had built an incredible sales network over the years.

I made the decision to apply for an executive position within the company. They eventually offered it to me and I accepted. Seemingly in an instant, I went from earning almost $350,000 a year with all my benefits as a sales executive to $100,000, plus another $50,000 in bonuses and commissions to manage a new team. Although the pay was disappointing, I loved the people and was not going to let my new team down.

So I faced my fears, buried my anger, and decided to give this new opportunity a chance. For some reason, I have always liked the adrenaline rush that accompanies challenge, adversity, and uncertainty; meeting uncertainty with certainty has always been a game changer for me.

Wanting to prove that I could succeed in this new position, I applied the mindset of winning I was proud to possess. But I also learned the importance of having an exit strategy—whether you have a job or own your own business, nothing in life is certain, other than the thoughts you have and the choices you make. When I lost my sales position, I had few options and faced several roadblocks, and there didn't seem to be a favorable exit ramp in sight.

LIFE LESSON 69:
CHOOSE YOUR GOALS AND OBJECTIVES CAREFULLY

When I lost the senior marketing job at Comcast that I loved so much, I was at the top of my corporate career. I was making a lot of money—more than I ever had before. I had earned a few million in less than nine years. The problem was that I had started to value money so much that I forgot who I was; that poor, hungry kid from Brazil was lost. This problem was one I recognized in myself and numerous others I have mentored over the years: we often choose the wrong goal and ask ourselves the wrong questions. We start our journeys with the wrong definition of "success."

The key question I should have asked myself when I was poor and forming my vision of future success should have been this: What level of professional success do I need to achieve to support myself and my loved ones, enjoy time with my family and friends, and achieve self-fulfillment? Instead, I had started my journey with the wrong goal in mind, focused primarily on material success. As a result, I reached my destination, but it wasn't where I needed or wanted to be, since it was the wrong destination. Because I had the wrong goal to start with, when I was on my journey to success, I lost sight of what truly matters—personal relationships, family, health, spirituality, self-fulfillment, and so on.

So, when I lost my sales executive position, I felt as though I had lost everything, because that is all I really had (or thought I had). Had I attended to those other, more valuable aspects of my life, the loss of position would have been much less devastating.

As I pushed forward with my new executive manager position in corporate America, I was aware what the reason was my previous position had been eliminated and why hundreds of people had lost their jobs. This new position demanded a lot of my time because I not only had to train an entirely new team, I also had to ensure that our company didn't lose business during the restructuring of our department, I had to assure our existing business referral partners that everything was going to be fine.

Most people resist change, especially when the system is working fine as is; if it's not broken, why fix it? So it made everyone uneasy that we were eliminating entire departments with people who had established close relationships with our outside partners, partners who were responsible for a huge percentage of our business. The restructuring was maddening, but I remained calm and focused and kept pushing forward.

Finding out that I would be losing my sales executive position was a shock, but I didn't want to pass that to Angie. She had enough dealing with lack of sleep and our Isabella still tossing and turning all night long. I was the pillar of the house, and they both needed me. But I was so consumed with disappointment over having to take a position that paid much less that I lost sight of what was going on with Angie's health on a deeper level. I had assumed everything was going to be okay at home after the operation, but my work had created a blind spot. Everything was not okay.

More Fallout

Angie remained in guardian mode, on high alert and unable to sleep, terrified that something would happen to Isabella during the night. At that point, Angie had been dealing with the problem for four years, and her health was starting to deteriorate. The chronic stress and sleeplessness had taken its toll on both her mind and body. Her thinking had turned negative, and she had fallen into a dark depression.

I wasn't much better off. I was still working long days, and I was exhausted from four years of frustration from having a sick child doctors couldn't help. We had spent $100,000 on medical tests and treatments, but the money didn't matter—what irked me was having to pay so much for so little. I was in a business that paid for results, yet we received virtually none. I also found it increasingly difficult to keep my focus at work, where I had to train new teams and keep up with the whole restructuring of the business. It was a challenge, but I managed to do quite well, considering the circumstances.

In the meantime, Angie's health continued to decline. She didn't want to see a doctor for herself; she simply wanted Isabella to sleep, but her constant worrying contributed to her own sleep deprivation, making her spiral into a very dark place, both physically and psychologically.

One sunny Friday afternoon, I told my boss that I was going home an hour early to surprise my wife. But instead of surprising her, I found her sitting on the hardwood floor crying desperately for help. Trying to avert attention away from herself, she told me that she didn't want to stress me out with her problems, that she felt I already had too much on my plate. But after some concerned coaxing from me, she finally opened up and told me that she was becoming very sick. The sleep deprivation was causing her to have numerous health problems. The miscarriage, which was very difficult for her, was only part of it. She had developed anxiety and thyroid problems, and she had several thoughts of not wanting to live. "I don't feel like living anymore," she said to me tearfully. "I just wish God would take me and end all this suffering."

I sat there completely shocked. I had never expected to hear anything like that from her. It was then that I realized how blind I'd been about what the prolonged sleep deprivation, as well as dealing pretty much alone with our daughter's suffering, was doing to her. Tears welled in my eyes as I thought about all I was doing for people at work, yet I had not been paying enough attention to my own family. I had believed that by working hard, I was doing everything I could for Angie and Isabella, but I was focused solely on providing financially for them. It was a tough truth to face that I had neglected their need for my physical presence and emotional support, pouring my heart instead into my employees.

LIFE LESSON 70:
IN A RELATIONSHIP, COMMUNICATION IS KEY
• •

A critical mistake that Angie and I had made in our relationship was having poor communication. We were married and should have been operating closely as a team, sharing our thoughts and feelings so we could support one another. Instead, we were living separate lives—mine at work and hers at home. We had separate goals that were not aligned, and we failed to realize that if any single member of our family suffered, we all suffered. With clear, open communication, we could have worked together as a unit to ensure better outcomes in all aspects of our lives—together and separate.

It took me two decades to realize that my decision—at the age of six and a half—never to cry again, was a mistake. Nothing good comes from holding in your feelings. Not communicating your needs and feelings, especially to your life partner, can lead to multiple problems in all aspects of your life, including marriage, family, business, and health. Your subconscious will deal with those feelings, but not always in the most productive way. In the worst case, people often turn to drugs and alcohol or get trapped in a vortex of negative internal dialogue.

It was clear to me that Angie and Isabella needed me far more than anyone at work did.

"Baby," I said to Angie, "would you like to go see a therapist or a coach?"

"No," she said. "I don't want to go see anyone. I just need you here."

I nodded, resolute. "No worries," I said to Angie. "You don't sleep, I won't sleep. I'll stay up with you all night if need be. I'll become your chef and housekeeper . . . and I'll learn to be a therapist or coach or whatever I have to do. I'll figure this out, my love. I'll do whatever it takes to help you to never again feel this way."

I asked her for some quiet time and went out to the garage. Sitting inside my car, I told God for the first time in a long time that I felt lost and powerless, that I didn't know what to do, and that I needed help and guidance. I started meditating and praying and asked God for a sign. After about twenty minutes of meditation, I opened my eyes and saw, on a shelf in my garage, the book *Awaken* the *Giant Within*, by Tony Robbins. It was exactly what I needed to start a new journey to help my precious family, since we weren't getting the help we needed from doctors. They still couldn't tell us why Isabella was tossing and turning all night and waking up every thirty minutes. The screaming and terror had thankfully stopped, but it was still extremely stressful for both of us. We knew how important it was for children to get a full night's sleep because their bodies and brains developed at such a rapid pace; fortunately for us, with all the attention we paid her while she was awake—constantly reading to her, playing fun games, and spending time in the park—she showed remarkable intelligence, despite the consistent interrupted rest.

Shifting Focus

I decided to leave my position as executive manager so that I could spend more time with my family. My supervisors were shocked, but they understood. I told my supervisor at that time that I had the rest of my life to make money, but I didn't have the rest of my life to save Angie's life.

In my lightbulb moment, I realized that we are either hurting the people we love or we are helping them; we are making them stronger or weaker. I finally saw how we often make the mistake of thinking we're being a great husband or wife or parent because we're "working so hard," but we're often working hard at the wrong things. What we're thinking we're great at may not be what that person actually needs from us. As such, we always need to be asking ourselves whether we are truly giving the people in our lives what *they* need to achieve happiness and fulfillment.

It starts by being sensitive and asking questions. You can usually tell when someone close to you is unhappy or unfulfilled, even when they cannot see it themselves. They may have fallen into a comfortable pattern, or they may be adopting habits that are not in their best interest. By asking them the same questions I encourage you to ask yourself, or by having them read this book, you (and they) can start exploring more about what they want out of life—or perhaps why they are disappointed or why they have given up—and begin to shift their thinking. Once you listen to what they truly need, you can figure out what you can do to help them and what they need to do to help themselves.

My corporate peers from my previous career had known me for almost a decade, and they were aware that I hadn't been acting like myself for a while. So when I told my boss I was quitting, he suggested a senior marketing position. It was a downgrade from executive management, but my schedule would be lighter and more flexible, allowing me to go home whenever necessary. I accepted the position and took some time off, but I knew that I couldn't keep living that life anymore if I wanted to save my wife and family and support them at the highest level.

In the midst of all the instability at work and concerns about Angie and Isabella at home, I started seeing everything at its worst instead of seeing the reality of my life. I slipped into focusing on the problems rather than on creating solutions. I was zeroed in on the fact that I was making less money and that my wife and daughter were continuing to suffer with no end in sight, and I felt helpless to do anything about it. Trying to hide my internal strife and not talking to anyone about it only made it worse, and I felt hopeless and lost. Drawing on my youthful positivity, I continually reminded myself that I was capable of doing much more than my mind was telling me, that my family situation was not as bad as my mind had led me to believe, and that my work situation wasn't as bad as my mind had been telling me.

Even though my job was not entirely to blame for everything bad that was happening in my life, I knew that the health of my wife and daughter were my top priority, and I knew that I needed to focus all of my time, energy, and effort on helping them. So only a few days after accepting the senior marketing position, I quit. Then I called Tony Robbins's corporate office to find out what it would take to quickly learn what he knows.

After explaining the situation I had going on at home with Angie, I was redirected to their Coach University where I enrolled in the Robbins-Madanes coaching program to become a master coach in strategic intervention methods. My main goal was to coach my wife, because I knew she needed to talk to someone about her problems, and she didn't feel like talking to anyone other than me. This decision was a breakthrough for me—that young giant who grew up in Brazil not knowing how to achieve his dreams was about to be transformed into a coach who could help others achieve theirs.

LIFE LESSON 71:
PROBLEMS PILE UP

When you forget to detach from the problems you're facing at home or work and bring them back to either environment, those problems start to pile up and cause new problems. Because the mind is powerful, it will attempt to solve all of your problems at once, which can make you feel overwhelmed, frustrated, and anxious, and the intense pressure can cause you to snap or make mistakes that sometimes are irreversible. The mind is very tricky. Do not let it control you.

I encourage you to write down all of your problems, prioritize them, and then deal with each issue one at a time. When you're ready to tackle a problem, write it down again, followed by the tool or the approach you will use to deal with it, followed by the desired outcome. Then, stop focusing on the problem; instead, focus more on the desired outcome and how you will achieve it. Remember what I quoted earlier from Tony Robbins: "Where the focus goes, the energy flows." If you focus on your problems, that focus will pull all of your energy and attention away from solutions.

In sum, focus on work issues at work, and leave them at work. Focus on family issues at home, and then leave them at home.

Based on his book and his track record of helping millions of people, I firmly believed that Tony Robbins was the best master coach in the world, and I wanted to know what he knew.

I told Angie, "I've got good news and bad news."

Her eyes grew wide.

"The good news is that I'm quitting my job to spend more time with you and Isabella, and I'm enrolling in a Tony Robbins master coach program. We'll live on our savings and investments for the next five years if we have to."

Her eyes remained wide.

"The bad news is that because you don't want to see a doctor, coach, or therapist, I'll be your coach. I'll learn what the doctors and therapists know, and I'll study and practice relentlessly to become better than Tony freaking Robbins if I have to. But I'll save your life, my love. I'll stay up with you and we'll figure this out."

Angie fell into my arms with happy tears. She could tell I was confident about ending our suffering, and as I started on my journey to help my family, I too felt my conviction and confidence were at their all-time highs. I immediately began investigating and learning about all of Robbins's most effective methods:

- Health coaching
- Relationship coaching
- The six human needs
- Life and business coaching mastery
- Neuro-associative conditioning
- The seven master steps to creating lasting change

At home with my loving wife and daughter, I tried all of those techniques, along with additional techniques I had learned from other mentors and doctors. One of them is Master Zhao, who taught me qigong (pronounced "shee-gong"), a Chinese system of physical exercises and breathing control related to tai chi ("tie-chee"). I was determined to spend every single dollar I saved over the years to help my loved ones, so I poured myself into learning and applying numerous methods of Eastern and Western medicine, coaching, therapy, meditation, and home remedies from around the world. I also coached (for free) as many people as I could find to practice on.

After three months of taking Robbins's certification program, I was able to help Angie with her self-esteem, happiness, and stress. But that wasn't enough; we still had a long way to go. There was no quick fix for the sleep deprivation that had gone on for years, so I set a goal for my wife and daughter to feel better and sleep through the night by the end of 2016, which was about a year down the road.

Later that year, Angie and I learned that Isabella had some methylation problems, which affects her sleeping at night and, because of that, it also affects how her body absorbs certain vitamins, which then affects her sleep patterns. We also learned through research that since Isabella had lost so much blood in the operation and because she was a picky eater for so long, she needed certain vitamins to make up for the methylation issue, which we would have to supplement for life. So we added vitamins, minerals, and alkaline water to our routine, and we also embraced ongoing personal development, mentorship, and meditation, all of which have improved the health of our entire family.

I am proud to say that we achieved Angie and Isabella's sleep goal and that my first two clients (out of the hundreds I have coached since 2015) are catching up on their sleep as well.

Concerns About My Health

During the time I was struggling with work-related issues and family illness, I started to eat and drink more. I was living in a constant state of worry and stress, and my monthly expenses were extremely high, partly because of my family members in Brazil who depended on me to survive. To add to my problems, I was holding everything in. The only person I talked to about my stressors was the doctor who performed my annual checkups, who was surprised I didn't have a heart attack. My blood pressure was through the roof, and my doctor told me that I needed to find a way to control my stress levels.

My poor health didn't surprise me. When I came to America, I was somewhat fit, but over the years, I had partied and eaten my way to obesity. When I was living in Brazil, I would tell myself that when I made a lot of money, I would eat everything I wanted to. In Brazil, for example, McDonald's was only for middle- and upper-class people, and they didn't have a value menu. In America, however, food is cheap, and it's everywhere. When I first saw a double cheeseburger for a dollar, I bought four of them! I would also go to fancy restaurants and order double portions of everything. Because I still had a scarcity mindset from growing up in Brazil, I subconsciously thought that I wasn't getting enough food. Now that I am a mentor of mentors, though, I understand that I was thinking all wrong. I needed to shift from thinking that I wasn't getting enough food to the reality that I needed only a small amount of food every two hours or so to remain healthy and to function at my best.

The medical exam showed that I had a lot of weight-related health issues: high blood pressure, pre-diabetes, and a fatty liver. My doctor told me that if I didn't change something, I would probably die between the ages of fifty and sixty. Finding out that I was slowly killing myself was a scary conversation—he was basically telling me that I wasn't going to see my daughter graduate high school if I didn't make some serious changes. I couldn't imagine my daughter growing into a woman without me, so I had a choice to make right then and there: either I could change my lifestyle, or I could continue to suffer and eventually die young. It sounds easy, and from a logical standpoint it was. But it meant I had to completely change all of my bad habits, which included drinking alcohol and overeating, especially high-calorie meals, and I needed to start exercising regularly.

Over the two years after the birth of Isabella, I lost a hundred and fifty pounds, and a new checkup confirmed that I had managed to eliminate all of my prior health issues. I was receiving compliments from my wife and others, which led to weekends of overconfidence that extended to an entire summer of overconfidence. In short, I overate all summer long, and I started drinking again. By the end of the summer, I had gained back sixty pounds. The seesaw of weight gain and weight loss lasted for several years until I eventually lost patience with myself. At that point, I made a final decision to adopt a lifestyle that would forever change my life.

LIFE LESSON 72:
YOU NEVER WANT WHAT YOU ALREADY HAVE
• •

When they are down and out, many people like to remind themselves, "Well, at least I have my health." But it's not typically what you have that drives you. It's what you don't have. When you're sick, for example, health becomes your number-one priority. When you're unemployed and broke, all you want to do is get a job and earn some money. When you're hungry, food takes precedence, and if you're hungry enough, you may even risk your health and safety to get food.

When you already have something and lose your desire for it, your risk of losing it rises, which is why you should replace desire with gratitude for everything you have. Every day, give thanks for what you have, whether it is your health, a job, a place to live, food, people who love you, whatever. It's also prudent to be careful about risking what you have to pursue something you want. In most cases, you can have both, but in order to do so, you must continue to strive to keep what you have (your health, marriage, relationships with your children, and so on) while pursuing what you desire.

Choosing the Path to a Healthier Me

Over the years, I had learned numerous techniques for improving my overall health and fitness from books, personal trainers at the gym, and several friends who are into weightlifting, bodybuilding, and martial arts. Although the health and fitness knowledge I accumulated was certainly helpful, something I learned while studying to be a life coach and a mentor of mentors proved to be even more effective: the ability to associate bad foods with various diseases when I was about to eat something unhealthy. I associated sweets with diabetes, deep-fried foods with heart attacks, alcohol with liver damage, and so on. That approach helped me to lose my appetite for unhealthy foods and appreciate healthier foods, including healthy proteins, vegetables, fruits, and nuts.

I also noticed that when I was anxious or nervous, even when I experienced nervous excitement watching a soccer match, I would eat more, and the foods I ate during these episodes were usually high in sugar, starch, and unhealthy fats. So I started applying a technique I used when I was six and a half, when I decided to flip every negative feeling into a positive.

After gaining all of that weight (the negative), I decided to be physically fit (the positive). I had been putting myself through a lot of unnecessary pain. My legs and back were hurting so much because of the load they had to carry that even pain pills didn't help. I realized then that I needed to stop focusing on the pain and discomfort of being out of shape and focus instead on health and fitness.

To fight the battle of the bulge, I developed mind-over-matter fitness techniques that I would later use as a coach. One technique was to envision two paths and imagine myself following each path for ten years. On one path, I would practice my current lifestyle (eating whatever I wanted and not exercising), and on the other path, I would adopt a healthier lifestyle. At the end of those ten years, I imagined how I would look and feel. At the end of the first path, I was obese and experienced severe chronic pain that made me wince simply thinking about it, and my wife and daughter were sad. At the end of the other path, I was fit and trim, standing tall, full of energy, and enjoying a pain-free life with my wife and daughter (both smiling). That vision made it easy for me to choose the path to health and fitness.

LIFE LESSON 73:
LONG-TERM CHANGE REQUIRES
A FINAL DECISION

Whether you're trying to quit smoking, lose weight, stop drinking, or put a halt to any other unhealthy habit, relapse is common, and coming up with excuses to justify it is easy. To prevent relapse, make your decision to change final and link it to a reason that's compelling enough for you to hold you to your promise.

Choosing the path of least resistance (which usually means continuing old habits) is human nature. Why? Because it's typically much more attractive and looks like the more pleasurable of the two paths. The other path looks like it will require commitment, perseverance, and hard work, which is why you need to envision yourself traveling down each of those paths for ten years. Although one path seems more attractive at present, it takes you to a place you don't want to be. At the end of the other path, you're exactly where you wanted to be all along.

It's not always easy, but we have to condition ourselves to replace old habits with new ones. I conditioned myself to look at healthy food as amazing because it's good for my body, rather than as bad because I don't like the way it tastes. Over time, those new habits and thought processes become your norm.

LIFE LESSON 74:
THE PATH OF LEAST RESISTANCE MAY NOT BE THE PATH YOU THINK IT IS

We often think of the path of least resistance as the path that requires the least amount of work, but that can be deceptive. The path that requires the least amount of work often leads us to a destination of pain and misery that requires even more effort and energy to undo. For example, instead of choosing to not to exercise—which may seem easier—you might end up overweight and then have to work hard to get it off. Had you chosen to exercise all along, you may have avoided what's now the more difficult task of losing the excess weight. Another example is breaking up with someone over a text message— the "easier" path—yet creating a lot of heartache between you and that person. In speaking to them thoughtfully in person— which, yes, entails a bit more "work" on your part—you do right by them and potentially lessen the pain of a difficult situation. In short, what may seem "easier" at first may, in the long run, reap the less desirable outcome for everyone involved.

Appreciating the Value of a Good Coach

Becoming a certified master life coach through the Robbins-Madanes coaching program, understanding the foundation of strategic intervention, and helping others achieve a breakthrough in any area of their life regardless of their situation was life changing. That training not only helped me save my wife and marriage and help our daughter, but it also enabled me to inspire and help others to get back in the game.

In December of 2015, I told my story of Angie and Isabella to Tony Robbins during one of his live events in front of an audience of a few thousand people. (This annual six-day event is called "Date with Destiny," and I highly recommend it.) On the last day of the event, Tony invited me to join him on stage. Being in front of such a large live audience with my idol felt like a dream I didn't want to end. And with thousands of people chanting and applauding me, I knew at that moment that I wanted to become an inspirational speaker and a great mentor like Tony Robbins. In achieving that status, I could share my stories and wisdom to help countless others in need.

After being on stage with Tony Robbins, I started getting calls and messages from people around the world who felt inspired and who thanked me for being so vulnerable and for sharing my stories. Many of the callers said that I had inspired them to stop thinking about suicide or to reconnect with their spouse and kids, their business, and/or (most importantly) themselves. These calls reinforced my belief in the importance of enjoying life, celebrating victories, and living every day with a sense of purpose and joyful execution. I felt so grateful to have ignited my best self, the one who knows there is more to life than what my mind was able to see as I watched my loved ones suffer and felt powerless to help.

Taking leadership academy training under Tony Robbins and going through all his programs and events gave me a tremendous amount of knowledge and experience, along with a deeper understanding of human psychology and what it takes to be a great leader like Nelson Mandela or Steve Jobs. It requires a much higher level of mastery and understanding of the human psyche to help others achieve their "aha moment" and get their mojo back. During the process of developing that understanding, I became fascinated with combining my twenty-plus years of life experience, struggles, reading, events, coaching, consulting, breakthroughs, performances, marketing, leadership, and sales experience to deliver powerful mentorship to others from diverse backgrounds in a way that is fun and memorable, and that brings them lasting business- and life-changing improvement.

Helping Clients Achieve Their "Aha Moment"

The thing I love most about coaching, consulting, and mentoring is when I see my client's turning point, when they have their "aha moment" and get their mojo back—especially the ones who were struggling to make money and were fed up with not having time to spend with their kids, spouse, or friends. When people come to me, they're often stressed out because they have tried other coaches or consultants, but they continue to feel stuck in several areas of their life or are not where they want to be financially. Often times, they have quit their job and have gone into business for themselves, but are struggling to make ends meet. This happens to numerous coaches, consultants, and speakers who immerse themselves in courses and earning certifications, and then don't make enough money or achieve the results that were promised. Some may be near the point at which they say to themselves, *enough is enough* and decide that they need to do whatever it takes to succeed; others are not quite at that point; and both may be unclear on what "whatever it takes to succeed" truly entails. Because this is a challenging crossroads, we strive to make it easy by teaching our clients what the top experts in the world are doing—"cracking the code" of their success so we can share it with others.

People often think it will be easy—that they can simply set up a website and a Facebook page, and clients will start lining up to pay top dollar for their services. What I remind them, however, is that that approach rarely works, that they have to look at their businesses as entities that require innovation—or rather, doing what others are not willing to do. Each business is a bit different, but that willingness to take your thinking to the next level is where the success usually lies. For example, unless you are prepared to spend some serious cash on marketing to build your brand and attract clients with deep pockets, you must get back to the basics, especially when you're first starting out. In many cases, "hitting the streets"—as I used to say in my door to door sales days—means hitting the businesses in your town to find out what their needs are, as well as attending events and meet-ups where local business owners gather. It's almost always advantageous to leave the confines of your home or office and talk to people. This is how you make strong positive impressions and deliver value. And you need to do it over and over again, unceasingly. When you do, those "aha moments" tend to become quite frequent!

LIFE LESSON 75:
COACHES DON'T WIN GAMES, PLAYERS DO, AND THEY CAN ONLY WIN WHEN THEY FOLLOW THE COACH'S DIRECTION

If you persist in doing what winners do, you will win. You simply need to be disciplined and coachable, and you will get results. That's what I tell my future clients who struggled with their last coach or consultant. I ask them, "Is this your dream, your mission? Is it aligned with your purpose in life? Are you willing to put in the time and to work hard and do what I tell you to do in order to achieve the outcomes you desire? If so, let's talk."

I love coaching someone new who comes in with a hunger, knowing it's their calling to become a coach, consultant, or speaker. While helping someone begin to build their legacy is a long road and not easy at times, everyone has the capacity to work hard to achieve their dreams. They merely need to know it's possible, that they need to dream big and envision their dream as their reality. The dream, and the commitment to achieve that dream, are all the motivation they need to do whatever it takes to bring that dream to fruition.

An Important Lesson

Tony Robbins taught me that every time I learn something from him or from other coaches and consultants I admire, I should ask myself, *If this were my event, my inner circle, my retreat, or my mastermind:*

- *How could I make this better?*
- *How would I handle this intervention?*
- *How would I handle this client?*

This has pushed me to rise to even higher levels than I had ever experienced before, and I now do the same with my coaching and consulting staff. I feel empowered to ask myself and my team better questions every week in our team meetings, such as:

- What value curve can I create in my business that will separate me from my competitors?
- What do I have to do to convert an unhappy client from someone else's business into someone who raves about my business?

- What can we do today that our competitors won't do, can't do, or will not think of doing?
- Which strategies are we going to apply that will give someone results in a way that is fun, fast, and memorable and that results in a lasting, life-changing experience?

When you ask better questions, you get better results on a consistent basis, and you develop a habit of breaking away from anything that fails to deliver the desired outcomes.

LIFE LESSON 76:
IF YOU ARE NOT IMPROVING, YOU ARE FALLING BEHIND

Progress is persistent, so if you aren't moving forward, you're falling behind. You should always be engaged in self-development—working to improve your health and fitness, your career, and your relationships; deepen your spirituality; seek greater levels of fulfillment; and improve your community. Never accept anything as good enough. It can always be better.

Finding the Right Clients

As I gathered experience as a coach, I discovered that the first step to coaching is to find clients who are ready to burn their boats, something Hernán Cortés ordered his men to do when they landed in Mexico in 1519. He did this so that they would have only two options—conquer or die. Likewise, clients who are ready to burn their boats (give up the comfort of their old patterns) and try bold new ways to achieve success in all areas of their life have the added motivation to listen to and act on advice. All they need is direction.

I always tell the coaches I mentor not to accept any payment until their clients know what they want, are clear about the value they offer others, and are ready to follow instructions and do whatever's necessary to succeed. I tell these coaches that only when a client meets all of these conditions should they agree to work with the client, and then they should give the client all they have—which means everything that has worked for them in the past. I take this same approach when working with my clients:

1. Start with the end result in mind, or the desired outcome. In a business, for example, I work with my client to nail down the brand—the mission and vision that makes the business unique and represents the value the customer can expect.

2. Reverse-engineer. I look at where my client wants to be and where that person is, and we draw up a systematic plan with action steps tailored to enable the client to achieve the desired outcome. The goal is to align all activities with the desired outcome, so the client wastes no time or effort on hit-or-miss activities, such as online advertising or trying to create a sales funnel. Merely hiring a funnel or webinar consultant is not going to cut it if the face of the business is not in true alignment with all marketing and sales activities.

3. With a mission, vision, and plan in place, my client and I can work on execution, or putting the plan into action.

LIFE LESSON 77:
PUT OBJECTIVES BEFORE PRACTICES

• •

Many entrepreneurs make the mistake of engaging in practices before they have a goal or objectives in place. They launch a website or Facebook page, set up a sales funnel or other lead-generation system, start blogging, and so forth before they have a clear idea of what they are selling and the outcomes they expect from engaging in those practices. As a result, they engage in low-impact marketing and are surprised at the disappointing results.

For this reason, I always help my business clients figure out 1) what they want, and 2) what they have to offer of value that is unique to their market. Any lead-generation technology is useless unless a business has a mission, a vision, and a message that resonates with the targeted clientele.

I love to help others who are struggling to overcome challenges, because—as I've shared extensively throughout this book—I've struggled in key areas of my life: health, career, family, self-fulfillment, and so on. I've been hungry, broken inside and out, defeated, lost, overweight, hopeless, without sales or clients, and about to give it all up. Through it all, I had to keep reminding myself that I'd been in dark places before and always managed to emerge stronger. I also emerged better able to help others overcome their challenges in ways that are fun, exciting, and lead to lasting positive change.

Getting Unstuck

In August of 2016, I had the same experience that numerous entrepreneurs share with me. I wanted to scale my coaching business faster, so I consistently attended events, read books, took courses, and obtained more training and certifications. But I got stuck. The truth is, the amount of information and the number of courses and training opportunities available are overwhelming; a person could read and train forever without actually getting anywhere. In my case, I spread myself too thin, reached a plateau, and started to burn out. Despite all I knew and all of my experience, I struggled to scale my business. I simply couldn't break through the six-figure mark.

This is a common occurrence among solopreneurs, coaches, and consultants I have met. Why? Because we tend to want to do everything alone, so we stop seeking help and mentorship from other coaches who are doing the same thing, even if they're producing great results.

These people often become entrenched in activities that don't pay the bills, and they get stuck there for a long time. In operating all alone, solopreneurs frequently enter a danger zone where the mind is focused on thinking, which causes the body to remain stationary. The problem with this is that thought without action doesn't deliver the desired outcomes.

In my case, I wanted to separate myself from the pack in a market that is flooded with coaches and consultants. Finally, it dawned on me: I was stuck in my head and not acting on what I already knew. For example, I found that I had to take hourly five-minute breaks to close my eyes, breathe, meditate, and let go of the thoughts that were stressing me out. I would then stretch and move around, shadow-box, play air guitar like a rock star, or jump in place for a couple minutes to restore my focus and energy. After rebooting my mind, I could then enter my "must mode," focusing on what I *must* do to get clients, earn money, pay my bills, give to my charities, spend more time with my family, and live fully and joyously every day. In must mode, I was able to get out of my head, stop thinking, and *take action*.

I also discovered that I needed to do what I did best and what brought me the most joy, then hire or partner with others to do the rest. To do this, I found people who complemented my expertise with their own. Because my strengths were in marketing, sales, and coaching, I focused on those areas. I am also good at connecting with people, talking to them, and delivering results, so I capitalized on those gifts. For example, I would take my clients to events and *show* them how to do what they needed to do. By following up my instruction with a demonstration, I gave them something that many coaches don't offer.

Once I discovered that the majority of my clients learn best by seeing these processes in real-time, they wanted an even deeper level of "done-for-you" mentorship. This was when I got "unstuck" even further and came into my true gift of offering one-on-one, hands-on instruction, for which I was able to raise my fees. Being able to give advice strategies for key moments in my client's life—such as just before walking onstage to speak at an event or making an offer to attendees, or before an important meeting with a corporation to secure a six-figure deal—completely upped their game, and mine. As a result, I was able to work with fewer clients one-on-one for six months at a time, which gave me more time to spend with my family, as well as to travel, speak, and contribute to causes.

Stepping It Up

To take my business to the next level, I sought help from other coaches and consultants who were the best at their craft in obtaining results for others, so that I could learn their best practices. You already know that I enrolled in programs with Tony Robbins, but wanting to be a well-rounded mentor, I also pursued studies in life coaching, strategic intervention coaching, consulting, business strategy, and online marketing. I also received my certification as a high-performance coach.

As I learned from all of these leaders, I became aware that I had more in me than what I was utilizing, and I looked for ways to do what *they* do even better—a technique I had learned from Robbins himself. My goal was to master a multitude of skill sets, developing a system to train other mentors so that they could use my methods to coach their clients.

LIFE LESSON 78:
ACCOUNTABILITY INCREASES
COMMITMENT AND MOTIVATION

One of the key benefits of having a coach, or mentor, is that you become accountable to another person, preferably someone you regard highly. Not wanting to disappoint this person, you have a stronger sense of commitment and more motivation to succeed. As such, I strongly encourage you to work with a coach, a mentor, a consultant or ask someone you know and respect to hold you accountable for achieving a goal or objective. You may consider partnering with someone so you can hold each other accountable. And it doesn't matter if you have different goals. What's important is that you tell the other person what your goal or objective is and then keep that person posted on your progress.

Finding someone to hold me accountable was essential in helping me achieve success in those areas of my life I found most challenging: health, business, and relationships. With my coaches and accountability partners, I embarked on a transformational journey. I lost the excess weight I had gained again and redefined my eating habits. (The change was permanent this time—I made a vow to myself that I would never go back to my old lifestyle, and I went on to lose another forty pounds the following year. Being healthy feels amazing, and my new lifestyle is a great accomplishment.) My marriage was on fire again, and my businesses were growing and prospering more than ever. I also became a role model for my family, friends, and clients who wanted to lose weight, adopt a healthier lifestyle, earn more money, sell from the stage, scale their business, reconnect with loved ones, and optimize their performance and productivity.

Working in America, I had gone to several seminars and read a lot of books. However, what I learned from Tony Robbins gave me a whole set of tools to help me with my personal and professional challenges. I thought I was a great husband, father, and leader, because I had always made learning a priority, but having a mentor to motivate and guide me through the tough times made a huge difference.

A Wrong Assumption

Setting a price for my services was a discovery process for me. I was always reluctant to charge clients for the real value I delivered, because I was afraid that charging more would burden them financially. Interestingly, I found the opposite to be true.

My clients who paid more actually paid closer attention to my advice and were more likely to act on that advice. They also attended to both the big and small things and adopted healthier habits. Over time, they experienced real improvement: they were happier, their businesses were growing, they had more satisfying and productive relationships, their loved ones were happier, and their colleagues were more satisfied. In short, they were more successful. What's more, these clients were more likely to recommend me to others. Everybody won!

I experienced this personally as well. The more I paid an accountability coach, a consultant, or mentor to help me develop in areas where I was weak, the more I paid attention and got stuff done. I knew I needed to continue to take courses and receive training, but not until I started paying higher fees for someone to mentor me and to hold me accountable did I truly start making significant progress. After all, when you're paying for something that depletes your savings, you want to make that investment work for you! It's like prepaying for a gym membership, which motivates you to work out to ensure that the money you spent doesn't go to waste.

LIFE LESSON 79:
TO DO WHAT IS BEST FOR YOUR CLIENTS, FIRST DO WHAT IS BEST FOR YOU

For quite some time I was undercharging my clients, because I assumed that charging more would strain their finances, even when I realized it would help to motivate them as it did me when I paid for higher-priced coaching or consulting services. But by undercharging my clients, I was hurting both them and myself. Charging less was demotivating.

When you launch your own business, charge a price for your product or services that enables you to live the lifestyle you desire and deserve. You are doing your customers no favors by charging less than you deserve—as long as you're delivering value that is proportionate to the compensation you receive. Selling yourself short will only lead to disappointment and bitterness that can negatively affect your ability to deliver top-quality products and services to your clients. It can also damage the industry in which you work by undercutting the prices that others in your field are charging.

It took me a while to understand that charging less than I deserved was a mistake. When I finally raised my rates, I not only didn't *lose* clients, but I *gained* clients and it benefited everyone. And it was not solely the increase in the rate I charged that attracted better clients—my rate reflected the value I brought to the table.

Having All I Need

I remember waking every day and anchoring in my brain phrases of empowerment. I always remind myself, "Everything I need to succeed or to start over is with me now." Throughout my life, whenever I felt like giving up or felt tired, stressed, sad, depressed, anxious, or worried, I would repeat that mantra. I knew that wallowing in negative feelings would not help me achieve what I desired. Yes, I had my downfalls where I became engulfed in negativity and made some poor choices, but I'm a firm believer that I am alive for a reason and that I'm part of something bigger than myself so that I can serve a greater purpose. When that guy held a gun to my head so many years ago and pulled the trigger, I believe a divine power kept that gun from going off. That and other experiences led me to make the commitment to help everyone in my path live a happier, more fulfilled life. The truth is, I had been repeating some version of that to myself since I was seven years old selling bread on the streets of

Brazil. When I got older, I realized that all of my experiences and learning have aligned with that purpose.

LIFE LESSON 80
"IF YOU CAN DREAM IT, YOU CAN DO IT." —WALT DISNEY

It doesn't matter what you want out of life. If you can write it down and you have a compelling enough reason to achieve it, then you can. Your purpose will raise you from the lowest depths, fill you with energy, and sharpen your focus. Even if you have bullets flying over your head or some other form of adversity hunting you down, you can still find something more powerful than yourself. That's when breakthroughs happen! Life seems to reboot like a computer, and you end up with a new outlook.

Once I realized I had all the tools to help anyone with a problem in their personal or professional life achieve success—courses, programs, training, and experience—it didn't matter whether clients were seeking to improve sales, breathe new life into a dying relationship, find the love of their life, get a promotion, become a better leader, or get their mojo back, I had been there. But perhaps what made me most valuable to my clients was that I truly care about them and their success and fulfillment. Because I have had so many blessings, I wanted to be a blessing to others. God gave me numerous second chances to bring me to a point at which I live every day with intention, love, gratitude, joy, and a hunger for helping people live happier more fulfilled lives, and I was determined to give that zest for life to everyone I worked with.

As I quoted at the beginning of this chapter, "Success without fulfillment is the ultimate failure," and to achieve fulfillment, we must achieve success in all aspects of our lives, including career, family, finances, health, relationships, and spirituality.

Part 2

NINE KEYS TO UNLOCK YOUR POTENTIAL, ATTAIN TRUE FULFILLMENT, AND ACHIEVE YOUR LEGACY TODAY

Part 2

NINE KEYS TO UNLOCK YOUR POTENTIAL ATTAIN TRUE FULFILLMENT AND ACHIEVE YOUR LEGACY TODAY

STEP 1

Control Your Mind, Control Your Destiny

If you can dream it, you can achieve it.
—Zig Ziglar

The New Thought movement, which began in the early to mid 1800s, can best be summed up by the belief that "all of life happens through us, not to us." To New Thought proponents, the mind is a spiritual force that creates whatever reality it imagines, either consciously or subconsciously. Imagine the perfect mate, and that person will find his or her way into your life. Imagine being wealthy, and you will receive the money and possessions you envision. Imagine yourself being the perfect parent, and you will be that parent. On the other hand, if you think, consciously or subconsciously, that money is the root of all evil, you will have more expenses than income. If you suspect your spouse of having an affair, he or she will likely cheat. If you worry that your business will fail, it probably will. If you read an article in a magazine about an illness, and you are susceptible to the power of suggestion, you may get that illness.

While I don't believe that the mind itself creates the world around us, I do believe it is a powerful force that shapes our reality—good or bad. I also believe in the Law of Attraction (another concept at the heart of the New Thought movement)—that every thought is a force that draws positive or negative energy and experiences into one's life. The Law of Attraction was most recently popularized by the book and video entitled *The Secret* (2006, by Rhonda Byrne), which cites numerous references to New Thought authors, including Prentice Mulford, *Thoughts Are Things* (1889); Wallace Watters, *The Science of Getting Rich* (1910); Charles Hannah, *The Master Key System* (1912); and Robert Collier, *Riches Within Your Reach* (1947). Other popular writers in this tradition are Geneviève Behrend, *Your Invisible Power* (1921); Napoleon Hill, *Think and Grow Rich* (1937); and Joseph Murphy, *The Power of Your Subconscious Mind* (1963).

But even if you aren't a card-carrying member of the New Thought movement, you will reach the conclusion, through your own experiences and observations, that optimists are generally much more successful and happier than pessimists, that people who set their sights higher achieve more, and that those with the most imaginative minds and the strongest convictions have the greatest impact on human history. Whether thoughts are actually energy doesn't matter; those who imagine and who endeavor to bring their vision to fruition will always attract other like-minded individuals, find a way to procure the necessary resources, and join together to create a force that changes the world, for better or worse.

As I've quoted several times, "Where focus goes, energy flows." Focus is entirely a product of the mind, a thought, and it is what drives your choices and actions. Focus on the positive, and your energy will flow toward productive ventures that deliver mostly positive outcomes. Focus on the negative, and your energy will flow toward destructive choices and behaviors resulting in mostly harmful outcomes. I know, because I have traveled both paths.

When I focused on my problems, I found plenty more as the problems piled up and my worry inhibited my ability to deal with those problems. When I focused instead on solutions, I began to make progress. When my thoughts turned to darkness, unhealthy results followed. I made poor choices, abused alcohol and drugs, and actually brought myself closer to that which I was thinking about most—death. But when I set my mind on my objectives to achieve wealth and help others, I achieved both beyond anything I had imagined.

The power of positive thinking impacts every area of your life. Think about it: If you get caught up in negative thought processes about your job or your business, how can you possibly perform at the level required to succeed? If you think about everything your significant other does to make you miserable, how can you possibly love that person and build a deeper connection? If you focus more on a child's negative behaviors than on the untold gifts they have, how can you develop the type of parent-child relationship that leads to positive change and helps that child achieve his or her full potential? If you believe that money is the root of all evil, where will you find the motivation to achieve wealth?

I cannot say this strongly enough: control your mind, and you will control your destiny. Become more aware of what you're thinking. Feed the positive thoughts and starve the negative ones. If this is the only step you take, you will be well on your way to achieving health, wealth, happiness, and fulfillment.

Dream Like a Child

Children imagine and pretend with abandon. They may dream of becoming an astronaut, a rock star, a superhero, a race car driver, president of the United States, a doctor, a teacher, or even a wizard. Sometimes, they create a pretend world in which they act the part and truly believe, in the moment, that they are what they dream. At an early age, good parents and teachers encourage children to dream, that they can be whatever they want to be. Certain books, movies, and TV shows reinforce this valuable lesson.

Unfortunately, by the time we are twenty or thirty, we are expected to grow up and stop dreaming. We are inundated with messages that make us start to wonder whether we're smart enough or talented enough or rich enough. Some of us grow up thinking that the deck is stacked against us—that unless we belong to a specific group or know the right people, we will never be able to rise above a certain level, so why dream beyond that? Others grow up believing that "life is cruel," and they tend to perceive everything through that distorted lens.

I want you to return to your childhood for a moment. How awesome was that? Hopefully, in your circumstance, you had no responsibilities or worries. Maybe you even rode your bicycle without a helmet. You pretty much lived in the moment, right? And you probably dreamed of being something or doing something incredible one day.

Now, recall a dream you had as a child that you abandoned as an adult. How vivid was it? How strongly did you believe at the time that one day your dream would come true? Did you have even a sliver of doubt? When did you start to question the practicality of it? Who or what led you to abandon that dream? What lies did they tell you or lead you to believe about your potential?

Now I want you to begin dreaming like a child again, with complete abandon, without doubt. Ask yourself the following questions:

- **What do I want in life?** Your answers can (and should) be related to all aspects of your life—health and fitness, education, career, spouse, family, travel, and so on.
- **Why do I want to achieve these goals?** If you want a certain amount of money, for example, why do you want it? To support your family, travel the world, retire early? Having a compelling reason to want what you want significantly increases your drive to get it. If you have a hard time finding

your compelling reason. As you answer each question, for example "to support your family," ask why you want to support your family and keep going a few layers deeper as you will gain clarity of your why and compelling reasons.

- **If I had everything exactly the way I wanted, how would I feel physically and emotionally?** How would you look, breathe, walk, and talk? Where would you be? What would you be doing? Who would you be with? How would others interact with you? Are you happy? Are you proud? Attaching emotions to your dream will make it a deeper impression on your subconscious mind.

- **How would I see the world?** Do you see the world any differently now that you have everything exactly the way you wanted? Has your attitude changed, and if so, how?

By asking these questions, you place yourself in visualization mode, conditioning your mind to produce the vision that will ultimately become your reality.

Now imagine waking up every day with this vision of your awesome reality in your mind and the certainty of ultimately living it. How do you think that would change your attitude? How would it change the way you think, act, and conduct yourself? How would it affect your thoughts, your decisions, your relationships?

Flipping the switch from negative to positive thinking is not that difficult, and it is up to you to do it; nobody can do it for you. The trick is to continue to hold the vision in your mind until *you* believe it without question.

What Would You Do, If . . . ?

Minister and speaker Robert H. Schuller, in his book titled *You Can*

Be the Person You Want to Be, begins the second chapter with these three questions:

> What goals would you be setting for yourself if you knew you could not fail?
>
> What dreams would you have on the drawing board if you had unlimited financial resources?
>
> What plans would you be making if you had thirty years to carry them out?

These questions are interesting in that they serve two purposes: 1) Each question engages your imaginative faculties, and 2) each removes a key obstacle. For example, the first question removes the possibility of failure, the second removes the common excuse of "not having enough money," and the third removes the barrier of insufficient time. In short, these questions liberate your imagination from any practicalities that might restrain it.

When you engage your imagination, take the same approach. For each of your goals, remove any obstacles that may get in the way or that you may put in the way. These obstacles are the negative thoughts that shackle your imagination and prevent you from fully exploring the most amazing possibilities. Remember that many of the obstacles standing in your way could have been placed there by others long ago. You may have been led to believe that you're not smart enough or strong enough or talented enough or disciplined enough to do what it takes to achieve your dreams.

With this in mind, try to pair your dream with any obstacles that you believe are standing in your way, and then formulate your own questions, such as the following:

> Where would I choose to live if I could speak any language?

What would I do with my life if I didn't worry about what other people would think?

What subject would I study if I could find a well-paying job in that field?

What career would I pursue if I had the talent and knowledge to be successful at it?

With whom would I spend time if it were entirely up to me?

Daily Vision

In addition to imagining the big picture—your ideal career, family situation, residence, and so forth—spend time each day envisioning what success will look like on this particular day. Every morning, as soon as you wake up and before you get out of bed, ask yourself the following questions:

What will I accomplish today?

Why do I want to accomplish this? (How will this accomplishment further my larger goals?)

What will I get for accomplishing this?

How will I feel after accomplishing this?

Answering these questions gets you revved up for the day ahead. You will know exactly what you need to accomplish, be more committed and motivated to producing the end result, and be more focused on what must be done, so daily distractions are less likely to drag you off course.

Keep the Faith

The most successful people in the world are those who have no doubt they will succeed. They don't *believe* they will succeed; they *know* it. In fact, they can see it before it happens, know the outcome before they even start. That's the true definition of faith. We see this in top athletes and teams who never step onto the field thinking that they might lose or are willing to accept second place. They go for the gold with the single-mindedness and knowledge that they will achieve it. Weightlifters are also well known for using faith to increase their strength; before they lift, they envision themselves having lifted it. This eliminates their sense of doubt.

If you consider that thought is the vision, faith is the heat that brands that vision onto your subconscious mind. And your subconscious, in full faith, is what brings that vision to fruition, doing whatever it takes to make it happen.

For this reason, I encourage you to develop a crystal clear vision of your goals and objectives. Imagine what you want, then take the next step and create a vision board—a collage of words and pictures to feed your imagination and provide inspiration. Look at that board several times a day and imagine, with all of your five senses, achieving what you see there. Imagine how it feels. You can also carry a picture that reminds you of your dream and look at it several times a day. You will be amazed at what a positive difference it makes.

Recognize Your Negative Thoughts

Negative thoughts may creep into your mind, even when you're highly successful, which is perhaps when you're most vulnerable—when your mind is complacent and not populated with a sufficient density of positive thoughts to crowd them out. Although I advise against focusing on the negative, you must focus on these negative thoughts at times to identify them and replace them with positive ones.

Imagine your mind as a field of lush, green grass, which represents positive thoughts. Occasionally, a weed pops up in the middle of the field. If you don't remove it, it eventually spreads and the weeds take over. In the same way, you need to recognize and remove negative thoughts before they become deeply rooted and begin to spread.

Unfortunately, when it comes to negative thoughts, this analogy falls apart, because unlike weeds, negative thoughts grow faster as soon as you turn your attention to them. Their roots dig deeper into the soil of your mind, and all the attention you give those thoughts act like water, fertilizer, and sunlight to make them grow and spread even more aggressively. To eliminate these weeds of negative thought, you have two options:

- **Starve them.** Shift your attention from the negative thought to a positive one, think about something else, or engage in productive activities that draw your attention away from those thoughts.
- **Replace them with positive thoughts.** Visualize uprooting the negative thought and planting the seed of a positive thought in its place. For example, if you're thinking about a problem, replace that with thoughts about possible solutions. If you're thinking about an uncomfortable relationship issue, replace it with a thought about what you can do to strengthen or deepen your relationship. If you're annoyed because you're stuck in traffic, reframe that thought as an opportunity to listen to music or come up with a million-dollar business idea.

Problems generally come in four categories: those you are committed to solving, those you don't want to put the effort into solving, those you create by having a bad attitude, and those you have no control over, such as something in the past that you can't go back in time to change. Therefore, you have four options:

- **Fix it:** Solve the problem, resolve the issue, or repair the relationship.
- **End it:** If you're in a situation or relationship that is making you unhappy, and you cannot or do not want to put the effort into fixing it, end it. For example, if you're unhappy with your job and cannot change what's making you unhappy or change your attitude about it, then start looking for another job.
- **Change your attitude:** As Maya Angelou once wrote, "If you don't like something, change it. If you can't change something, change your attitude." We often create our own problems by having a negative attitude. Consider the example I just gave about being stuck in traffic: you can choose to look at that as an inconvenience or an opportunity. By viewing it as an opportunity, you can do something positive rather than wallow in misery.
- **Let it go:** Negative thoughts can often be attributed to past events that cannot be changed and worries about future events that we cannot possibly know will happen. Letting go often means choosing to deal with the present and letting go of anything we have no control over.

Thinking about a problem you can't fix or one you decide is not worth the trouble to solve is senseless. It wastes focus and energy that could be better spent in more constructive thought and activity.

Here's an activity I want you to do a couple times a day to become more aware of what you're thinking and feeling and to strive to weed out negative thoughts:

- Step out of your mind to observe what you are thinking.
- Write down your observations.
- Create a two-column list, label the columns Positive and Negative, and record your thoughts in the appropriate column.
- Assign any negative thoughts to one of the following four categories: Fix It, End It, Change My Attitude, or Let It Go.
- Choose one of those negative thoughts and fix it, end it, change your attitude, or let it go.

Challenging Limiting Beliefs

We have all grown up with limiting beliefs—thoughts that convince us to give up without ever really trying. Some of these beliefs have been drilled into us from a very young age by teachers, parents, and society in general. Others we have created ourselves, typically by basing a belief on a single observation or experience; for example, we failed once, so we'll fail again. Here are just a few of the numerous common limiting beliefs people have:

- I'm too old (or too young).
- There's not enough time in a day.
- Business people make their money by cheating people; I can't be like that.
- I'm not smart enough.
- I don't have enough money.
- It's just poor timing.

- I'm not worth it, or I don't deserve it.
- I don't want to work that hard.
- Why would anyone want to hire me?

I once read a story of a fifty-year-old woman who wanted to be a doctor. She told a friend that ever since she was in her twenties, she had dreamed of being a doctor but was now too old to return to school. Her friend said, "When you're eighty and look back to when you were in your fifties, will you be saying the same thing?" The woman applied for and was accepted to medical school, worked her way through, and became a doctor. The moral of the story is that you need to find a way to challenge any limiting beliefs you have, which may simply require having a different perspective.

Here are a few ways to challenge limiting beliefs:

- State the limiting belief in your own words and then ask, "Really?!" or "Seriously?!" or "Are you sure about that?"
- Ask yourself when the conditions will be right. For example, if you think that a certain opportunity is merely poor timing, ask yourself, "When will the timing be right?" "If not now, when?"
- Look for solutions. If your limiting belief is centered on a problem or an obstacle, start thinking about ways around it. For example, if you think you don't have enough time, analyze how much time you really have in a week—time that you may be wasting.
- Look at the facts. Many limiting beliefs are based on lies or false information. For example, if you think that business people make their money only by cheating others, look for instances in which that may not be true. Never accept as true anything that lacks evidence to back it up.

Conducting Your Daily Interview of the Truth

In moments of extreme stress, disappointment, or loss, you may be overcome with emotion, which can cloud your thinking and make your mind imagine that things are much worse than they are. When I begin to sense that my emotions are clouding my thinking and undermining my ability to make wise decisions, I conduct my daily interview of truth by asking the following questions:

- Am I focusing on the problem so much that I'm actually making it worse?
- Am I focusing more on the problem than on solutions?
- What's the worst that can happen?
- What's the best I can hope for?
- Do I have all the facts and information I need to make a wise decision?
- Do I truly know what that person thinks, or do I need to ask?
- Am I thinking and acting in ways that align with my core values?

In the absence of truth, our minds often try to fill in the blanks, and when the mind is overcome with emotion, especially negative emotion—such as hate, jealousy, greed, fear, anger, frustration, or resentment—it can fill in lies to complete the picture we want to see instead of the picture that actually is. For example, if you hate someone, you start finding reasons to hate them, and you filter out any redeeming qualities that might challenge your belief. But by conducting a daily interview of truth, you begin to think about the facts that might be missing—the facts that can help you develop a more objective view.

What Else Can This Mean?

Bad things happen—natural disasters, war, illness, the death of a loved one, job loss, divorce, financial loss, and so forth. One way to shift your thinking from these negative events is to try to see the good in the bad—but in the midst of tragedy, that may be easier said than done.

Many people rely on their religious beliefs for support. They may say things like, "Everything happens for a reason" or "This is just part of God's plan" or "God doesn't make mistakes." But when you are the one suffering, such phrases can bring more pain than relief. They can make you feel that somehow it is in God's plan for you to suffer, which is highly unlikely. So whenever adversity strikes in my life, I prefer to ask the question, "What else can this mean?"

Asking that question enables me to keep my emotions in check and look at the situation in a more positive light. It shifts my focus from what happened to the opportunities made possible by what happened. For example, when I was first robbed at gunpoint in Brazil, I asked, "What else can this mean?" and I started coming up with answers, such as, "Maybe he needed the money to feed his kids" and "Maybe I need to figure out what to do if this ever happens again so I can avoid getting killed without losing all my money."

However, you need to be very careful with this approach to keep your answers positive. If your answers are, "Maybe this means I need to quit" or "Maybe this means I'm not smart enough to do this," then shift your thinking to more positive answers. Think in terms of solutions and opportunities, not in terms of problems and failure.

The next time something bad happens to you, I want you to ask yourself, *What else can this mean?* or *What good could possibly come out of this bad situation?* and start thinking in terms of opportunities. If nothing else, every bad situation and loss is an opportunity to learn, grow, and strengthen your character. Eventually, you will look back at these times as pivotal points in your life that prepared you to take advantage of an amazing opportunity, or to fulfill your purpose or destiny. It is up to you to discover their meaning.

Turning from Problems to Solutions

Much of our negative thinking centers on problems. Unfortunately, we tend to spend more time and energy focusing on problems than we do solving them. In addition, we often ignore problems until the problem pile is so high that we feel too overwhelmed to dig through it. To prevent problems from taking over your life, here's what I want you to do:

1. Write a complete list of your problems.
2. Prioritize the problems, listing them from most to least serious.
3. Choose the problem at the top of the list.
4. Write down the desired outcome. In other words, describe what you want the situation to be after the problem is solved.
5. Brainstorm solutions. Be creative; do not rule out any solution, even if it sounds crazy.
6. Rank the solutions from most to least promising.
7. Choose the most promising solution.
8. Implement the solution you chose.
9. Evaluate the outcome. If the solution produced the desired outcome, you are done. If not, proceed to the next step.
10. Determine why the solution did not produce the desired outcome; was it a good solution improperly executed or a bad solution? If the solution failed due to improper execution of it, try it again. If the solution simply didn't work, head back to Step 7 and try the next most promising solution on the list.

Another method I often use to solve problems is the problem-tool-solution approach:

1. **Problem:** Define the problem as specifically as you can.
2. **Tools/Resources:** Consider the tools and resources you have at your disposal to solve the problem.
3. **Solution:** Develop a solution that uses one or more of the tools and resources you have.

Here's an example:

1. **Problem:** My wife, Angie, was ill. She was worn out from years of lack of sleep and from chronic worry over our daughter's insomnia, with no promise of a solution. Even after doctors discovered the root cause of Isabella's insomnia, which we are still treating, Angie's physical illness, depression, and anxiety were deepening, and I had to figure out how to restore her health and well-being.
2. **Tools/Resources:** Doctors, my ability to learn quickly and develop multiple skill sets, my love for Angie, Tony Robbins's teachings, strategic intervention coaching strategies that provide lasting positive change, time management, money, journaling.
3. **Solution:** Take time off my job (I eventually quit my job), learn how to make Angie feel better, and coach Angie through her difficult times.

Daily Rituals: The Triple Trizzo Carlito's Way Technique

People who are successful in any field of endeavor have daily rituals and healthy habits—structured routines that bring them incrementally closer to achieving their goals. Athletes have special diets and exercise regimens. Salespeople have systems, such as making a certain number of sales calls every day. Couples may have a date night or a shared hobby or activity. Parents may read to their children every night or play a board game once a week. And we all have weekends and vacations that help us rest and restore our minds and bodies.

In addition to the obvious practical benefits that come from healthy habits and rituals is the fact that they help us maintain our focus on the positive thoughts that crowd out the negative ones. My family and I have a three-times-a-day ritual that I designed specifically to feed our positive thoughts, a technique I share with all of my clients: The Triple Trizzo Carlito's Way Technique.

Three times a day, morning, noon, and night, when you're in a calm, quiet place (relaxing music may help), list all of the following (by writing them down or at least saying them out loud):

- Three things for which I am most grateful
- Three things that will make me happy today, especially if something goes wrong or not as expected
- Three essential things I can do to move myself toward my goals

As you think about each set of three items, visualize them as if they already exist or as if you're already doing them. Then, visualize yourself living all of your dreams as if you had accomplished them. By taking time throughout the day to engage in this exercise, you bring your attention back to what matters most, regardless of how hectic or chaotic your day has been. If you take the time to pump yourself up, nothing can stand in your way!

During the time that Isabella wasn't sleeping and I wasn't as present as I should have been for Angie, I allowed myself to get so caught up in work that by the time Angie was sick herself, the problem had already taken a serious toll on our marriage.

To remind myself how important Angie was and to think of ways I could restore my awesome marriage, I used The Triple Trizzo Carlito's Way Technique:

- The three things I was most grateful for: 1) Angie's internal beauty, 2) Angie's love, and 3) Angie's ability to light up a room.
- The three things that will make me happy today: 1) Spending time alone with Angie, 2) Spending time together with Angie and Isabella, and 3) Having dinner together as a family.
- The three things I can do to move me toward my goals: 1) Spend time with Angie and be fully present during that time, 2) Listen to Angie and sincerely pay attention to what she is saying, 3) Find out more about what Angie really wants in life and cheer her on to achieve her goals—whatever she would like to accomplish.

When Angie was struggling, I coached her through her difficult times using several techniques and strategies. But this Triple Trizzo Technique was one of our favorites because it became a daily family exercise among the three of us and was such an effective tool. It helped Angie, in particular, calm down and focus on what truly mattered in her life instead of focusing on the problems we were having. Isabella quickly picked up on it and would gather kids at the park, telling them, "Okay guys, put your hands on your heart and think about three things you're grateful for. Then, take them in, hear, see, feel, and know that everything you want is within, and you'll feel happy. Shout the word *yes!*"

The first time I saw her do this was with a little boy who was shaken up about something and cursing in the park. I almost cried with joy. She was not even four years old yet, and here she wanted to break his pattern! I was able to record it and post it on my Facebook page, and I received wonderful comments. That's when I realized it wasn't simply a cute kid video that made people smile—it was a topic I needed to speak and write about more so that I could spread the word about educating our future leaders of the world.

It became clear to me that if we all taught personal development and prayer or meditation to our kids at home and in school, they could be more present and calm when things don't go their way. We could also plant seeds to help reduce bullying and violence in school among children—promoting character building that would serve them their entire lives. I was a victim of bullying when I was a child growing up in Brazil, and I wanted to keep other kids from suffering the way I did—and worse. These techniques, I knew, could help to achieve that.

Awaken the Warrior Within You

I like to think of myself as a warrior, and I encourage you to do the same. Imagine having two warriors inside you—a negative warrior and a positive warrior. Which one is controlling your mind? If the negative warrior is winning the battle, awaken your positive warrior— the one with the spirit that will not be defeated. Your positive warrior will emerge victorious.

Decide today that you will no longer settle for less than your best self. You will spend your valuable time doing the things that truly matter, because that's what a warrior does. Decide to have a crystal clear vision of what you must do and be so committed to achieving your goal that you're 100% sure of the outcome. Promise yourself that you will do whatever it takes, in accordance with your warrior integrity and principles, to achieve your goal.

Pump Yourself Up with Affirmations

Some people think affirmations are corny, and I must admit, they can sound contrived, but they work. In fact, the funnier they are, the better they seem to work. The mere act of speaking an affirmation blots out any negative thoughts and derails the train of negative thinking. You simply cannot think of anything else, let alone anything negative, when you speak an affirmation.

One of my favorite ways to use affirmations is to give myself love. Try it: Close your eyes, and imagine looking at yourself as a baby who's smiling at you because you're being kind and loving to yourself. Now say to yourself:

"I love me."

"I am a love champion."

"I love myself so much, I am tattooing my name on my chest, and I am about to give myself a hug."

Now, hug yourself. It feels good, right? I'll bet you even laughed. Personally, I love this affirmation because it gets my whole being into it: I think love, I speak love, I feel love, and I even hug myself.

It doesn't take much to feel good and to love others; you simply have to practice daily until it becomes automatic. Remember, "Where focus goes, energy flows." Focus on love, and your energy will go there.

I also love to pat myself on the back a few times a day and say, "Great job, Carlos! You're awesome!" Some people may think it strange when they see me celebrating a small win in public, but it instantly makes me happy. In fact, one of the best ways to give your mood an instant boost is to rapidly change your physiology—jump, skip, wave your arms, sing, or do anything physical that gets you out of your head.

I've come to realize from my own experience and coaching clients from all over the world who are feeling down that silliness provides quick relief. I have had clients from abusive relationships, people with suicidal thoughts, and business owners and coaches who lost their passion for what they do get an instant boost simply by going against the norm and not caring what others will think or say.

Try it: Do two or three silly things now to make yourself laugh or smile. Walk silly, dance, talk like Mickey Mouse or Donald Duck, whistle a tune, whatever. Better yet, do it in public where everyone can see you.

Now, I challenge you to take it a step further. Over the course of the next thirty days, I want you to pat yourself on the back every time you achieve even the smallest accomplishment, such as exercising in the morning when you don't feel like it, brushing your teeth for the second time in a day, or cooking a meal. Tell yourself, "Great job!" and remind yourself how awesome you are. If you're down, your mood will instantly shift and become positive.

Remember, you've been loved since the day you were born. Any seeming absence of it is only temporary. You don't have to seek love from others to feel loved; it comes from within you and will always be there. And the best way to start feeling the love is to give it away, even if the only person around to give it to right now is you.

STEP 2

Harness the Power of Purpose and Passion

Passion is energy. Feel the power that comes from focusing on what excites you.
—Oprah Winfrey

Life is supposed to be fun and joyful, but many of us are too busy trying to survive to be truly alive. We do what we think we are expected to do instead of doing what we love to do. And, in today's world, doing what we love to do is becoming increasingly more difficult. Personal income is flat, at best, and for many of us, our take-home pay is shrinking while our cost of living soars. And the future doesn't look any better, as companies increasingly use technology to replace workers with artificial intelligence and robots. You'd think life would get easier; with robots doing all the heavy lifting and taking on the drudgery of the daily grind, we should all be out there doing what we love, right? But in practice, we are losing jobs and upward mobility, and the chasm between the rich and poor is widening.

Remember the good old days when only one parent needed to work a nine-to-five job to support a family, make a better life for the children, and build a respectable retirement nest egg? Remember when nearly everybody had weekends and holidays off for rest and relaxation and quality time with family and friends?

When is the last time you gathered with family and friends to play board games, dominoes, or cards? When is the last birthday you received a phone call or a real birthday card instead of birthday emails, emojis, and virtual cards on Facebook? When was the last time you went camping or had a vacation without thinking about work or being tethered to your smartphone or tablet? And even when we get that time, many of us are so worried about paying bills, keeping our jobs, building a better life for our children, and having enough money for retirement that we can't fully enjoy it. So, what do we do? We work harder at jobs we hate, and we don't even do that very well because we're so miserable. Or we turn to drugs and alcohol to forget about our problems or to at least minimize them—or make the pharmaceutical companies richer by popping pills.

What if I told you that you can have both, that you can have all the money you need to live the life you always dreamed of *and* all the time you need to enjoy it? What if I told you that you can have even more than that—health, wealth, happiness, *and* fulfillment? You may be thinking, "Yeah, right, Carlos, what are you smoking *this* time?" But I make this claim with the honesty and clarity of a clean and sober mind, and from the experience of having lived such a life and successfully coached others to do the same. The truth is, you can have everything you ever imagined, and perhaps even beyond what you imagine, by creating a life around your passion.

While I painted a bleak picture of the current reality and future prospects at the beginning of this chapter, I did so only to convey the reality of the lives and attitudes most people have. The fact is that the world is better now than it has ever been. If you look back hundreds of years ago, even the rich lived less luxurious lives than do today's poor in most developed countries. We have nice places to live, heat in the winter, air conditioning in the summer, and food in abundance.

Most of us have cars and numerous other forms of transportation that enable us to travel anywhere in the world in a matter of hours or a single day. The quality and selection of entertainment we have now was unimaginable only a few decades ago. We don't even have to step out of our homes to get a quality education because learning options abound online. And opportunities are more plentiful than ever. As artificial intelligence and robots take on more and more of the work, it's actually allowing the world to move closer and closer to a time when people can harness the power of their imaginations and have the time to engage in more creative endeavors—those they are truly passionate about.

But the possibilities unlocked by advances in technology also pose an enormous challenge. Because at some point we will no longer be able to rely solely on social norms and business constructs to provide us with jobs and incomes to support ourselves and our families, each of us will need to define our own essence and figure out what our purpose is in life—and we will need to find a way to earn money fulfilling that purpose. And we're not talking about some far distant future; this shift is happening right now, and that is why so many people are struggling in multiple areas of their lives. The transition from the information age to the automation age is a huge challenge, because it requires people to be self-directed and self-motivated. In the absence of that, people don't know where to turn for answers—the answers can be found only within themselves, a place where few of us are accustomed to looking.

In this chapter, I encourage you to look within yourself to find your inner passion—the only force in the universe that can tell you what you should be doing with your life. I will provide techniques to help you do this, as only by creating a life around your passion will you be able to achieve health, wealth, happiness, fulfillment, and the life you imagine on your terms.

Discover Your Purpose in Life

Rick Warren's advice to live a purpose-driven life resonates with most people, but because he's a Christian minister, "purpose-driven" life seems to imply predestination—that God has had a plan for you, a purpose for your life, even before the day you were born. This "plan" is up to you to discover what that purpose is, perhaps through prayer.

Although this is certainly one way to interpret Warren's message, you don't have to be religious or to believe in predestination to benefit from the concept. In other words, you don't have to believe that God defines your purpose in life; it can be whatever you choose to make it. But the process of discovering or defining one's life purpose seems elusive to most people. They simply don't know how to go about it.

One excellent method is to take a job or career assessment to find out where your personality, interests, skills, and other qualifications align. Plenty of these assessments exist online, and while they are mostly directed at matching you with a suitable job or career, they can also be highly useful in determining the type of business you may be good at and the best role for you in that business. Further, they may provide some clues as to what you're most passionate about. After all, most people are passionate about something they excel at.

Another method I recommend is to look back at your past—your experience, education, what you're good at, what comes naturally to you, and what you enjoy. Closely examine the people and events that have influenced you. For example, my father—although he died when I was only three months old—was dedicated to helping underprivileged children, and my mother and grandmother carried on his work. Their examples had a tremendous influence on my goal to help others, particularly children and teenagers, realize their potential. I had a natural gift of being able to talk to people and lift their spirits, and I had a great deal of sales and training experience that taught me even more about communicating and interacting with others. People often came to me for advice, even when I was young. But when Angie was struggling, I didn't have all the answers. So I sought the guidance of a life coach and discovered the teachings of Tony Robbins. My entire focus shifted to learning what he knew in order to coach Angie through her difficult time.

I reiterate this part of my story to illustrate that when I looked back at my past, I could see my future—I was created to be a mentor and people's coach. Everything I had done in my life pointed me in that direction, and then when I was called upon to refine my gift for Angie's sake, my life purpose became even clearer to me. If I had placed a dot at each important event in my life, and then drawn an arrow through the dots, the "arrow" at the end of that line would have pointed directly to being a coach for various people and mentors.

I recommend that you follow the same process:

1. Look back at your life and draw a timeline from your birthday up to the present moment.
2. List all people and key events in your life, including incidents that reflect your interests, skills, knowledge (education), influences, accomplishments, challenges, what comes naturally to you, and what you enjoy.
3. Look for a pattern. Where is your "arrow" pointing?

Another way to identify your purpose is to look at the intersection of your values, talents, passions, and skills/expertise. Draw a cross like the one that follows, and list the various pieces in the boxes around the center. Where your passions, talents, skills/expertise, and values intersect is likely where you will find your purpose.

	Passions	
Talents	Purpose	Skills/Expertise
	Values	

Discover Purpose in Problems

I spend very little time thinking about problems, because 1) I try to instantly shift my focus from a problem to possible solutions, and 2) to me, most problems are opportunities.

When I have a problem, for example, I see it as an opportunity to develop a solution that may help someone else. And when someone comes to me with a problem, I see it as an opportunity for me to help them. As a business consultant and coach, I find that people rarely seek me out when business is booming and when everything is going okay. They seek me out when they have problems.

Often, a person without a sense of purpose will discover their purpose in life when they encounter a problem or a significant challenge. For example, when my wife Angie was ill, my purpose in life became crystal clear to me—making her feel better. And think about inventors: the majority make a good living from identifying problems, inventing a gadget that fixes the problem, and selling it. Some people who've dealt with certain challenges make it their life purpose to help others through their struggles.

In other words, instead of letting your problems get you down, look at them as opportunities, and try to find a purpose in those problems.

Explore Your Skills

An excellent start in determining your skills is to list twenty things you're good at, know a lot about, or that come naturally to you. Some examples are:

- a particular hobby
- resolving conflict among friends or family members
- negotiating deals
- organizing closets and storage spaces
- planning parties
- working on your own car
- preparing meals and/or desserts
- making people laugh
- numbers and managing a budget

Whatever you're good at, regardless of whether you consider it to be marketable, is a valuable skill. And don't be humble in doing this exercise—brag about your gifts, even if only to yourself. If you can't think of twenty things, ask your friends and family members; they may have more insight into your skills than you do. You can also ask yourself, *When people come to me for help or to answer a question, which of my skills are they asking for?*

I urge you to write all the skills you come up with on index cards and lay them out on a table. This way, you can group them in different ways to see whether the juxtaposition of various skills points to an area you're passionate about.

You can also use your skill cards to evaluate what you're currently doing. For example, how many of your skills do you use at your current job? If you're using most of them, chances are pretty good that you're fairly happy with what you're doing. On the other hand, if you're using only one or two of these skills at your current place of employment, you probably need to change jobs or consider business ideas that will make better use of your skills. Otherwise, your valuable assets are going to waste.

Your skill cards will also come in handy when you discover what you're passionate about by helping you identify skills you may be lacking. This doesn't mean you should give up on a dream. It simply means you need to acquire the skills or collaborate with someone who already has them.

Celebrate Your Accomplishments

It may be easy to forget that you have accomplished quite a few things to get to where you are right now. You had to work hard to finish high school and maybe even college or trade school. Maybe you survived a difficult childhood or had to overcome the challenge of living with a serious physical or mental illness. Perhaps you worked hard to build a good relationship or get out of a bad one. Maybe you managed to transition from living at your parents' home to living on your own. You may have also figured out how to build credit and buy a car or a home. Regardless of how big or small they may be, all of these are accomplishments.

Even the mistakes you made in the past are accomplishments of a sort because they have helped create the person you are today. Those mistakes are part of your story. Hopefully, you got from them what you needed, so you never need to make those mistakes again. In the best case, they made you grow and you're glad they are behind you.

Now I want you to jot down a list of all your accomplishments. Think back to how passionate you were when you were pursuing these goals and how determined you were to accomplish them. Chances are good that at the time, you were laser focused on achieving each goal—so focused, perhaps, that all you thought about was the desired outcome. In fact, you probably gave little thought to the obstacles that stood in your way.

Consider how much of what you know now can be attributed to those lessons you learned from your younger self. You should see that you have accumulated an incredible body of knowledge and skills simply by living your life—not from what they taught you in school.

Now, perform the following exercise:

1. Close your eyes and recall your top three accomplishments.
2. Choose one accomplishment and relive it for sixty seconds. Visualize that moment and engage your senses to re-create the experience in your mind. Repeat this step for the other two accomplishments.
3. In your mind, pat your younger self on the back for accomplishing so much to make you the person you are today and for bringing you to this point in your life.
4. Give yourself a big hug and tell yourself "I love you" and that you will be more considerate and appreciative of yourself going forward.

5. Make the commitment that from now on, you will approach every task with the passion and courage of your younger self. If you hold to that commitment, you will see an improved outcome in everything you do, whether it's related to health and fitness, your job, your business, your relationships, your personal finance, or any other area of your life.

Find the Right Match

When I was selling cable TV and Internet door to door, I told my friends and family members my stories, including the stories of being harassed by gang members and frisked by criminals who thought we were the police. They asked me how I could continue selling after so many dangerous encounters, which was a fair question since I never knew who would be behind the next door. But I told them I wasn't focused on that. I continued doing it because it's what I loved to do.

When you're doing what you love, *nothing else* matters. In contrast, if you aren't doing what you love to do, *everything else* matters. In other words, you find fault with everything—your boss, your coworkers, policies, procedures, corporate leadership, even the customers! Yes, misery loves company. Then, you come home from work and start finding fault there. Your spouse doesn't understand you, the kids are lazy, the dog won't listen. And it doesn't stop there. Before long, you start finding fault with yourself. You decide you're not qualified to do anything else, and you grow to believe you're a failure at work and at home, perhaps as a spouse *and* as a parent. In short, you see nothing as going right.

Face it, continuing to do a job you hate or working for an organization or a boss you don't respect is not doing anyone any favors. For your own sake and for the good of everyone around you, you need to fix it, end it, change your attitude, or let it go (as discussed in the previous chapter, Step 1):

Fix it: Spend some time writing down the issues that are getting in the way of your being passionate about your job and what changes would be required to bring you to where you want to be. Then, discuss the situation with your coworkers, boss, boss's boss, or anyone else in the organization who may be able to help. Don't complain or blame. Keep the focus on solutions and the discussion positive.

End it: Look for the nearest exit. I'm not suggesting you quit immediately, because that's rarely a good idea. To *get* a job, it's best to *have* a job. However, you should make it your number-one priority to find a new position in the company, a similar position with a better company, an alternative job, or a fresh line of work that will enable you to make a living, because this job will kill you.

Change your attitude: The problem may not have to do with your job but with your attitude toward it. Try shifting your thinking and focusing on positive aspects of the job, the organization, the people you work with, and the customers. Start looking at what you love about your job instead of what you hate about it. Look for ways to do your job even better, to improve the organization, and to enhance customer value. (The great thing about this step is that you can still look for a different job while you start feeling better about the job you have.)

Let it go: Whatever is getting in the way of your being passionate about your job, let it go, especially if what bothers you is something you cannot change, such as a coworker's personality. Although you may be able to influence change in another person, you can only truly control what you think, feel, and do.

My life has been chock-full of adversity, but I've always pressed forward until I found something I loved and that aligned with my core values. Even when I encounter challenges in my work, I refuse to become a prisoner of my own negative thoughts. I add joy to my life by dancing, singing, climbing trees, and making people laugh. I take the scenic route to work. I try to see the good in everyone. Only by maintaining a positive mindset can you clearly see the source of your dissatisfaction—whether the source is your attitude, your workplace, your boss, your department, or something else. With a negative mindset, however, you will see problems in everything.

Keep in mind that you may need to try different careers, organizations, or businesses before you find the right fit. Think of it as dating around; you probably won't find your soulmate until you've dated a few people. Likewise, while you may get lucky and find the right match with your very first job, it's not likely.

Dream Big, Then Make It Bigger

I encourage my clients to dream big, because big dreams stir passion. What's exciting, too, is that you can use your dream to stir up even more passion by making that dream more prominent in your mind. How does this work? The greater your passion, the more drive you will have to plow through adversity. To take it a step further, convince yourself that your dream will benefit the world a hundred times beyond what you originally thought. You can do this by extending the dream out from yourself to encompass your circle of family and friends, and then out from that to encompass everyone in the world and generations to come.

For example, I imagine building a worldwide network of schools for disenfranchised children around the world, having all of those students graduate, and then seeing them build a world of unmatched peace, intelligence, creativity, and beauty.

Such a dream makes billions and billions of people now and in the future stakeholders in your success. As I pursue my dreams, for instance, I fuel my inner drive by thinking about the people who depend on me to achieve that dream. I start with my wife and daughter, and I think about how I would feel if I saw my child without something to eat, or how I would feel if I didn't have a way to get my wife to a doctor if she were injured. Then, I think about my extended family back in Brazil. What sort of life would they have if I couldn't afford to send money back home? These motivational drivers keep me focused and determined that I will accomplish whatever I set my mind to. They make me fully invested in accomplishing my dream—the bigger the dream seems to me, the more passionate and motivated I become.

As a result, I find that I operate from that higher state of mind at all times and engage in continuous learning to push myself further. Although I maintain a healthy work-life balance, I still work long hours when necessary to meet my objectives and those of my clients. I am able to do that by finding ways to pump up my passion to the level at which no obstacle can drive me off course.

By focusing on the end result and pursuing the desired outcome relentlessly, and by doing whatever it takes within the boundaries of your core values, you can consistently excel beyond the average person in work ethic and production. I have seen this happen time after time with the many people I coach. Once you tap into that inner power and combine it with a singularity of purpose, you can accomplish anything you set your sights on. Nothing can stop you.

Prime Yourself Daily

I always start my day off on the right track by programming my alarm to play a heart-pumping tune. I wake up smiling and singing and hop out of bed dancing, which sets the tone for my entire day. I encourage you to wake up in a way that sets a happy tone for your day as well.

To stay pumped up throughout the day, try to see the fun in everything you do. When you're doing what you love every day, everything becomes much more pleasant—but that enjoyment can sometimes become clouded if you start seeing what you love as a to-do list on which you merely check things off. Savor each project, each client, each challenge. Life is too short, and opportunities are too abundant for you to be unhappy. And you don't have to wait until you're making money or on vacation to feel happy and to truly experience life to the fullest. Happiness is within you, and you can evoke it at any time.

Try the following exercise for five minutes twice a day:

1. Close your eyes.
2. Breathe softly and deeply.
3. Think about three to five times in your life when you were super excited, full of joy, or laughing hysterically.
4. Choose one of those experiences at a time and spend sixty seconds imagining it as if you were reliving it.

Whenever negative thoughts or limiting beliefs start to creep into my mind or when I start to miss my family, I perform this exercise and usually conjure up a funny incident in my past. In a matter of minutes, my mood shifts, I'm smiling or laughing, and I'm more productive as a result.

Make a Bucket List

I highly suggest you feed your passion by creating a bucket list—a list of everything you want to do and everywhere you want to go before you kick the bucket. Think of it as providing you with reasons to live, to wake up in the morning, and to work harder doing what you're passionate about. Once you make your list, write a compelling reason for each of the items. Then, read and update your list regularly, being sure to cross items off as you do them.

For example, one of the items on my bucket list was to write a book about my life, so I could share my adventures and what I learned with others (check!). Having a compelling reason to pursue a goal gives you additional motivation to achieve it.

Beware of Dream Killers

Why is it that you don't you have health and fitness, wealth, happiness, or fulfillment right now? I'm sure you have asked yourself this or similar questions more than once, and you probably came up with a lot of answers, many of which might be valid. However, I think the main reason most people are not living the dream is because they have underestimated the power of their minds and have let their thoughts control them instead of controlling their thoughts.

Were you ever told when you were growing up that a certain career path wasn't good for you, or that you were not smart enough or talented enough or good looking enough or not whatever enough to do what you had always dreamed of doing? Maybe the person who told you that or led you to believe that was right, but you should never accept another person's opinion about you until you analyze it carefully.

Ask yourself the following questions:

- How does this person know I'm not a good fit?
- Who is this person? Is he or she an expert?
- Has he or she ever helped others succeed?
- What could possibly have motivated this person to say such a thing?
- Has he or she ever mentored others to help them find the right career paths?

Many people never ask those questions. Instead, they merely accept or reject the person's opinion without giving it much thought or knowing where the other person is coming from. You can listen to their opinion, analyze it, and decide for yourself whether their observations are accurate and their conclusions are reasonable, but never let someone else blatantly kill your dream.

I find it interesting to observe highly successful people in various fields of endeavor, because they are often not the people voted most likely to succeed in high school. They are also not always the prettiest, the smartest, or the most talented. What they *are*, however, are those who pursued their dreams and tuned out the naysayers. They are the people who believed in themselves.

The Moment of Truth

Most of us cruise through life on autopilot, living a life that conforms to a social or cultural norm. A typical life, for example, may go like this:

1. You are born.
2. You go to school.

3. You get a job and work hard.
4. You get married.
5. You have kids.
6. You retire.
7. You die.

We go through life thinking that if we do all of those things, everything that is "expected" of us, we will be happy. But instead of leading to happiness and fulfillment, living a conventional life frequently makes people feel like they are in a rut.

I don't want this to happen to you! So for the next twenty-one days, I want you to conduct a daily self-assessment by asking yourself the following three questions:

- Am I happy?
- Am I fulfilled?
- Do I truly love my mind, body, and soul?

I call this "the moment of truth." It's the moment when you take an honest look at yourself instead of getting caught up in doing what is expected of you or what you think is expected of you. If you're not on the right path, it could be because you let another person—a family member, friend, teacher, or even your spouse—make choices for you that derailed your dreams. The worst part is that you probably were living on autopilot and didn't even realize it was happening.

To get back in touch with who you are, what you think, and what you want out of life, you must disable your autopilot and silence whatever thoughts or beliefs may be holding you back from pursuing your dream.

After performing this self-assessment every day for twenty-one days, evaluate your results. Then, if you feel like you've fallen short somewhere, know that it's never too late to pursue your dreams. Whatever you have done up to this point in life has served you and has become a part of who you are. If you want something different for yourself, start by believing that anything is possible. If you feel that others have derailed your dream, forgive them. They probably didn't know any better. But you must never allow someone else to put limiting beliefs in your head again.

Fuel Your Inner Drive

When I talk about passion, I am most often referring to doing something you love so much that you would do it regardless of the compensation. But passion can also be looked at as a drive to succeed, in which case you can manufacture passion for something you're not all that passionate about, such as a job you don't particularly like. In other words, you may need to work at a job for a while that you don't love, but you drum up passion for it because it allows you to pay the bills and fund the education you need to pursue the career you are truly passionate about.

In situations such as these, especially if you're feeling not so thrilled about your current position, strive to convince yourself that succeeding at whatever endeavor you're engaged in will ultimately benefit the world a hundred times beyond what you can imagine.

Convert "Would" and "Should" to "Must"

Another way to maintain your inner drive is to convert "would" and "should" to "must." This helps keep you from thinking you can back out or back down when you meet an obstacle or a challenge. For example, when I was seven years old and selling my mother's bakery items off the back of my bicycle, I never allowed myself to think that I *would* or *should* sell all the items by the end of the day. My attitude was that I *must* do it—that I must sell all the items before returning home, and I must return safely. I did the same when I was selling cable TV and Internet services door to door. I decided that I *must* make at least seven sales a day to earn $350, and I would not stop until I reached that number. Many times, I didn't stop there and made ten or more sales.

In sum, never make failure an option; doing so makes failure far too easy.

Stay on Purpose

Because life is full of distractions, it can be easy to lose sight of your purpose. If you find yourself wandering off track, perform the following exercise.

For three days straight, write a minimum of one page daily about your purpose using the following routine.

In the morning, write down your answers to these three questions:

1. What is my purpose in life?
2. What three things am I going to change from a "should" to a "must" to further my purpose?
3. How can I stay on purpose when something goes wrong?

In the evening, write down your answers to these three questions:

1. Did I live up to my purpose today?
2. What can I do tomorrow to stay more connected to my purpose?

3. If today were the last day of my life, could I honestly say that I truly lived, loved, and made an impact aligned with my purpose?

Do It—The Plan and The Process

*Goals are pure fantasy unless you have
a specific plan to achieve them.*
—Stephen Covey

Numerous quotes about planning exist. Some of the best I've found
are:

Failing to plan is planning to fail.

—Alan Lakein

*Productivity is never an accident. It is always the result of
commitment to excellence, intelligent planning, and focused
effort.*

—Paul J. Meyer

Never look back unless you are planning to go that way.

—Henry David Thoreau

*In preparing for battle I have always found that plans are
useless, but planning is indispensable.*

—Dwight D. Eisenhower

Adventure is just bad planning.

—Roald Amundsen

*Planning is bringing the future into the present so that you can
do something about it now.*

—Alan Lakein

I particularly like the quote by Eisenhower, because life is complicated. Things rarely go as planned, but it's true that the planning and preparation processes are indispensable for keeping your mind focused on the steps you need to take to achieve your goal. They not only keep your thoughts and actions aligned with your goal so you continue to drive forward, but they anchor your goal and break down the steps required to achieve it, so that the goal, however ambitious, does not seem overwhelming.

Plan—Break It Down

You can look at planning and preparation as a simple process of breaking down goals into objectives (measurable, time-bound outcomes) and breaking down objectives into specific actions or activities. For example, suppose you have a goal to be healthy and fit. Your objectives may look something like this:

- Lose seventy pounds by the end of the year.
- Bring my blood pressure down to 120/80 by the end of the year.
- Increase the amount of weight I can lift by 25% within the next ten months.
- Stop smoking by the end of the month.
- Run a 5K within the next six months.

Note that each objective is measurable and time-bound, which is important, because it provides you with a deadline and a way to determine whether you have achieved your objective.

To achieve your objectives, you would need to perform certain actions or engage in certain activities. For example:

- Consult with my doctor.
- Perform challenging cardiovascular exercise for thirty minutes every other day.
- Lift weights every other day, increasing the weights by 5% every two months.
- Enroll in a smoking-cessation program.
- Choose and adopt a weight-loss diet.

Schedule Your Days

With a goal and objectives in mind, you can build a schedule to ensure that you stay on track. I find that writing the daily activities you must perform in a planner or calendar is the best way to stay organized. Also, keep in mind that if you have a longer-term objective, such as losing a certain amount of weight by a certain date, you want to set shorter-term milestones. This allows you to have small wins that lead up to the larger one. In addition, having a schedule for achieving each of your goals allows you to see the big picture, so you know what you need to do every day, week, month, and year to further your progress toward that goal.

Focus on "The Process"

University of Alabama football coach Nick Saban is one of the greatest college football coaches of all time, leading Alabama to three Bowl Championship Series (BCS) wins in 2009, 2011, and 2012. Although his team's goal is to win games, Saban discourages his players from looking at the scoreboard during the game. Instead, they focus solely on each and every play, something Saban refers to as "the process."

When Saban was coaching the Michigan State Spartans in the late 1990s, he befriended a psychiatry professor at the university by the name of Dr. Lionel (Lonny) Rosen. At the time, Saban was interested in psychology and how he could harness the power of the mind to win games. In November 1998, the team was scheduled to play the undefeated, number one–ranked Ohio State Buckeyes, and Saban sensed that his team lacked the confidence to win, so he turned to Rosen for advice.

Rosen recommended that the team adopt a form of step-by-step thinking—commonly used in Alcoholics Anonymous—developed by Aaron Beck, a pioneer in cognitive therapy. Rosen pointed out that each play in the game lasted about seven seconds. Each player had a role, and the players were to commit to doing their best in their respective roles during those seven seconds only, for each and every play, without worrying about the score or the outcome.

When game day arrived, the Buckeyes started out strong and were leading the Spartans 17 to 3 at the end of the first quarter. By the end of the half, the Spartans battled back to close the gap to 17 to 9. But nearly ten minutes into the third quarter, the Buckeyes' Damon Moore returned an interception seventy-three yards for a touchdown, putting the Buckeyes up 24 to 9. The Spartans were not concerned, however, because they didn't care about the score or the time remaining. They were focused on the process, not the outcome. Later, it was reported that the players felt as though they had an infinite amount of time to come back—and they proved it. In the last two quarters, the Spartans scored nineteen points and won the game 28 to 24.

The moral of this story is that after you have a plan in place with a well-defined goal and objective, you can stop worrying about the goal and objectives, be completely present in the moment, and focus entirely on the actions you need to achieve them.

Strive for a Healthy Work-Life Balance

Although I talk mostly about success in career and business—because that is such a big part of people's lives and an area in which people commonly struggle the most—there is much more to life than just work. As Tony Robbins says, "Success without fulfillment is the ultimate failure." Although I tend to agree with him, I think the word "success" includes fulfillment, and success applies to all aspects of a person's life—health, career, relationships, family, and so on.

I particularly like Zig Ziglar's Wheel of Life Approach to Life Balance and Goal Setting that covers seven areas of life:

1. Physical/Health
2. Personal & Social
3. Work & Career
4. Family
5. Spiritual
6. Financial
7. Mind/Intellect

To achieve self-fulfillment, you must attend to each and every area of your life. Although your ultimate goal may be to achieve self-fulfillment (or self-actualization), you must set a smaller goal for each area of your being.

Take some time right now to write down the seven areas of life, and next to each write down your goal. Here, I provide some questions that may help you start thinking of goals in these areas:

1. **Physical/Health:** Do you have any health issues you need to address? Do you have any fitness goals you would like to achieve? How would you like to feel physically? Do you have any habits that negatively impact your health and fitness?

2. **Personal & Social:** What do you want to spend more time doing alone or with friends? Do you know anyone you would like to be friends with but are not? Who would you like to spend more time with? Do you spend too much time with people who waste your time or are a negative influence? How could you be a better friend?

3. **Work & Career:** Describe your ideal job or business. Are you happy at your current job? If not, why not, and what changes could you make, if any, to bring your current job up to what you would consider ideal? If you own a business that is struggling, what would success look like?

4. **Family:** Do you have a healthy relationship with a spouse or significant other? Do you have any relationship issues that need to be addressed? Are you spending time nurturing your family relationships or simply dealing with problems? If you have children, is your relationship with your children what you want it to be?

5. **Spiritual:** Do you set aside time to study and grow spiritually? Do you spend time communing with nature? Do you have and live by a certain code of ethics? Do you treat others as they would like to be treated? Are you reaching out to help others?

6. **Financial:** Are you struggling just to pay the bills, living paycheck to paycheck? Would you consider yourself buried in debt? Are you saving and investing enough money? How much money would you need to earn to fulfill all of your obligations and do everything you would like to do? Where would you like to be in your finances one year, five years, and ten years down the road?

7. **Mind/Intellect:** Are you reading or listening to books, taking courses, attending seminars, consulting with a

mentor or coach, or engaging in other learning activities to improve your knowledge and skills? What would you like to be better at? Which skills would you need to achieve other goals? What other activities could you engage in to sharpen your mind?

Envision what success looks like in each of these seven areas. You can then break down each of those goals into objectives and activities.

Keep in mind that each of the seven areas requires your time and energy, which are fixed entities. Spending more time on health and fitness, for example, leaves you with less time to focus on family and on your career. In other words, in the midst of a family crisis, you may need to focus entirely on your family at the expense of other areas in your life. What often happens, however, is that in the hustle and bustle of daily life, we focus only on one area and neglect the others until something goes wrong: we focus on health only when we become ill; we focus on our careers only when we lose a job or fail in business. Instead of being proactive, we live our lives in reactive mode and are constantly dealing with problems.

This is why it is so important to devote time every week and, when possible, every day, to each area of our lives. When we are strong in every area, we encounter fewer problems and achieve a healthy balance that helps us avoid the chaos that knocks us off track.

Find Time

Many people complain that there are not enough hours in the day to get everything done. You likely work an eight-hour day; sleep for eight hours; spend a half hour to an hour getting ready for the day; commute an hour or two; cook, dine, eat, and clean up afterward;

and spend some time on daily and weekly chores. That leaves you with only about four or five hours a day during the week. However, multiply four or five by five, and you have twenty to twenty-five hours during the week to devote to other productive endeavors—and they don't necessarily have to represent hard work. In addition, you may have another twenty plus hours on the weekends. Add it all up, and you're looking at forty to forty-five hours a week!

Now, if you shaved an hour off the standard eight hours of sleep, you would gain another seven hours a week. You're now up to forty-seven to fifty-two hours a week. Suppose you invested forty hours of that into improving yourself, your health, your relationships, your family, and your finances. That's an entire forty-hour workweek. Just think about how much you get done at work over that same amount of time!

When we break it down this way, it doesn't seem so impossible to find more time. But the trouble is that many of us waste most of that time. We're watching three or four hours of TV every night, reading and posting content on social media, texting and emailing, and engaging in fruitless conversations. You're likely not immune to wasting time in one of these ways, so I have an activity that will help you see where your extra time is actually going. For the next week, I want you to log everything you spend time on. Then, I want you to go back through your log and total the time you spent on various activities. You may have several categories, such as work, sleep, cooking, cleaning, personal hygiene, exercise, family time, and entertainment. Look at that list and highlight areas you can reduce or eliminate to find more time for productive activities.

Another exercise I would like you to do is experiment with your sleep schedule. Many of the most successful people I know function best when they sleep only four or five hours a night. Now, I am not recommending sleep deprivation. A lot of people absolutely need the recommended seven to eight hours a night—especially since this is the time our bodies are rejuvenating themselves. But because some people need more and some need less, it's crucial that you find your sweet spot—the amount of sleep you need to feel rested and function best during the day. As in the previous exercise, I want you to record the results of your experiment. Log the number of hours you slept, and note how you felt in the morning and how well you performed during the day. You may be surprised to find that you function better with *less* sleep.

Make Time

People who claim that they have only twenty-four hours a day to get everything done are usually thinking that they need to do it all. The fact is you do not need to *do* it all; all you need to do is *make sure* it gets done. This is why the most successful people hire assistants. You can hire people to clean your house, cook for you, shop for you, run errands, mow your lawn, manage your finances, watch your kids, and even perform some of the work you need to do related to your day job. By outsourcing some of your daily duties to assistants, you can accomplish much more in a day and free up time to invest in yourself, your family, and your community. In addition, by hiring assistants you are providing jobs to the numerous people who need them.

If you think you cannot afford to hire assistants, consider that without their help, you may not have the time you need to engage in the productive activities required to boost your income—and attend to all seven aspects of your life. Look at it this way: If you can hire someone to take on one of your chores for less than you earn, you're paying yourself too much to do that chore.

Achieve Time Mastery

By studying highly successful people, I have observed that they all have one thing in common—time mastery. They wring every minute out of every day by constantly engaging in productive activities.

Here's what you need to do to achieve time mastery:

1. Master the art of positive thinking (skip back to the Step 1 chapter for details). People waste considerable time and energy engaging in negative thinking.
2. Plan ahead. You should have at least a daily and weekly plan so that you don't need to spend time wondering what you need to do next.
3. Focus on the task at hand. Distractions will make you less efficient.
4. Reduce or eliminate time wasted on unproductive activities.
5. Delegate—outsource some tasks/chores to trusted assistants.
6. Consult experts (see the later chapter, Step 7, on collaboration). Experts typically know better, faster ways to achieve a goal or objective or to perform a task.

And one final tip: Every evening, I want you to look at your schedule for the next day to see what needs to be done. As you sleep, your subconscious mind will process your schedule and may come up with ideas for performing certain tasks better or faster. You will wake up knowing what must be done and motivated to achieve your daily objectives.

In sum, time mastery, combined with a plan and a focus on the process, provides you with everything you need to achieve your goals. Now, you simply need to do it.

Invest in Yourself

> *The best investment you will ever make is in yourself.*
> —Warren Buffett

We think of our assets as stuff we own—our house, our cars, our savings, our investments. Rarely do we list our most valuable asset— ourselves. Even more rarely do we invest in ourselves. In fact, if you are like most people, you spend the least amount of time, money, and other resources on yourself. Instead, you spend it on your job, your loved ones, your government, your possessions, your entertainment, your pets, and so on.

But the truth is that *you* are your most valuable asset. Without your imagination, desire, skills, knowledge, and other amazing gifts, you would not have any of what you have today. So, how do you get more?

You must invest more in yourself, especially in areas that improve your knowledge, skills, understanding, and relationships. The time and money you invest in yourself will never go to waste, and it will increase your value even if the stock market and the housing market both crash.

Embrace Continual Purposeful Learning

I attribute much of my ability to help people in their careers, their businesses, and their lives to the great amount of knowledge I acquired over the years from other people and from my own experience. I have used this knowledge to be successful in every career I have ever had, from selling my mother's baked goods on the streets of Brazil to selling cable television and Internet service door to door, from my years as an executive at Comcast and over the course of my career as a high-performance consultant and coach. My lifetime of education has improved every area of my life, including my physical health, personal relationships, family life, spiritual life, and finances. None of what I have learned has ever gone to waste, and all of it has enriched my life.

I knew at a very young age that learning would be my ticket to health, wealth, happiness, and fulfillment. That is why I have always been passionate about getting involved in other people's lives and asking them questions, and about inviting people into my life, including mentors and coaches, so I could learn from them. With every experience, every book I read, and every question I asked, I learned more. Not only do I appreciate the value of learning, but I also truly enjoy it. Everything fascinates me, and the more I know, the more eager I become to learn.

Regardless of how much you know, how many diplomas or certifications you have, or your age, I encourage you to become a lifelong learner. And you don't have to enroll in college or even take classes on the Internet. Learning can be as simple and enjoyable as engaging in a conversation about a topic that interests you, joining and participating in a club, taking a trip to a foreign country, starting a hobby, reading books and magazines, watching educational videos, or listening to podcasts.

Although all learning is valuable, regardless of whether you intend to apply it, I have found that the best way to learn is to find something that interests you and connect it with a compelling reason to learn about it. This is the approach I took to learn English. To achieve the level of success I desired in the United States, I knew I needed to learn English, which gave me the drive I needed to immerse myself in the language. When my wife was struggling in life and so depressed she was thinking about suicide, I knew I needed to develop the knowledge and skills to coach her.

I want you to take some time now to perform the following exercise:

1. Write a list of ten things you sincerely want to learn or learn how to do. These can be topics that fascinate you or relate to some area of your life, such as your career, family, health, relationships, finances or investing, or spiritual life. Your list may also include skills you would like to develop, such as speak Portuguese, play the guitar, build a website, start a business, or invest wisely.

2. For each item on your list, try to think of a compelling reason to learn it—something that makes you feel as though you *must* learn it to survive or save the world. (As you do this, remember that you never need a reason to learn anything, and nothing you learn will ever go to waste. So try your best to come up with a reason, but don't feel bad if you can't. Sometimes, to satisfy your own curiosity is reason enough. Curiosity can provide the motivation you need to learn.) Write down your reason next to each item on your list.

3. Rank the items on your list from 1 to 10, with 1 being the topic you want to learn most or have the most compelling reason to learn about.

4. For the top three items, set a deadline and note how you will know when you have achieved your learning objective; for example, I will have a degree of fluency in Portuguese when I can interview Carlos entirely in Portuguese.

5. Type your list, print it out, and carry it with you. Also, hang it somewhere in your home or apartment where you will see it every day, so you have a constant reminder of what interests you and what you want to learn.

As your learning needs and interests change and as you cross an item off your list—after having completed it or as a result of losing interest in it—update your list. Don't be concerned if your list grows beyond three items, but as you update it, reprioritize so that what you need or want to learn most is at the top. Don't be afraid to have a hundred items or more on your list!

Ask Questions

I have learned a great deal from others simply by asking questions. When you communicate with people, try to find out what they do and why, what they would do differently if they had a chance to start over, what mistakes they would avoid, and how they felt about what they have accomplished. If a person you're speaking with has a successful career, business, marriage (or other close long-term relationship), or is successful in other areas of life, ask, "What's your secret?" If the person has failed in some area of life, ask, "Why do you think it didn't work?"

Here's a challenge: For the next seven days, I want you to ask one person a day (family member, friend, colleague, acquaintance, complete stranger) the following four questions (which I always asked people when I was growing up):

- Why do you do what you do?
- What would you do differently if you could start over?
- What mistakes would you avoid?
- How did you feel once you accomplished _____?

Explore Different Ways to Learn

As I've already illustrated, education is not restricted to books, classes, and seminars, although these three modes of education are certainly effective.

I, for example, learned a great deal of English by listening to rock and roll songs. When I arrived in the U.S. and improving my English became more urgent, I bought a Portuguese/English dictionary and read books and newspapers in English, looking up unfamiliar words; I left the apartment to talk with people in the neighborhood who helped me enhance my knowledge and skills; and I watched movies in English. Although my English wasn't perfect back then, it improved every day and it was sufficient for me to achieve my other goals.

As you choose topics to learn about or skills you would like to develop, write down specifically *how* you will learn them. Will you read books, talk to experts, enroll in a course, take classes online, attend seminars, find a mentor, hire a coach, seek an internship, join a group that shares your interest, engage in relevant educational activities, and/or receive specialized training? You'll find that writing down all the ways you plan to learn about a topic or develop a skill will enhance your motivation and give you direction.

Use It or Lose It

You may have already experienced that learning does not truly take hold until you apply it in some way. There is a vast difference between reading a book or watching a video and actually doing something yourself, right? You cannot, for example, learn how to play the guitar by reading a book or watching a video about it. You cannot learn a language merely by studying vocabulary and grammar. You can learn some of what you need to know to fly an airplane through study and the use of a flight simulator, but you still need to fly a plane to master that skill. Even if you read a book about how to improve your relationships or your health, you must apply what you learned in order to make that knowledge work for you.

A great way to have this three-dimensional learning experience is that as you learn, think about how you will apply it, then write it down. I encourage you to take notes like this for two reasons: 1) so you have a record of your thoughts, and 2) because the physical act of writing helps you retain your knowledge. Another excellent method for retention is to discuss what you learned with at least one other person. If you cannot find someone who will listen or who shares your interest, seek out blogs and discussion boards online.

Last, put it into practice. You may feel a little clumsy at first, and you may even fail in your early attempts, but trying out your new skills creates valuable learning opportunities. The more you apply what you learn, the better you will get at it, guaranteed.

Invest in Your Career

You probably invest a lot of time in your career already, and you learn a great deal simply by engaging in your daily work activities. Even so, you should be spending some portion of your workday or some time outside of work to improve your knowledge and hone your skills. The pace of change in the world is accelerating, and you must remain competitive in your field or, if you're no longer passionate about what you're doing or your field is being phased out, you must start training for another more promising career. Here are some suggestions on how to get started:

- Join groups in your field on LinkedIn and Facebook and start engaging with other group members to add value as well as learn.

- Join Toastmasters. Public speaking is one of the top skill sets to master—even if you're not planning to be a speaker—because you will need to communicate your message well, whether during an interview, sharing your business with others, or talking to your team.
- Join a professional association related to your career. This is the best way to keep up on changes in your field and to find out about courses, classes, conferences, and seminars.
- Attend conferences and networking opportunities. If they cost more than you can afford, offer to be a volunteer crew member, which organizers will often accept in exchange for attendance. If you can't reach anyone before the event, you can show up the day before and offer your time. This can also result in a free ticket, as most events can use extra hands.
- Enroll in relevant webinars and pay close attention to how they are being presented. Ask yourself how you would you present it if it were your webinar, and how you could make it better based on what your competitor might *not* be doing.
- Read the latest books, magazines, and industry publications.
- Subscribe to and read e-mail newsletters related to your field.
- Learn from a more experienced mentor in your field and mentor someone who is less experienced. Both mentoring and being mentored are valuable learning experiences.

No matter your career path, think of yourself as a craftsman or craftswoman and continuing education as a way of honing your craft. People in every field are figuring out better and faster ways to work, which may or may not involve new technologies. When you're practicing your craft at work but not further honing your craft, you can easily miss out on the latest advances.

Invest in Your Health and Fitness

We often categorize the money we spend on health and fitness as an expense, but it is actually an investment. Just think about how much money we would save as a nation if we spent as much money on health and fitness as we do on health insurance and medical bills. How much money would we save if everyone in the nation took their health seriously and simply ate healthy diets, became more physically active, and avoided unhealthy habits, such as doing drugs, smoking cigarettes, and drinking alcohol? With less demand for medical services, medical costs and health insurance premiums would drop. Not only would the amount of money saved be enormous, but we would have a nationwide increase in productivity, because everyone would be more alert and energetic. Students would do better in school. We would even see a drop in crime and other social issues.

Of course, this is a pipe dream. Try as we might, we cannot control other people's choices and behaviors. However, you can invest in your own health and reap many of the benefits for yourself and your family in any of the following ways:

Learn about your health. Doctors tend to focus more on curing illness than making patients healthy. They don't always have the time or make the time to educate patients, and patients are often unreceptive to such advice. Therefore, you must take the initiative to educate yourself in the areas of nutrition and exercise.

Consult with a doctor who is more focused on health than on illness. Look for a practitioner with specialized training in functional medicine, naturopathy, osteopathy, integrative medicine, or nutrition.

Invest time, effort, and/or money in becoming more fit. Fitness doesn't need to cost a lot of money, but it does take time and effort.

Pay the farmer instead of the pharmacist. Spend money on quality food, or you will probably need to spend even more money on medication.

Identify unhealthy habits and work toward reducing or eliminating them. Some unhealthy habits make life more enjoyable, and they may even be healthy if done in moderation, but if the habit is negatively impacting your health, you need to find a way to let it go.

Invest in Your Relationships

At the beginning of any relationship, personal or business, there is often a short courtship phase during which we devote a great deal of time, effort, and attention. Afterwards, we tend to get comfortable and complacent and stop investing in the relationship. As I point out in Life Lesson 72, "You never want what you already have." Over time, it's easy to start taking the other person for granted and vice versa. As a result, the relationship starts to wither.

Friends, mates, children, parents, colleagues, and other people in our lives are valuable assets, second only to ourselves. Treat them as such. Many of us give more attention to our possessions—maintaining our homes, our cars, and our boats—than we do to our loved ones and to others who help us on our journeys.

To maintain and deepen valuable relationships, you need to give them time and attention. Here are some suggestions:

Become more aware of the goals and objectives of others in your life, and look for ways to help those people achieve them. You can also approach this as becoming more aware of their needs and desires. Sometimes, all that is needed is some advice on how to solve a problem or remove an obstacle.

Become more aware of how the people in your life express love and like to receive love. In his book *The Five Love Languages*, Gary Chapman points out that people in a relationship often value different expressions of love. Some appreciate valuable time spent together. Others value gifts. Some value acts of service, physical touch, or words of affirmation. Learn to speak in all five languages.

Learn about communication, conflict management, and problem-solving. If this is the only step you take, your relationships will be well on their way to being awesome.

Focus on building the positive and not so much at eliminating the negative (or what you perceive to be the negative) in others. You cannot change anyone until that person feels your love and respect and knows deep down that the change is in their best interest.

Make all of your decisions about how to act and what to say from a foundation of love and genuine appreciation for the other person's awesomeness.

If you encounter problems in a relationship, avoid the urge to blame. Problems have solutions, and blame is not a solution. The other person's behavior may be the primary source of the problem and may need to change, but blame will only increase resistance. If the source of the problem is the other person, tell him or her how you feel, give the person an opportunity to change, and then make a decision to either end the relationship, change your attitude, or let go of the issue. And if you choose to let it go, really let it go.

If a relationship is valuable enough to save, and you see no way to fix it, consider making an appointment with a relationship counselor or coach. Relationships can be complicated, especially when more than two people are involved. When the dynamics become difficult to figure out on your own, don't be afraid to bring in an objective third party to help you sort it out.

Many of my clients come to me for help in growing and scaling their businesses, never realizing that certain relationship issues are having a negative impact. When we uncover and resolve the relationship issues, it is amazing to see the positive transformation both in the individual and in his or her business. It's as if a brand new person is born.

Imagine having no relationship problems or being able to resolve any issue without it becoming an argument. How would you feel on a daily basis going to work and communicating with prospects? When you master your emotions and become a champion influencer, you have the confidence to approach anyone at any time. What's more, your ability to network and to close deals skyrockets.

Invest in Your Financial Future

You work hard for your money, but how hard is your money working for you? Would you like your golden years to be truly golden, or are you settling for copper? Would you like to have another source of income that you don't have to work for?

Rich people may work for a living, but they can afford more of what life has to offer (both in time and money) because they put their money to work for them. You should be doing the same. The best way to do this if you haven't already is to start thinking about saving and investing, then start learning about it, then start doing it. The earlier you begin, the more time your money has to grow, and the more you benefit from the exponential growth from *compounding*— earning money from the money your investment already earned.

Part of investing in yourself involves investing in your money, so you're in a better position to live your life on your terms. Here are some techniques that have helped me over the years:

Pay yourself first. You have probably heard this numerous times, but a reasonable goal is to invest 10% of your pre-tax income toward retirement—more if you're over the age of forty.

Borrow money only for things that improve your productivity and income. For example, you can borrow to buy a house, because it will probably cost you less than if you had to rent and because the home will probably appreciate, earning you money over time. You can borrow to buy a car to get to work so you can earn money. You can borrow to buy a computer if you need it for education or to perform a job that generates income. But be careful not to borrow money to finance a lifestyle you cannot afford. If you are buried in debt, you will have little money to invest. All you're doing at that point is putting your money to work for your lenders, not for you.

If you are buried in debt, make a plan to reduce and eliminate your *consumer debt* (debt used to purchase items that do not appreciate in value). Consider speaking with a credit counselor. You may have options, such as consolidating debt to reduce the total amount of interest you're paying, and negotiating with lenders to reduce the amount you owe. Carrying some debt on a house or car is okay, but do not get into debt by spending beyond your means.

Build an emergency fund. Most people are unprepared for unexpected financial setbacks, such as job loss, expensive home repairs, or serious illness. You should have at least enough money saved up to cover six months of expenses.

Take out a home equity line of credit. If you owe less on your home than it is worth, a bank may approve a home equity line of credit that enables you to draw from it only when you need the money (and pay interest only on the money you draw). This can save you from losing your house in foreclosure in the event of a major financial setback. It can also buy you enough time to recover your financial footing or to list and sell your home. Be careful, though, not to draw funds from your line of credit unnecessarily. In other words, don't use your home as an automatic teller machine (ATM).

Take full advantage of tax deductions and credits. For example, if the government lets you deduct up to $5,500 in contributions to your IRA for the year, try to invest that much money. By making pre-tax contributions, you have more of your money working for you than going to the government.

Invest Wisely

Even if you're fortunate enough to have a savvy financial advisor, don't place all of your trust in one person or one company. You need to know what is going on with your money and how it is being invested, so be sure you're receiving regular reports from all persons you're working with. If you're not so savvy yourself, you can find plenty of books, websites, and videos that offer valuable insight into investing. Two authors I highly recommend are Warren Buffett and Ray Dalio. I love Buffett's rules for investing:

Rule #1: Don't lose money.

Rule #2: Never forget Rule #1.

In 2007, Dalio predicted the global financial crisis of 2008. When most people lost half of their nest eggs, he barely lost anything. To learn more about Ray Dalio, visit his website at www.economicprinciples.org and watch the video called "How the Economic Machine Works."

Here are a few generally accepted rules about investing that have served me well:

Diversify: You can easily diversify by investing in index funds. Another option is to invest in stocks and bonds, and to invest across multiple industries, so if one industry suffers, your return on others can make up the difference.

Pay attention to dollar-cost average: Invest on a regular schedule, so you're investing when markets are up, down, and in between. Ideally, you want to buy low and sell high, but predicting market fluctuations is challenging.

Reduce costs: Look for investments with low or no management fees, such as no-load funds that don't have hidden costs. Every dollar you spend on management fees is a dollar less you have in your investments.

Review and rebalance: Review your investment portfolio at least once a year to be sure it is aligned with your investment goals. For example, as you age, you may want to shift more of your investments from stocks and mutual funds to fixed-income investments that are less risky and provide you with a steady cash flow.

If you have children, I strongly encourage you to "implant the hard drive," as I call it, by teaching them how to manage their money and invest wisely. Most parents don't discuss finances with their children because they think they're too young or they don't want them to be concerned about money at such a young age. But few schools teach these important lessons, so you must ask yourself, *When do I think it will be the right time? Where will my children learn how to earn, save, and manage their money and investments?* Fewer and fewer companies are offering decent retirement plans to their employees, and numerous companies encourage employees to sign up for their 401(k), which is mainly an incentive for the company to get a tax write-off from Uncle Sam.

In sum, you can't rely on anyone to invest for you or your children, so educate yourself and then educate your children.

Invest in Your Business

Owning a business is an excellent way to invest in yourself and take control of your own destiny, assuming your business is as successful as you want it to be. The sad fact, however, is that 96% of all companies are out of business within ten years after they start. Hence, if you own a business, you must strive for continuous improvement. Here are some suggestions:

- Maintain close contact with your customers, so you stay current with their needs and desires. Many people say that owning a business is great because you can be your own boss. Not true. Your customers are your boss. Listen to them. Follow the trends. Know what the competition is doing and keep asking, "How can we do it better?"

- Do not micromanage, but be aware of what is going on in every department so you have better insight and can implement change when necessary. You may need to put even more effort into staying in touch with departments that don't interest you, such as accounting.
- Pay attention to even the smallest details. Those details can become astronomical problems if you're unaware of them.
- Review your goals and objectives annually, as everything is changing rapidly in technology and the world of business.
- If you don't have a board of directors, create one, or consult with a business advisor or trusted mentor. It's difficult to see everything related to your business from the inside; therefore, it's crucial to have someone outside your company provide you with an unbiased view of your business, the market, the competition, and so forth. Remember that a true coach and mentor will tell you what you need to hear, not what they think you want to hear.

Invest by Teaching Positive Thinking

You are already taking a valuable step toward investing in yourself by reading this book and adopting some of the practices I recommend. And you can do much more by sharing what you learn in this book with the people around you—your family, friends, coworkers, employees, customers, and so on.

The people we surround ourselves with often succumb to negative thinking patterns that can adversely impact not only their lives but also ours. If you can convince them to flip the negative into a positive, you will be giving them one of the greatest gifts you can give to anyone—empowerment—while freeing yourself from negative influences and the burden of other people's problems and poor choices. And when you create a community of positive thinkers, that community lifts all of its members to new heights.

Although you can certainly hand a person a copy of this book, they may not be receptive at first. A better approach may be to simply suggest one of the exercises in the book. For example, if you own a business and productivity begins to dip or you notice that an employee seems distracted, suggest that everyone take a five-minute break every hour to center themselves and be present. Suggest that they simply close their eyes and focus on their breathing, or imagine an experience from their past in which they were happy and excited, or recall something that made them laugh. Because some people don't know how to disconnect from their personal lives while they are at work and vice versa, and they often let their problems follow them, this five-minute break enables them to press the reset button and let go of distractions.

Be sure to remind them that smartphones are off limits during this break; this time is meant to help them regain focus and clarity. You can promote unity in your workplace by having everyone place their cell phones in a bag or box. You can also make it fun by having them pretend they are living back in the 80s when there were no cell phones. Even better, tell them you're giving them the gift of connecting to their inner selves and spending a moment in peace and tranquility.

While this is a great practice in the workplace, it's also effective at home. You'll find that performing this same exercise with your spouse or significant other—and with your children if you have them—will improve their mood and bring focus back to the time you're spending together as a family.

STEP 5

Persist: Continuous Joyful Execution

Have you ever been "in the zone"? It is the point at which your purpose, skills, and consciousness align so perfectly that your performance exceeds what you thought was humanly possible. You are so focused, so absorbed in the present moment, that you lose any sense of the past or future. Your actions are effortless, and your energy is endless. You lose your sense of self in a cloud of exuberance. You feel at one with the universe.

When an athlete is in the zone, they are invincible. Instincts take over, and they seem to be in the right place at the right time doing the right thing. You almost feel sorry for anyone who is competing against them, except for the fact that they usually know the feeling themselves, and they understand and appreciate that person's level of performance. Similarly, when a writer is in the zone, he or she is in a trance-like state, writing without consciously thinking about it. When a business owner is in the zone, he or she knows what to do without thinking.

When you're in the zone, you are engaged in what I like to call "continuous joyful execution." You perform the activity or task in which you are immersed joyfully and effortlessly.

Persistence = Continuous Joyful Execution

How do you get in the zone? How do you persist in the face of adversity and failure? How do you operate in continuous joyful execution? You can find the answer to all of these questions in the following three-step process:

1. **Be present.** Focus entirely on what you're doing at every point in time. You are not thinking or trying, you are doing. As Yoda from *Star Wars* said in *The Empire Strikes Back*, "Do or do not. There is no try." I would say, "Don't think. Don't try. Do." When you are present, you are immune to negative thinking.

2. **Function in a state of gratitude.** Be thankful for everything in the moment, including the work you have been given, the ability to do that work well, the energy and time you have to do it, and your ability to exert your full focus and maximum effort. Functioning in a state of gratitude is most important when you may be least capable of it—particularly when the day is long and you are struggling. Remind yourself that you're grateful because that is who you are. Your best self is full of gratitude at all times.

3. **Bring the joy.** Being present and engaged in activity is naturally joyous, especially when you have an attitude of gratitude. What often brings us down about our work are factors outside the work itself. We don't like where we're working, we don't like our pay or position, we are worried about other things. Don't let all that junk get you down. Let the joy of doing flow through you.

I urge you to challenge yourself to live every day enthusiastically from the moment you wake up. Be grateful for everything. Find the good in all situations. You know what you need to do, and you can do it feeling miserable or happy or somewhere in between. Why not choose happy? Keep in mind that a smile brings on a serotonin release, which serves as an antidepressant to lift your mood. Your joy will lift the moods of all those around you, causing them to feed off your energy and you off theirs.

I also urge you to take every opportunity to practice being present. If you're having a conversation, remove all distractions. Turn off the TV, step away from the computer, mute your cell phone, and stop thinking about what needs to be done as the other person talks. Truly listen to what the other person is saying, and when you speak, be deliberate in the words you choose. Likewise, when you are at work, clear your mind of all thoughts about home. When you are home, clear your mind of all thoughts about work. When you are spending time with your mate or your children, focus on them.

Researchers from the University of Michigan have looked into the notion of multitasking and have concluded that people are not very good at it. In shifting their attention from one thing to another, their performance for each task suffers. So unless you're in a situation where you can sincerely put one activity in the background while focusing on another (which usually results in the background activity being ignored or being a distraction), I suggest you avoid trying to multitask.

Know Your Why

I want you to go deep into your heart and ask yourself:

What is my why?
What drives me?
What lifts me up?

What makes me happy?
What am I known for?
What is the purpose of my life?
What is that big why that will remind me to keep moving when I
am failing and there isn't anyone there for me?

Journal your answers to those questions over and over until you're clear about your mission on this planet. Once you discover it and before you do anything to achieve it, however, you must believe in yourself. You must grasp with your whole heart that your mission is what you were born to do and destined to become, so there is no question that you are capable of achieving it and no doubt that you will. You may fail many times and your motivation may dwindle; at times, you may even consider giving up. But listen to me, there is greatness in you. As long as you continue to move forward, any "failure" will result in forward movement, bringing you closer to your goal. You *will* win.

I want to remind you that you can choose to walk with fear or faith. I choose to walk with faith, and you can too. Knowing I will achieve whatever I set my mind to, that I will overcome any obstacles, and that as long as I don't quit, I *will* win is incredible motivation. I also want you to keep in mind that when you are tired, alone, feeling hopeless, or experiencing setbacks, all of that means you are making an attempt at something, that you're going for it. You can't feel tired if you're exerting no effort, so keep fighting your way through it. As T.S. Eliot wrote, "Only those who will risk going too far can possibly find out how far one can go."

So here's your assignment: I want your *why* to be so clear that even if you put on headphones and blast the music, you will hear your *why*. When you take the headphones off, you still hear your why. You have the worst day of your life—you lose your job, your car breaks down, someone steals your identity, you break up with the person you thought was your soulmate. Somewhere in all of that mess, you see your *why*. You fail a dozen times, and your *why* remains. Your *why* is the one thing that stands by you at all times, and it is not going anywhere, ever. Your *why* is who you are. Your *why* is your soul and your salvation. And, ultimately, when you feel fear, you feel your *why* even more intensely, pushing that fear away.

Plan and Prepare for the Future, but Act in the Present

Before you drive somewhere, you probably think about how you're going to get from your point of departure to your destination. But when you're driving, you focus on driving. You keep your eyes on the road and not on the map. This is the approach you want to also take with your life plans.

When you set goals and objectives, milestones and deadlines, and make a schedule, you know what you will be doing from day to day. However, be aware that when the time comes to execute your plan, don't become too entrenched in those milestones or deadlines. Allow them to be fluid; you may be ready sooner than you thought, or you may need a little more time. But if you know where you're going, and you focus on driving and putting those miles in, eventually you will achieve the desired outcome.

Likewise, when athletes train, they may focus on developing certain skills or abilities. For example, a runner may have different training sessions to focus on technique, endurance, strength, and speed. During a race, however, the runner runs. If he or she thinks about *how*, losing is almost guaranteed.

Success in any endeavor requires preparation in the form of study and training. During these sessions, focus solely on those activities. All of your preparation will pay off come game day.

Be Patient

As English playwright John Heyword once wrote, "Rome wasn't built in a day." Later, motivational author James Clear revised it: "Rome wasn't built in a day, but they were laying bricks every hour." I like the revision, because that is exactly what success takes. You will probably not achieve success overnight, but that doesn't mean you should stop laying bricks. Unfortunately, that is exactly what many people do. They set goals and objectives, and when they don't see results as soon as expected, they stop. Even more tragic is when people achieve success, and then they stop doing what they did to achieve that success, causing it to fade.

I see it all the time. Two people start out having a great relationship. They are fascinated with one another. They pay attention to each other. They respect one another. They spend time together doing fun, interesting things. Then, they stop. One or both of them becomes stagnant, and they stop learning and growing. Soon, they become bored with one another, so they stop paying attention to each other and doing fun and interesting things together. If any passion is left, it often becomes redirected and focused on problems or perceived weaknesses in the other person. Before long, the relationship explodes or fizzles out.

I also see it in business. An entrepreneur comes up with a great idea and pours all of his energy into making the business a success. He attends to all details, motivates workers, connects with customers, and markets with a passionate belief in the products or services he provides. Then, he gets comfortable and stops doing all that. He forgets that he succeeded because he was innovative and passionate and worked hard, so he and his business become stagnant. Over time, the market changes, competition stiffens, and other people continue to innovate while his thriving business becomes yesterday's news and loses its relevance. If he doesn't get his mojo back—and quick—closure of the business soon follows.

Stagnation can occur in all areas of your life—your mind, relationships, career, family, finances, and so forth. That is why you need to be patient and continue to lay bricks. Remember, as another author wrote, "Rome wasn't built in a day, but it fell in one."

Another Perspective

As Stephen Covey wrote in his book *7 Habits of Highly Effective People*, you should "begin with the end in mind." While I recommend that you set goals and objectives and then focus exclusively on what you're doing in the present, other experts suggest that you focus on the goal—or keep your eyes on the prize. This is certainly a valid approach, especially when you encounter adversity or are not getting the results and rewards you expected. Reminding yourself of the goal can give you the motivation to press on. However, I maintain that after you remind yourself of the goal or check your progress, you shift your focus back to the present. Only what you do right now will bring you closer to achieving your goal.

Failure Happens

Of course, when you set out to achieve a goal, you never want to do so with a shred of doubt. However, failure does sometimes happen. As humans, we are apt to make mistakes, unfavorable choices, and poor decisions; we may lose motivation as forces outside our control sink our dreams. This is precisely when persistence is most necessary—and most difficult.

When failure occurs, you have several choices:

- **Give up.** Not recommended.
- **Regroup.** Realize you probably learned a valuable lesson, so you regroup and try again without making the same

mistakes. You may need to develop a different skill set, adjust your goals and objectives, change course, or take a different path to achieving the same goal.

- **Start over.** Even if you have little left after the failure, you have your most valuable asset—*you*. Your imagination, cognitive abilities, knowledge, skills, and abilities can help you gather the resources to start over. You always have options, even if those options require you to ask family members for help or seek government assistance.

Some successful entrepreneurs even celebrate failure as a necessary consequence of innovation. Fail Fest is a day-long celebration of failures, which you can find out more about by visiting failfest.us. As Fail Fest's founders point out, we only discuss the failures of famous inventors, not their successful inventions. Leonardo da Vinci, for example, failed at creating a flying machine. In school, Thomas Edison was told that he was "too stupid to learn anything." Walt Disney was fired from a job at a newspaper because he "lacked imagination and had no good ideas." Steven Spielberg was rejected *twice* by the University of Southern California's School of Cinematic Arts. After his first performance at the Grand Ole Opry, Elvis Presley was told, "You ain't goin' nowhere, son. You ought to go back to drivin' a truck."

Failure can often give us the kick in the pants we need to succeed. So when you experience failure, don't beat yourself up over it. Instead, turn it into a positive by asking yourself the following questions:

1. What did I learn from this experience?
2. What positive outcomes resulted from this experience?
3. How can I improve?

Take the Persistence Challenge

Before you leave this chapter on persistence, take the persistence challenge:

1. Think of a time in life when you gave up on something.
2. Imagine the outcome if you had been three times more persistent.
3. Imagine the outcome if you had been twenty times more persistent.
4. For the next three to seven days, I dare you to do something each day that is totally outside your comfort zone (because most of what we want is outside our comfort zones). As you do these things, don't give yourself an out; instead, imagine that if you don't do it, you won't bring food to the table, or that your entire future for your family, friends, or career is at risk. This will help you practice using yourself as leverage, which will serve you going forward on other areas of your life. As you do this, focus on being courageous, persistent, completely out of your head, fully present in the moment, not worrying about what anyone is going to say, and more joyful.

Here's what this might look like:

- If you're afraid of public speaking, sign up for a free class at a Toastmasters group in your town.
- Attend on day one.
- On day two, go live on social media and talk about it. (Tag me along with #worklikeanimmigrant so I can give you kudos!)

- On day three, go to a meet-up in your town and talk about how speaking in front of people isn't as scary as you thought, or share your story with three complete strangers.

Think of this exercise as resistance training. Whenever you travel outside your comfort zone, you will meet resistance, and you will need to overcome it to complete the task. The more you practice this exercise, the easier you will find it to remain persistent in the face of adversity. I sincerely want you pumping up your persistence muscle because most people fail to achieve their dreams not from lack of intelligence, talent, or skills, but from a lack of persistence.

STEP 6

Face Uncertainty with Certainty

As I related in Chapter 7, when I came home one night to find my wife sitting on the floor crying desperately for help, I was heartbroken at first and then afraid. I had not cried since I was six and a half years old, when I thought about stabbing myself to end the mental abuse and physical beating I had been subjected to. But that day, Angie's intense suffering brought me to tears. Because she had lost trust in doctors and wouldn't talk to anyone else about her problems or how she was feeling, I was truly afraid that one day I would come home to find her dead.

In the beginning, coaching Angie wasn't easy, because she was deeply depressed and we were both stressed out. Even though we shared the goal of being a healthy, happy, and productive family, our discussions often turned into arguments. To try to shift my mindset, I started reading the Bible daily instead of once every six months. I also read a book a week to learn about how to help Angie deal with her mental anguish. As you know, I also took multiple courses and began working with the best coaches in the world.

Imagine walking into your CEO's office and handing him or her a letter of resignation to quit a long-term growing career. That was me. Now fast forward a year and imagine being in an audience with thousands of others and your mentor selecting you randomly out of the crowd. He asks what you learned during the event, but instead of answering the question, you thank him for providing the mentorship, training, and techniques that helped you save the life of a loved one. That was also me, standing on the stage with Tony Robbins in December 2015, in front of three thousand people.

Imagining is a powerful technique that allows uncertainty to feel like certainty. It pushes your present self to not put off anything, because nothing is impossible for you. When you commit to your present self to do something every day, rain or shine, toward becoming your future self, your mind locks onto that vision. I remember dreaming that one day Tony Robbins would do an intervention on me. Instead, Tony and thousands of others were in tears and applauding me for letting everything go—status, ego, money, power—so I could be fully present and focused at home to save the love of my life. They congratulated me for going to extremes for Angie and for the bravery of sharing something so personal. Tony actually said, "I met someone as crazy as me and with even more energy and drive than my young version." There are no words to describe what an honor that was.

When you face fear and uncertainty, take this same approach—that of converting fear (losing Angie) into certainty and positive action (saving Angie). Embrace the challenge and don't give yourself a choice. Then, switch to *must* mode by raising the necessity. Call up your future self into your present every time you feel challenged or experience extreme difficulties in your life or business.

And as a last note: it's critical to understand that focusing on the fear will make it bigger than it already is. Instead of striving to fight that fear, turn your mind to positive thoughts by embracing certainty of the future outcome. If, however, you are having trouble letting go of the fear due to baggage from the past, I have an exercise at the end of this chapter to help with that.

Do It

Are you holding back? Are you afraid to do something you truly want to do? Do you quiver and shake during interviews or before delivering presentations? Are you afraid to knock on doors or make phone calls to generate new business? Are you reluctant to promote yourself, even though you are awesome? If so, all of that needs to stop. When you face your fears and uncertainty with certainty, you learn to smash those fears and reluctancies. And when you begin to feel uncertain, you simply need to remind yourself:

- I am awesome.
- Nobody is better than me or deserves success and happiness more than I do.
- I got this.
- The worst that can happen is not that bad.
- The best that can happen is amazing.

Also keep in mind that when people are on their deathbeds, they generally have more regrets over what they missed out on or didn't do than the failures or mistakes they made. So, if you're afraid to do something, consider how you will feel ten or fifteen years down the road if you don't do it—or don't even try.

Replace Uncertainty with Confidence

Uncertainty is often caused by thoughts implanted in us at a very early age or negative beliefs we have accepted, usually for no good reason—or any *reason* at all. We think we are not good enough, smart enough, strong enough, or deserving enough to get what we want or do what we want in life.

But you can't allow yourself to focus on these erroneous beliefs, especially when other people are the root cause of your negativity or when they stand in your way. You are pursuing your goals and dreams for yourself, not for them. Focusing on the negative doesn't serve you; it wastes your time and depletes your energy. When a problem or obstacle arises, it's natural for the mind to grab onto the negative first, but then it has a choice: it can travel down the path of worry and defeat or the path to solution and victory. You know logically that you won't achieve a positive outcome with a worrisome and defeatist attitude and a mindset that embraces limitations—being negative or in doubt only digs a deeper hole out of which you eventually have to climb.

The solution to this is that immediately upon identifying a problem or obstacle, take the path to solution and victory. Envision your goal vividly with the end result in sight to draw your attention away from the problem to the solution. Engage your imagination and your senses to see and feel yourself achieving your objective. Imagine touching, smelling, hearing, seeing, and enjoying all the things you want in life.

Remember that the mind always sees the problem or suffering first, and it must do so to identify whatever is causing discomfort. But then it is your choice and your responsibility to shift your mind's focus to positive outcomes—the joyful state when the challenge is behind you. It is all about rewiring the brain to choose the right path as early as possible in the process, so you don't waste time and energy following the path of worry and defeat. The guidance I provide in this chapter and in Step 1 of this book can help you make this shift.

Whenever you feel depressed or notice that you're beating yourself up, pause and ask yourself, *If my best friend were going through a really tough time right now and were deeply depressed, anxious, hopeless, stuck, or experiencing extreme difficulties, what would I say to lift him or her up to continue moving forward toward his or her dreams?*

Engage Your Higher Self

We hear a lot these days about robots and artificial intelligence replacing human beings. If the mind were merely a physical entity, such a futuristic scenario could unfold. However, the human mind is more than a biological computer. It is infused with a spirit that unites us all and provides inspiration that transcends mere thought. It is what makes us truly human. When we function in this transcendent state, we are capable of achieving whatever we set our minds to. We are what I like to call our "higher selves."

Sadly, when we experience adversity, we often become our lower selves. We make poor choices and bad decisions, worry ourselves into a state of anxiety and depression, make excuses, blame others, and may even act immorally or unethically out of desperation. By doing so, we relinquish many of our most powerful gifts, including the power of the imagination and the power of choice. We are telling ourselves that we are not to blame and that we have no power to overcome a challenge, even when we are the *only* ones who have the power to do so.

Your higher self would never allow this thinking because it has the imagination and resourcefulness to overcome any challenge. It does the right thing and makes the right choices. It focuses on solutions. It is certain in the face of uncertainty and comfortable in the most difficult situations. It is tranquil and unruffled, because it has the power to set the direction and make things happen.

Right now, I want you to engage your higher self. Give your higher self a name, one that represents for you someone who is confident, self-assured, creative, and powerful. You can Google something like "names of powerful women" or "names of powerful men" to get some ideas. For example, Bria is an Irish name that means "power, strength, and vigor," and Alexander means "defender of men." Names of Greek or Roman gods and goddesses are always good too.

Whenever you start feeling down or overwhelmed by a challenge, I want you to engage your higher self:

1. Imagine your higher self sitting right next to you, coaching you, reminding you that conditions are not as bad as they may seem.
2. Ask your higher self if you are missing something or have overlooked anything.
3. Imagine your higher self saying, "You got this. You're awesome. Don't settle for less than you're capable of being."
4. Do ten jumping jacks or pushups, or move your head up and down, breathing in and out of your nose as fast as you can for one minute, feeling the energy building in your body. While you're moving, remind yourself of your mission by asking yourself one or two of the following questions:
   - What do I truly want out of life? What is my life purpose?
   - Why do I want what I want? What will I feel having it?
   - What can my higher self do to overcome obstacles on the road ahead?
   - What would I like to be written in my obituary? What would I like others to say about me when I pass away?

Asking questions of your higher self is one of the best motivational and visualization strategies you can add to your arsenal when dealing with uncomfortable situations, or with the sensation that all is lost. The more you engage your higher self and ask it questions, the better the answers you will receive. I began asking my higher self questions when I was only seven, and it has helped me to stay focused on my mission and purpose in life. If I can do it, then so can you! All you have to do is condition your focus by reminding yourself of the reason you're on this journey, with the highest amount of certainty you've ever had.

Remember: Negativity breeds more negativity. If you expect bad things to happen to you, they will. If you are prone to negative thinking, I want you to take a stand right now. Imagine your higher self telling you, *Enough is enough! Get out there and create the change you so desperately seek. You are not negative. Your mind is tricking you.*

We know that the mind is so powerful that it can make you believe bad is good and good is bad. Think about how much suffering Adolf Hitler was able to inflict by tricking scores of his countrymen and women into believing that Jews were evil. Their beliefs were so strong that they committed crimes against humanity that were so atrocious, most of us cannot imagine having the capacity to commit such acts. Yet, in Nazi Germany, the leadership was able to make those acts seem perfectly acceptable to many of the country's citizens.

I also want to warn you not to fall for mind traps. If you think about something enough, whether it is true or a lie, you and others will eventually believe it. Control your "pink rubber" (your brain) and take your life back by planting the seeds of a strong mindset to fulfill your dreams. It is never too late to press the reset button, and if you happen to go negative one day, simply press the reset button again to reboot your brain. Forget about anything that didn't serve you the day before. By starting every day anew, you begin each day with eager anticipation—and the start of anything is always exciting. Buying a new car or home, starting a new relationship, beginning a new job, or launching a new business carries its own level of exhilaration. Strive to start every day with that same sense of eager anticipation.

Be Confident; You Can't Fake It

You cannot fake confidence. You can try, but any shred of uncertainty will show through. There's no "fake it till you make it." You are it. You move it, you breathe it, you dress it, you act it, you speak it. Confidence is you, and you are confidence. Believe and you will achieve.

This is it! *You* are it! Be who you were meant to be. Believe in who are and what you have to offer the world. Have faith that you are where you need to be, and embrace the moment. Be passionate in delivering your value to others and you can't go wrong.

Burn the Past

For many people, their biggest obstacle is what has already occurred and cannot be changed. They focus so much on past success, past failures, and past mistakes that they become frozen in the past. As a result, they cannot move forward, and they typically stop growing. This is even more ridiculous than it is tragic, because nobody can fix the past or relive it. Dwelling on the past is merely dragging around heavy baggage—like train cars loaded down with lead that keep the engine from roaring forward into the future.

As of this moment, I want you to commit to burning your past, and here's how.

1. Over the next three days, journal your answers and thoughts about these three questions:
   - What is your biggest fear in life?
   - Has that fear been holding you back to live the life you deserve? How so? Why? The idea here is to log your thoughts and feelings about the fear and increase your awareness of it, so you are better able to deal with it.

- What are you faking your way through because you're afraid of dealing with it or afraid of others knowing about it? Is it your finances, career, a business, a close relationship, an addiction? You have been ignoring the problem and stuffing down your emotions for too long. It's time to get real.

2. On the fourth day, burn those papers and celebrate the new you by writing down what will change going forward so you can live free from fear as your higher self and start enjoying your life to the fullest.

3. Forgive yourself and everyone you think has ever harmed you. Let go of any worries or concerns about what anybody else may say about your dream, and make a commitment to go for it.

4. On the fifth day, journal about what you can do for the next twenty-plus days of the month now that you have conquered this fear. What do you need to think about and focus on now that you have burned your past?

As a high-performance consultant, trainer, and coach, I remind myself and my clients that when something bad happens in life, what comes out of it can be something truly wonderful. It might connect you to new people and put you on a path toward a dream you had as a kid—a dream that you had put to sleep over the years. Maybe you were raised to do something you aren't passionate about, and you became comfortable with it and ended up settling for what you're doing now. But when something happens that we perceive as bad, it can actually awaken us from our trance to realize that we have bigger and more fulfilling options.

STEP 7

Collaborate

*If I have seen further, it is by standing
on the shoulders of giants.*
—Sir Isaac Newton

We are often taught to live our lives as a contest that produces winners and losers. My dream is to create a world of winners and winners—one where winners climb onto the shoulders of winners and rise to new heights, where people work together to develop and build a world rich in diversity and innovation.

Does that sound like a fantasy? I would argue that it is more realistic than a world of winners and losers. To believe in a world of winners and losers is to believe that health, wealth, happiness, and fulfillment are finite—that there is only so much to go around. From this perspective, one person's gain is another's loss; for you to become wealthy, another person must become poor; for you to be happy, another must suffer. But this is a fallacy, an all-too-common limiting belief. We know that wealth can be created, not necessarily at someone else's expense but through innovation, collaboration, and hard work. We can look back on history and see a steady progression in quality of life, health, happiness, and fulfillment, and we are living in an era of accelerating progress and growth.

This is not to say that the world is without problems. All around the world people suffer from poverty and injustice, and yes, the rich and powerful sometimes oppress the poor and humble. But this is not the result of insufficient wealth and resources to go around; rather, it is often the product of fear, greed, and limiting thoughts. It is the result of people being afraid of what they might lose if they give up some of what they have to help others achieve their dreams. It is a failure of the imagination.

Picture how amazing this world would be if we were all striving to be our best selves and helping others to become their best selves. Imagine how much we would accomplish if we focused on pursuing our dreams instead of wallowing in our own or others' misery. Imagine what we could achieve if all nations around the world redirected their time, energy, and resources from oppression to achievement and empowerment.

I also know that my dream is not a fantasy because it is how I have lived my life. I have been climbing on the shoulders of giants, continuously achieving new heights since my youth, and I have empowered others to climb on my shoulders to achieve their dreams, thus creating health, wealth, happiness, and fulfillment for those whom I have mentored—and at no one else's expense.

I want you to have the same advantages I've had. I want you to climb on my shoulders to rise to new heights in your life, and I want you to give a boost to others by sharing your knowledge and wisdom. Together, we can build the world of my dreams, a dream I think we all share. Whatever you do today in your business or toward your dream, I challenge you to ask yourself more often, *Am I creating better, faster, and newer conversations in my market to foster a new value curve and differentiate myself from my competitors?*

Find a Great Mentor

Many businesses have a board of directors and/or upper-level management who cement the direction for the organization, holding everyone accountable for executing its mission. Together, they set policies, develop plans, make the big decisions, and ensure that the business's strategies and operations align with its business plan, goals, and objectives. Few will argue against the necessity and value of strong leadership and direction in running a successful business, yet few of us have such direction in our personal lives.

In multiple ways, you are a business—You, Inc. You have policies (principles) that guide your decisions, goals you wish to achieve, a plan to achieve them, and objectives you must meet along the way (at least you should!). As your own "board of directors," you oversee operations in several departments—health and fitness, career, family, finances, human resources, community relations, marketing, and so forth—and you're in charge of making the big decisions and ensuring that your strategies and operations align with your plans, goals, and objectives.

With so much to do and so many balls to juggle, it's easy to lose focus, and when you do, you start dropping balls, lose sight of your goals, focus your attention on one aspect of your life at the expense of another, and spend most of your time putting out fires without making any headway. Certainly, if you're an outstanding manager—impeccably organized, self-disciplined, self-directed, self-aware, well-informed, wise, and completely honest with yourself—you may be able to handle all of these responsibilities yourself, but I cannot think of one person, myself included, who has all of those qualifications. The fact is that nearly every one of us is under-qualified to manage our own lives as they should be managed.

What most of us need and few of us have is an advisor or mentor, someone to help us set our direction, suggest ideas on how to achieve our goals better and faster, and let us know when we're drifting off course so we can make the necessary corrections.

If you don't have an excellent mentor, I suggest you seek out one—or more than one—as soon as possible. Think of it as expanding your personal "board of directors" so that you're no longer the sole member—one mentor to help you with relationships, another to help you with your career or business, another to help with your personal and spiritual development, and so on. After all, not all mentors are experts in all of the areas in which you may need guidance.

So where do you search for mentors?

You can start in the various circles in which you belong—friends, colleagues, business associates, your place of worship, parenting groups, and so on. Look for someone you admire, someone who "has her act together" in the area in which you need mentoring, and meet with the person to discuss your needs and explain the level of involvement you would like and the time commitment. Another option is to hire a professional mentor. You want to watch out for people who are more interested in serving their own needs than those of their clients, or who are simply unqualified to give the advice they are hired to deliver, but there are definitely excellent mentors out there. You can get a good sense in an interview or discovery call where you ask the kinds of questions that will help you know if the person is a good match for you.

Whether you choose to recruit from your personal and professional contacts or hire a professional, make sure the person (or people) you choose have the following qualifications:

- The skills and expertise in the field in which you need mentoring (By "field," I don't necessarily mean a professional field; for example, if you seek mentoring for improving your marriage, you may know a friend who gives valuable advice in this area.)
- Well accomplished in his or her field (he or she walks the talk)
- Highly respected in her or his field
- The willingness to share her or his skills and expertise

- A positive attitude, highly motivational
- A personal interest in you and in helping you achieve your goals
- Enthusiasm in the area in which you seek mentoring
- A commitment to continual learning in the field
- The capacity to be brutally honest with you (someone who won't simply tell you what he or she thinks you want to hear)
- Respect for the opinions and decisions of others
- Trustworthiness
- Perseverance and dedication to your long-term development (not someone who wants to merely give you a quick fix and send you on your way)
- Exclusiveness (someone who chooses his or her mentees carefully)

Before I sought guidance from a mentor, I frequently became overwhelmed with worry. I would go through cycles of earning more income than I had ever imagined and then being broke, buried in bills, and concerned about how I would care for myself and my family. I frequently drifted from the path I had set for myself and found myself making poor choices and losing ground. My number-one mistake was that I did not have a mentor or an accountability partner to offer guidance, hold me accountable, and help me find a way out when I became stuck. I often felt like quitting and giving up, something that happens to most of us at some point.

But imagine that in a crisis or in the midst of chaos, you had a tool like Amazon's Alexa, only smarter and wiser, that you could ask for advice on what to say, what to do, or how to do something faster or better, such as:

- how to create the ideal call to action during a presentation to provide instant results

- how to produce better videos
- how to build your own event
- how to create a program or course that provides massive results
- how to build and run a profitable mastermind
- how to get a high-ticket client
- how to become unstuck
- how to grow and scale faster
- how to overcome fear, anxiety, or depression

What if this tool could help you refocus on what matters most to you and ensure you didn't stray from your path to success? How would that change your life? That's the power of having a mentor—and not just any mentor, but one who has been there, done that, who knows the patterns of what it takes to win and advance fast, and who can help you produce life-changing results.

Be a Great Mentee

The mentoring relationship is a two-way street. Although part of a mentor's job is to hold you accountable, share strategies that provide quicker results, and get you out of your head when you go there, you should strive to make this role mostly a passive one for the mentor. In other words, you don't want the mentor to feel as though he needs to be a helicopter parent, hovering over you to make sure you do what you promised. Instead, you should hold yourself accountable, using your mentor as an added incentive to do so. This is why you want to choose someone you respect and trust; you will be more motivated to follow through on the person's advice.

Here are some tips on how to be a good mentee:

Optimize the time you spend together. A great mentor's time is valuable. Be prepared when you meet. Have a list of your accomplishments since the previous meeting and what you want to work on going forward. Be clear when asking for advice. Be specific when describing your challenges and desired outcomes.

Facilitate meeting times and places. If your mentor is doing this as a favor, make it easy and pleasant for him to meet with you. Go out of your way to choose a time and place that is convenient for him. Pick up the tab at cafes and restaurants.

Do what you say you will do. Not following through is likely to frustrate your mentor and may even result in an end to the relationship.

Be generous. Mentors benefit from the relationships they have with good mentees. They learn about new technologies and new approaches to doing things that they can use to achieve higher levels of success and to share with their other mentees. Grow your network and put your mentor in contact with other individuals who may be able to establish mutually beneficial relationships with him or her.

Provide frank and honest feedback. To improve, mentors need honest feedback. Let them know what's working and what's not and what you could use more or less of. Unless you tell your mentor what you think and how you feel, he or she cannot make adjustments.

Be a mentor. One of the best ways to become a better mentee is to mentor someone else, so you develop a better understanding of what it takes to grasp the challenges your mentor faces. In addition, being a mentor is a great way to engage in continual learning—your mentee is likely to expose you to things in your field you were not aware of and challenge you to be your best self. You also show *your* mentors that you are "paying it forward," which encourages them to be more generous with you.

Ask Yourself the Right Questions

Regardless of whether you have a mentor, and especially if you don't, you need to hold yourself accountable by asking the right questions. According to Drs. Linda Elder and Richard Paul in their book *The Art of Asking Essential Questions*:

> The quality of our lives is determined by the quality of our thinking. The quality of our thinking, in turn, is determined by the quality of our questions, for questions are the engine, the driving force behind thinking. Without questions, we have nothing to think about. Without essential questions, we often fail to focus our thinking on the significant and substantive.

To begin to hold yourself accountable, I want you to ask yourself the following questions and answer them with brutal honesty:

- Am I stagnant in any area of my life? If so, which area(s)? (See the Step 3 chapter for the areas of your life you must balance to achieve fulfillment.)
- Are there areas of my life I am neglecting? Why?
- Am I lacking drive in any area of my life? Is that the same area where I am stuck?
- What am I doing to get unstuck or to increase my drive?
- What outcomes do I want in the various areas of my life?
- What can I do (or do better) to achieve the desired outcomes?

- Who can provide guidance on how to achieve my desired outcomes?
- Who can help me achieve my desired outcomes?

I have you asking a lot of questions throughout this book, and I have a reason for that. Thinking travels a path, and often that path leads us in the wrong direction. If the path our thoughts are on is destructive, it frequently leads to a dead end. The only way out is to redirect our thoughts, and the only way to do that is to stop asking the questions that got us blocked, and start asking questions that redirect us down a more productive path. A good mentor will help you to start asking the right questions, but without a mentor, it's crucial for you to redirect your thinking on your own—by asking questions that draw your focus from problems to solutions.

Take the 99-Day Ignite Your Best Self Challenge

If you can't find a mentor or can't afford to hire one right now, I encourage you to ask a friend or your spouse to be your accountability partner and do this challenge together. This person will have one mission: to cheer you on and hold you accountable for the next ninety-nine days—no matter what occurs in your surroundings, in the economy, or in your life in general.

The goal for this challenge is for you to accomplish one to three things every day that will get you fired up and more excited—be it spicing up your marriage, working on fulfilling a dream, getting back into an old hobby, or doing something that will bring you one step closer to your ideal lifestyle. Progress equals happiness, even if little by little, and I want you to celebrate each step you take!

The way you'll execute this challenge is to document the entire experience in a journal or notebook. The reason we're going "old school" here by not using technology to keep track of our progress is because writing is connected to the thinking part of the brain. So, each evening, you'll write down the one to three things you plan to accomplish the next day and the "why" behind each one; you'll also call or text your accountability partner (or, if you live with that person, simply set time aside to talk at the end of each day). During that conversation, you'll let your partner know what you accomplished that day and celebrate together. Then, you'll share your goals with them for the next day.

One hint for success: Your morning routine will dictate how your day will go. So in the first fifteen minutes of your morning, I want you to review the one to three things you're going to accomplish for the day. Then, I want you to visualize completing the task(s) and celebrating with your partner.

For example, my wife and I are accountability partners. Here is what two sample days look like for me:

Day 1

- Doing, Not Trying — I am going to exercise and go for a swim at 5:00 a.m.
- My Why — So that I can build a strong, healthy body to have more energy and vibrancy, and so that I can live much longer to enjoy my family as well as work on my mission to make the world a better place.

- Doing, Not trying — I am going to spend 60 minutes creating mind-blowing new content strategies for my business.
- My Why — So that my clients and raving fans worldwide can apply additional valuable strategies to their businesses and get immediate results.

Day 2

- Doing, Not Trying — I am going to go for a power walk with my family for 45 minutes at 6:00 a.m.
- My Why - To stay healthy as a family and have extra time together having fun.

- Doing, Not Trying — I am taking a salsa dancing class with Angie at 5:00 p.m.
- My Why — To spice things up in our marriage even more!

The ideal scenario would be to have your accountability partner also participate in the challenge, but it's fine if that person solely encourages and supports you in your quest. Simply focusing on the one to three things that will improve areas you've been putting on hold for a while will be powerful. Whether it's your health, the quality of your relationships, an old hobby, and/or your business or career that you're seeking to ignite, I want you to celebrate even the smallest wins as you move forward on this challenge.

I also encourage you to join our Facebook group called "The Millionaire Mindset." When you do, share in an introductory post that you just finished reading the book and are going to take on the 99-Day Ignite Your Best Self Challenge (use the hashtag #99dayignite). Keep us posted on your progress every nine days for ten weeks, and then at the end, post what you accomplished during those ninety-nine days.

In addition to your daily goals, you'll answer the following fifteen questions once a week—ideally on a Sunday before you start your week. You'll want to keep these questions nearby throughout the day, looking at them a minimum of three times (during meals can be a good routine) to remind your best self what you are made of.

These questions are as follows:

1. What is/are your goal(s) or your mission for this week?
2. What is your purpose for this week?
3. List your wins and your losses over the course of the past week.
4. How can you create a new value curve in your life or business to separate you from your competitors, or cut the umbilical cord from past generations and start something new that generations from now will learn from you?
5. The next time you encounter a terrible situation, what will you do to make it better?
6. What can you do differently when something goes wrong again?
7. What did you celebrate this week?
8. What is your biggest distraction?
9. What can you do *now* to eliminate those distractions?
10. What can you do to your schedule to remove some of the distraction and whatever is blocking what is truly important in your life?
11. How do you feel about yourself at the end of the day?
12. Is there an area of your life where you are lacking drive? If so, what is it?
13. What would it take to reignite your passion in that area of your life?
14. In five words, what would you like to be remembered for being great at?
15. At the end of each day, are you living up to your five words?

To experience real, positive change in your life, you need to shake yourself out of your complacency and leave your comfort zone—and this challenge can be exactly what you need to do that.

Here's the thing: although I like to be right, I don't like saying "I told you so." I don't want you to write to me fifteen years from now to tell me you have regrets because you passed up a golden opportunity, or that you turned your back on a relationship that could have truly made you happy, or because you finally realized that you should have teamed up with a mentor or accountability partner long ago.

I cannot count the number of times I have heard people say, "I hate my life," "I hate my job," "I hate my relationship," "I wish I had _____ when I was younger." My response to that is, "When will be the right time to start living your life on your terms? If not now, when?" The truth is, today is the perfect time to start setting an example that will stand as a testament for future generations, showing them how they can live a fuller, richer, happier life. So I urge you to make the commitment today by saying, "Yes I can. Yes I will. Yes I must," so that fifteen years from now, you can say, "Yes I did, and I have no regrets."

Collaborate with Colleagues, Friends, Family, and Others

As Darwin pointed out, it is not competition that enables species to thrive but collaboration:

> It is the long history of humankind (and animal kind, too) that those who learned to collaborate and improvise most effectively have prevailed.

People are social, collaborative animals for a reason; these traits have ensured our survival and enabled us to adapt to and thrive in ever-changing conditions. Yet, we often choose conflict over collaboration to overcome challenges.

Of course, sometimes conflict is necessary, or at least it seems to be. For example, when someone infringes on the basic human rights of life, liberty, and the pursuit of happiness and won't listen to reason, conflict may be necessary. Conflict is also useful in debate, where it pitches ideas and opinions against one another for the purpose of testing their merits. And, of course, conflict is necessary and part of the fun in competitive events; it gives the participants motivation to rise to new heights. I have no beef with conflict itself.

I do, however, know that conflict that leads to negative outcomes or a stalemate is pointless at best. When people have shared interests, which they almost always do in situations in which conflict arises, collaboration is the better approach. For example, I often meet clients who are arguing with a business partner or significant other over a decision to be made. Obviously, they have shared interests, but in the heat of the argument, they lose sight of them. So, instead of identifying what the problem is and then exploring solutions, they blame and sometime ridicule one another. Communication shuts down, and collaboration ends.

In the interest of choosing collaboration over conflict, I would like you to do three things right now:

1. Make a list of the troubled relationships in your life and journal about how each may benefit more from collaboration than from conflict. Who are you in conflict with? What can that person do to help resolve the conflict? What can you do to help resolve the conflict? If you cannot answer either of those last two questions, then you may need to ask the other person, which may be just what is needed to open your line of communication.

2. Make a list of problems, challenges, or obstacles in your life and journal about how you may be able to resolve them

more efficiently and effectively through collaboration. Who can help you? What can they help you do that you're unable to do yourself?

3. Make a list of opportunities that you feel you cannot pursue without the help of someone else. What dream do you have that seems impossible to you? What goal do you have but are lacking the resources to achieve?

When we feel stuck, we often fall into the trap of thinking that if we can't come up with the answer or the solution, there must not be one. That is a limiting belief that reflects a lack of respect for others. To free yourself from that trap, think about other people who may be able to answer the question or think of a solution. Sometimes, the simple act of conversing with someone else or engaging in a brainstorming session reveals ideas that you would have never considered on your own. This is another great reason for having a mentor (or two or three).

If you're in business, don't hesitate to reach out to suppliers or to customers for advice and assistance. Remember that you have shared interests, and that you are all partners in one another's success.

Collaborate with Your Competitors

It may shock you to hear that I advise you to collaborate with your competitors. To be clear, I'm not suggesting that you share your trade secrets or specialized systems or new product ideas, but I do suggest that you work together to develop a learning community that lifts your industry. Trade publications, conferences, and seminars have been doing this for quite some time, so while this is not a new concept, it may be a new idea in your business.

For starters, monitor the competition and learn from them. Figure out ways to do it better, and then share those ideas. By not being stingy with your knowledge, you will become the thought leader in your field, and demand for you and your products will skyrocket.

Depending on the type of business you're in, you may also benefit from collaborating more directly with your competitors. For example, professional coaches often co-market their products or serve as affiliates to sell related products that don't directly compete with their own. I often recommend books and systems developed by other coaches, not because I want something in return but because I think my clients will find them to be of value. Coaches may even supply a testimonial or a foreword to a competing coach's book. Because we know there is plenty of work to go around, we want to promote the best professionals in the field.

Collaborating with your competitors can also involve making friends with your perceived enemies outside of your career or business. Simply because you disagree with someone in one area of your life doesn't mean that they have nothing to offer you in other areas. I often see people who hate each other personally enter into collaborations, precisely because both of them know it is in their best interests to do so. You can witness such alliances on the world stage when countries that have historically had an adversarial relationship join forces to accomplish a mutually beneficial mission. Sometimes, a productive collaboration is enough to turn a relationship around.

However you choose to conduct your life, I implore you not to be a loner. If you think going it alone is safer and less complicated, you may be partially right, but embracing comfort and simplicity poses the bigger risk and almost always leads to stagnation. If you want to live a fuller, richer life, you need to expand your circle to encompass others. As Helen Keller once wrote:

"Alone we can do so little; together we can do so much."

CHAPTER 8

Clarify and Communicate Your Mission

Regardless of who you are or what you do, you should have a *mission statement*—a summary of your goals, purpose, values, and what you do. A mission statement aligns and focuses your thoughts and actions to maximize their impact. In fact, you should probably have more than one—one for your professional life and another for your personal life. Some people even do a mission statement for every aspect of their life—health and fitness, social/community, business or career, family, finances, spiritual life, and intellectual development. Or, you may simply do a single mission statement with a broad scope that covers everything. If you own a business, however, or run any sort of organization, a mission statement is essential, because it aligns everyone's thoughts and actions with the mission, putting everyone "on the same page."

The benefits of having a mission statement extend beyond keeping you, your family, or your organization focused and aligned. You can also use it to guide your personal and professional decisions and quickly communicate your value to others. Here are a few practical applications of a mission statement:

Choosing opportunities to pursue: There are many more opportunities to pursue in life than your time and resources allow. Use your mission statement as a litmus test for every opportunity that comes your way to avoid wasting your time and resources on fruitless pursuits.

Choosing business partners, customers/clients, and employees: Be sure that the people you choose to work with—and for—are the right fit for your goals, values, and what you do. In business, a mission statement plays a major role in recruitment efforts.

Deciding what is right or fair: Use your mission statement as a moral compass to decide whether an action you are contemplating is right or fair. Does it align with your values? For example, one of the guiding principles in Starbucks' mission statement is "provide a great work environment and treat each other with respect and dignity."

Inspiring innovative ideas: Use your mission statement as a source of inspiration to spark innovation. Keep asking yourself what you (or your organization) can do to improve in the areas highlighted in your mission statement.

Marketing/public relations: Your mission statement serves as the cornerstone of your marketing efforts. If you have a website or blog, post your mission statement so that everyone knows what you do and what you stand for. Use it as part of the signature line in your emails.

Rallying the troops: A mission statement is a great way to unite your team. If you have a personal mission statement, share it with your mentor and others who will help you on your quest. If you have a business, share it with your partners, suppliers, customers, and employees. You may even want to give everyone on your team a mission T-shirt or some other friendly token of what you are all striving for together.

Write Your Mission Statement

A good mission statement is accurate, specific, and *actionable* (meaning you can look at it and know immediately what you must do). Before you start writing one, ask yourself the following questions to gather the information and insight you will need:

What is your purpose/goal? See the Step 2 chapter for guidance on determining your purpose. If you're writing a professional mission statement, think about why you chose the profession you chose. If you're writing a mission statement for your business, why did you start the business? What were you hoping to achieve? If you're writing a family mission statement, discuss with your family what you want to achieve as a family. What is your big dream goal?

What value will you bring? What types of products and services will you provide? How will you, your family, or your organization improve the lives of others? Why do others need what you have to offer?

Who are the people who will benefit from your mission? This may be customers, family members, community members, suppliers, partners, or others whose needs or desires you plan to serve or who will benefit indirectly from your efforts.

What do you want to be known for? What image do you want to convey? How do you want others to perceive you, your family, or your organization? What kind of example do you want to set? What do you want to have a reputation for?

What makes you distinctive and extraordinary? What makes what you have to offer different and better than what others have to offer? Why should the people you're trying to serve flock to you rather than to someone else who offers something similar? What makes you different and better?

What values or principles will you embrace? Think in terms of virtues—honesty, fairness, integrity, respect for others, and so on. Which principles will help you, your family members, or people in your organization decide to do the right thing?

What types of people do you want to attract or associate with? Try to envision the people you're working with every day to achieve your goals. Are they fun, creative, diligent, hardworking, trustworthy, dependable? Think about what you need to say in your mission statement to draw these people to you. What can you say to make yourself, your family, or your organization irresistible to the people you want to attract?

What is your overarching strategy? What is your strategy for achieving your goals? What is it for delivering distinctive value? What is it for being rich? Think about the unique way you will accomplish your goals.

Why does it matter? In the end, why does what you're doing matter to you, to those around you, and to the world at large? Why should it matter?

These questions are meant to stimulate thought about your mission and generate raw content for you to work with. You won't include all of your answers in your mission statement because you want it to be succinct—a few sentences at most. Think of it in terms of an elevator pitch, or something you can deliver in a twenty- to thirty-second ride in an elevator.

Now that you have some content, draft your mission statement. If you're writing it for your business, family, or organization, include everyone (or at least a few others in the group). Having additional input will help. Here are some guidelines:

Keep it simple. Be clear, direct, and succinct.

Cover the key points. Start with who you are, what you do, why it matters, and why it's better.

Make it inspirational. You want a mission that makes you hop out of bed in the morning in eager anticipation for the day and to motivate those who read it.

Make it distinctive. Far too many mission statements sound lifeless and boring. Be original. (A great way to give your creativity free rein is to separate the writing process into two stages: creation and criticism. Don't allow criticism into the creation phase—treat every idea that pops into your head as a great idea, and leave the editing for later.)

Here are a few examples of mission statements to get you started:

- **Honest Tea:** Honest Tea seeks to create and promote great-tasting, healthy, organic beverages. We strive to grow our business with the same honesty and integrity we use to craft our recipes, with sustainability and great taste for all.
- **Nordstrom:** In our store or online, wherever new opportunities arise Nordstrom works relentlessly to give customers the most compelling shopping experience possible. The one constant? John W. Nordstrom's founding

philosophy: offer the customer the best possible **service, selection, quality** and **value**.

- **Cradles to Crayons:** Cradles to Crayons provides children from birth through age twelve, living in homeless or low-income situations, with the essential items they need to thrive—at home, at school, and at play. We supply these items free of charge by engaging and connecting communities that have with communities that need.

- **Career:** To produce best-in-class motivational materials that inspire a revolution of positive thought, action, and innovation that sweeps the globe.

- **Family:** The purpose of our family is to be loving and passionate in everything we do for others and for ourselves. We treat others as we want to be treated, we engage in continuous learning and self-development, and we confront adversity as a family. We do the right thing no matter what, we help others in need, we face all uncertainty with full certainty, and we do something every day that makes the world a better place.

- **Personal:** The purpose of my life is to be loving, joyful, fully alive, and vibrant; to love everyone on my path; to appreciate every single thing; to inspire others to ignite their greatness; to live every second with intention; and to never forget that nothing is impossible in life other than what we convince ourselves is impossible.

Post your mission statement near your desk, on your refrigerator, or all around the house. Also carry it in your wallet or purse, and glance at it several times a day to remind yourself who you are, what you stand for, what you do, and why you're excellent at what you do.

You may even want to print it on the back of your business cards to broadcast it to everyone you meet.

In sum, your mission statement should be tattooed on your soul.

Speak Passionately About What You Do

Early in my coaching career, people came to me complaining that they could not find the job they wanted, the right life partner, or whatever else they desired in life. They were so down on life, what they were doing, and sometimes who they were (or mistakenly thought they were) that they were "unattractive" in the broadest sense. Who wants to hire someone like that? Who wants to spend time with a person who exudes repellent qualities?

I want you to ask yourself these questions:

- If I don't love myself, why should anyone else?
- If I don't care about what I do, why should anyone else?
- If I don't think that what I have to offer someone is worthwhile, why should anyone else think it is?

When you are passionate about what you do, that passion shows through, and it is sexy! People want to be with you. They want to hire you. They want to be closer to that source of high energy because it energizes them.

The first steps toward speaking passionately about what you do involve *being* passionate about what you do. If you're having trouble with that, skip back to the earlier chapters, Steps 1 and 2, to spark your imagination and discover what it is you are truly passionate about.

When you're finally doing what you love, work toward speaking passionately about it. Having a mission statement is essential, but at this point, it is less about *what* you say and more about *how* you say it. When you speak with passion, people hear it in your voice. They see it in your eyes and body language. And they feel the energy you project.

Part of speaking passionately is using gestures that are genuine. If you try to fake it, your gestures will appear cartoonish because they are contrived. So to come across as genuine, let your passion go when you speak; don't try to muffle it to sound more formal. Formal is boring and nobody will remember it. But when you speak with passion, people remember you—because your voice and your gestures resonate long after they forget what you were talking about.

Take the Passionate Speaker Challenge

One of the best ways to improve your speaking skills is to watch yourself speaking and then critique yourself.

Here's how to take the Passionate Speaker Challenge:

1. Video record yourself on twenty-one separate occasions speaking about different topics to various people in your professional and personal life. This does not need to be a presentation. You can simply record a normal conversation.
2. Watch the videos.
3. For each video you watch, rate yourself on a scale of one to ten—with ten being outstanding and one being even your mother would be ashamed—in three categories: sound, passion, and body language. Pretend you're watching a stranger as you assess each category.
4. Show the video clips to at least two other people—one male and one female—and ask them to rate you the same way.

This exercise will increase your awareness of just how passionate and engaging you are. You will hear your own voice and observe your own body language, which will allow you to recognize your strengths and weaknesses and identify areas you need to work on.

Sharpen Your Communication Skills

People who can communicate effectively with others tend to have better relationships and greater success in their careers or businesses. Keep in mind, however, that communication involves much more than an ability to express your thoughts and feelings verbally. It requires that you listen closely to what others say and take time to process it. The old saying, "We have two ears and one mouth so that we can listen twice as much as we speak," is as true today as when Epictetus wrote it early in the second century C.E. Keep in mind, too, that you have a brain between your ears so that you can process what people communicate to you.

Even more challenging is that excellent communication requires a knowledge and understanding of human nature—or what makes people "tick." What people say and how they say it, along with their body language, conveys subtle and sometimes not-so-subtle information about what they really mean and their motivation behind saying it. Cultural differences can also play a big role in how people communicate, influencing not only what they say, but also how they interpret your words and body language.

I cannot possibly in one short section relate all you need to know to become a master communicator. Thousands of books have been written on the topic, along with thousands of other books that address related topics, such as generational, gender, and cultural differences among people that can affect communication. I strongly encourage you to read one good book on communication and communication styles at least every two or three months. One I would highly recommend is *The Anatomy of Peace: Resolving the Heart of Conflict*, by the Arbinger Institute.

In the meantime, here are a few tips on how to become a better communicator:

Be present during conversations. Don't try to multitask. Block distractions. Focus entirely on the conversation.

Listen. Don't think about how you will respond to what the person is saying. Focus entirely on understanding what they are communicating to you. If it's appropriate, take notes to highlight anything you may wish to discuss after the person is done talking and you have had time to process what they said.

Ask. If you don't fully understand what the other person has said, ask—and keep asking questions until you fully understand. One of Steven Covey's seven habits of highly effective people is "Seek first to understand and then to be understood."

Look beyond the words. People are often poor at communicating their needs and concerns. Whatever they say, especially when highly emotional, can obscure what is truly bothering them or what they actually need.

Be deliberate, not reactive. Avoid the urge to blurt out what you're thinking. Choose your thoughts and expressions carefully. Think before you speak.

Model effective communication styles. If the other person goes negative, go positive. If the other person becomes highly emotional, go rational. If the other person gets loud, talk more softly.

Maintain a positive attitude. People tend to respond better to someone who has a positive attitude. When talking on the phone, smile. It may sound strange, but the person on the other end of the line will hear that.

Avoid criticism, judgment, demand, and blame. Any of these conversation crushers will either heat up emotions or shut down the conversation entirely.

In this age of texts and emails, the intended meaning and tone of a message can become twisted. Sometimes, you're better off picking up the phone and calling the person or paying them a visit. There is definitely no substitute for phone calls and in-person discussion.

With mission statement in hand and the skills to communicate it to others, you are well prepared to introduce yourself, your business, your family, or your organization to the world. Now, all you need is the courage to do it. So get yourself pumped up. You are on a mission! Let the whole world know about it.

Know Your ABCs: Always Be Closing

One of my missions is to show coaches and consultants how to close $3,000, $7,000, $15,000, and $25,000+ clients over and over and how to position themselves as the expert advisors in their industry, so they can stand apart from all the noise on LinkedIn, Facebook, Instagram, and Twitter. I set myself apart by walking my talk—by showing my clients exactly how I network and enroll clients. I became highly efficient by flying my high-ticket clients to local events where I live so that we can meet in person and attend the event together, as well as give them a live demonstration of how to network and enroll clients.

My skill actually developed out of a weakness: I was tired of not having enough high-ticket clients to pay the bills and provide me with time to enjoy my family. So I decided to find a way to fix this problem for the entire coaching and consulting industry. In my pursuit of a solution, I almost went bankrupt, and I even thought about quitting and returning to my corporate job. However, I knew that if I kept pushing and learning from the best in the business, I would figure it out eventually.

I received a lot of training and talked with numerous high-end consultants, constantly striving to find the solution. My mission was to combine everything I knew into one mentoring program to help others figure it out quicker. Because there are so many moving pieces in a coaching and consulting business, I was determined to develop a single system that would help everyone in the industry effectively manage all the pieces.

Here's what I discovered:

To separate yourself from the pack, you must master communications, sales, and marketing. You must become a world-class influencer, so you can always make an impact, create a new value curve in your industry, and stay ahead of your competitors.

You must be able to close clients from stage, in person, or over the phone. Some of my clients are highly skillful with technology, such as building sales funnels, landing pages, Facebook ads, webinars, websites, and coming up with great email sequences. However, if they don't have the expertise to close, then all of the time, money, and effort they invest in generating leads is wasted. I have been there, and I know how it feels to have invested so much in courses and still feel stuck, unable to attract and convert high-ticket clients.

Keep pushing to build a strong client base. Hire a mentor if you need someone to push you. You must love what you do, bring the joy no matter what, know your clients' needs and pain points, and put yourself out there wherever your target clients happen to be. If you run out of money to advertise on social media, go back to the basics—network with local business leaders, attend events and meet-ups, and call people who may be able to help you find clients.

Frame what you do in a way that sets it apart from what your competitors offer. Why should a client choose you over one of your competitors? To stay on top of your game, you need to answer this question every day. Everything moves faster than ever; what you invent today, somebody else will improve on tomorrow—so stay fresh, especially after you have achieved success. Many business people achieve success and then continue to provide the same service after it has become outdated. You need to stay current.

Be you. Don't try the "fake it till you make it" approach. Talk about your struggles, your beliefs, your values, your wins, and your setbacks. If you're genuine, people will trust you and want to work with you.

Invert the sales funnel. Don't pursue the entire marketplace. Instead, concentrate on a smaller number of people who are likely to benefit from your product or service and then contact them in a knowledgeable and personal way.

Keep an eye on your top ten competitors, including yourself. Compete against your top competitors, and then, when you're number one, compete against yourself too. That's how I managed to stay number one for five years straight as a sales executive in the telecommunications industry.

Offer your clients something exciting and extraordinary. I teach my clients exactly what I do. Some of my super-high-level clients want to meet me in person, so I make things fun and do hands-on demonstrations. (If I were a flight instructor, I'd have my students flying the airplane on their first day of class!) For example, suppose your niche is real estate. Every weekend in your town or within a few hundred miles is an event to help real estate professionals hone their skills. What if you were to meet your coaching clients at the event and spend the weekend together? Once you get to the event, practice what you teach in your group or during your one-on-one calls. Demonstrate your strategies right on the spot. Do that effectively, and you'll have a raving fan for life.

I started having coaches and consultants coming to me for help because they saw how effective I had become in less than two and a half years and the lifestyle I had achieved—gaining success in my career while still being present for my wife and daughter. I had quit my corporate job and coached hundreds of people internationally for free for an entire year before I earned a dime as a coach—not only to save my wife, but to gain massive experience in the marketplace. I admit that it was stressful living on my savings and running out of money due to mistakes I had made, including following bad, outdated advice from wannabe coaches and consultants I had hired.

However, I was patient and knew that if I kept learning and helping people, my time would come. I had done several interviews, and I was featured in a magazine in the same year my grandma passed away. Prior to coming to the U.S., I had promised her that

I was going to be on magazines and TV someday, and that I would use entertainment to help people overcome their problems and make the world a better place, with less poverty and violence. As I've shared, I took multiple courses, went to assorted events, and spoke on masterminds. I read a book a week, stayed up to date on what was happening in my market, and collaborated with others. I went to my mentor's events and added value, and I progressed from coaching people who wanted to quit their nine-to-five jobs to coaching leaders, network marketers, and sales executives—and then to doing all that plus mentoring coaches and consultants worldwide.

People often ask me, "How did you it?" But what they are really asking is, "How can I do it?" Here's the answer:

Be patient. Rarely do people achieve overnight success.

Create a plan with a goal, strategy, objectives, and tactics. Your goal is what you want to accomplish; your strategy is an idea of how to achieve your goal; objectives are measurable milestones on your path to success; and tactics are specific actions.

Stay at the top of your niche. Constantly seek to create a new value curve in your marketplace.

Work hard. Do three things every day to move yourself closer to your goal. Find the time or make the time to grow your business and build your brand.

Don't quit. Failure and setbacks are acceptable. Quitting is not.

When I decided to become a coach/consultant, I didn't give myself a choice; I raised the necessity and shifted to must mode. Although I was taking on a lot of debt, working crazy hours, and earning minimum wage, I decided to pay whatever it took to hire the top coaches and consultants and learn their best practices so I could offer the highest value to my clients. I took advantage of those who offered free calls. I watched webinars, attended events, paid a small fortune in fees, and soaked up all the knowledge and insight they had to offer.

I know this may sound extreme, but my goal was to learn from them so I could help others like me transition from their corporate jobs to become a coach/consultant without having to suffer the setbacks that I had experienced. To that end, I kept learning and implementing the best tools and eventually figured it out. Once I did that, I started enrolling clients as case studies at a lower rate, delivering results, and getting referrals. Increasingly, I was recognized for consistently delivering high value, and I increased my rates accordingly.

Success didn't happen overnight, but it *did* happen.

CHAPTER 9

Contribute!

> *Success is not a function of the size of your title but the richness of your contribution.*
> —Robin S. Sharma

Two hundred years from now, none of us will be here. Whether you owned a mansion or rented a tiny apartment, drove a Ferrari or a Ford Fiesta, died a pauper or a millionaire, it won't matter. What *will* matter is what you contributed to the world—the impact you had on the planet and on other people's lives that continues to give long after you pass from this life. As Stephen Covey has written, "Life is not accumulation, it is about contribution."

To preserve your legacy, you don't necessarily need to build corporations or institutions; have your name on schools, libraries, or endowments; donate millions of dollars to charitable organizations; or come up with incredible inventions that are long remembered after you die. Although those are certainly positive ways to impact the world, your contributions can be the products of your mind and creative imagination, such as art, music, poetry, plays, novels, performance, or films. You can contribute by raising children who are valuable members of society and by working to strengthen your community. You may even leave a lasting positive legacy through your everyday acts, such as by coaching or mentoring, helping your neighbors, volunteering, sheltering the homeless, feeding the hungry, visiting the sick or lonely, or providing jobs to those who need them.

All of the positive energy you project and the good you do have a positive and lasting impact on the world.

As you know, I was only three months old when my father died. But hearing stories of his good deeds and witnessing my mother and grandmother carrying on his legacy with their contributions to the movement he started was a huge influence on me. Instead of hanging out with his friends on his days off or heading home after work to relax and watch TV, my father walked the streets in our neighborhood in Brazil, looking inside dumpsters for infants abandoned by parents who could not afford to raise them. He would visit supermarket trash areas to find abandoned kids looking for food. He would often find children living on the streets, because they'd been sent out to find work or beg for money, and from fear of being abused or mistreated by their parents, they didn't return home.

My father did that over and over during his short life on this planet; it's truly tragic that he died when he was only in his early twenties. When he found those babies and kids, he would pick them up from the trash and invite the older ones to take them to shelters and churches. After he had them checked in to a safe place, he went above and beyond by visiting them, playing sports with them, reading to them, and even learning to play instruments so he could teach those kids to play. He loved those children as if they were his own.

His legacy continues to live in me as I seek ways to help underprivileged children. It comes naturally to me because I know firsthand how the power of positive thought and action can leave a legacy that lives on long after a person passes from this life.

Give with No Expectation of Return

Although your contributions to the world need not be in the form of selfless acts of kindness, some of your contributions should be.

As Tony Robbins has written, "Only those who have learned the power of sincere and selfless contribution experience life's deepest joy: true fulfillment." Giving of yourself with no expectation of receiving recognition or reward is the ultimate contribution. It is true giving. And the funny thing is that there is *always* a reward, even if it is nothing more than a warm fuzzy feeling that you did good. Often, you receive much more than that, especially when your good deed results in building a relationship that enriches your life, as relationships almost always do.

The key is to give without expectation, which for many people can be difficult. We almost always give expecting to get something, such as an expression of appreciation, payback, or a favor in return. But that is not really giving, because to give is to let go of what you have. When you truly give, whatever you gave belongs entirely to the other person. When you give with an expectation of receiving anything in return, even a thank you, it is almost as though you're still holding on to whatever you gave. That type of giving is more like a transaction, or like loaning the gift until you get what you want in return.

The definition of "give" is "to freely transfer possession of something to someone."

When you give anything, imagine yourself letting go of it; it is no longer yours to give or to receive anything back from. It is not an investment; it is a gift. If you see the person who benefited from your gift, don't think about it—remember, you let it go. It is now in the sole possession of the recipient. If she wants to think about it, mention it, or thank you for it, that is her prerogative, not yours.

I have received many gifts and favors over the years by well-intentioned givers, and I truly appreciated whatever they gave me. However, I could tell that many of them gave for themselves. They would act superior, as if I was some lesser being for needing their help. The favor could be something as small as driving me to work. It didn't matter how small the favor was, they saw me as inferior for needing them and themselves as superior for helping someone in need. That, my friend, is not giving.

I hate to criticize anyone who gives, even if they give for the wrong reason, because when I am in need, I'll take help however it is offered. The truth is that I care very little whether someone feels that helping me makes them superior. What I do care about is that such an approach to giving cheats the giver out of the fulfillment that comes from giving selflessly. In other words, that giver never experiences the unfettered joy of giving without expecting something in return, or rather, they give with their hand still on it.

I want you to experience the total joy of selfless giving, and you can do that by sincerely letting go of whatever it is you give.

Preserve Your Relationships by Giving and Lending the Right Way

Giving with the expectation of getting something in return is a great way to create bad feelings and ruin relationships. Have you ever given love without getting love in return, only to find yourself growing bitter and resentful toward the other person? The old saying, "Hell hath no fury like a woman scorned" captures the feeling pretty well (and it is often true of men as well). Have you ever given a present and received no thank-you card or even a verbal thank you and thought, !? Giving with even a thread attached makes us vulnerable to bitterness and resentment.

I suggest that you even be careful about loaning something with an expectation of getting it back, because if the person is unwilling or unable to return it, or simply forgets, what began as a good deed can trigger frustration and anger in you and make the other person feel guilty or ashamed—all feelings that can drive a wedge between lender and borrower. A good rule of thumb is to loan something to someone only when you're certain that if the item (or money) is not returned, you will harbor no ill will toward that person, and he will feel no guilt or shame for not having returned the item (or the money). Losing a relationship is a much bigger loss than losing whatever you loaned the person.

Give Yourself

When asked for a donation, people often say they can't afford it, which may be true in terms of money. You can't give what you don't have. However, everyone has something of value—time, talent, effort, knowledge, expertise, emotion . . . I could go on. So don't limit yourself; contribute what you have, whatever that may be and at whatever level you can. If someone calls for a donation, and you have no money to give, instead of simply telling them no, let them know that you give in other ways—maybe you watch a neighbor's house when she's in the hospital, help at your church or your child's or grandchild's school, serve as a Big Brother or Big Sister, coach a Little League team, or read to kids at the library. When you give yourself, you give much more than money.

Giving of yourself may also involve fighting for a worthy cause, such as a clean environment, overpopulation, an end to poverty or a certain social injustice, a cure for a serious illness, an end to terrorism, access to clean water for all people, or honest food labels and claims. Giving yourself to a worthy cause has the added benefit of giving you a purpose in life, a mission.

When you give yourself, you engage with life, which is much more rewarding than being passively entertained by TV or the Internet. In giving of your time, talent, or passion, you learn, gain insight, develop new skills, and forge new friendships. Your network grows. While you hopefully don't give yourself to reap these benefits, they are benefits nonetheless, and they are highly valuable.

Look for Trouble

If you cannot find a worthy cause, look for trouble—because wherever you see trouble, you will find a problem that needs to be fixed, and human beings are great at solving problems. You can probably find plenty of problems to keep you busy within your existing circle of family, friends, colleagues, business associates, and community members. All you need to do is take an active interest in their lives and encourage them to open up to you about whatever issues they struggle with.

When someone shares a problem they're having, you can often help by simply listening. The person may not need (or want) any more than that, and you should never push your advice on anyone. Ask what you can do to help or let them know of any knowledge, skills, or expertise you have that may contribute to solving their problem. You may have encountered the same or a similar challenge in your life and found a solution for it. Sometimes by simply describing your own experience, you can help the person solve their problem. Life is funny that way—people are often drawn together for the sole purpose of allowing one person to help another. By actively engaging with other people, opportunities to solve problems are often revealed. At that point, all you need to do is listen, observe, and be receptive.

Be Generous

Part of contributing involves being generous in all areas of your life. You may give yourself time and space, give your spouse attention and presents, give your children time and impart your knowledge and wisdom, contribute to your colleagues' success, offer forgiveness to people who have done you harm, and even send business to your competitors when it makes sense to do so (for example, when a competitor is better suited than you are to serve one of your client's needs). In addition, a lot of professionals contribute their knowledge and insight to others in their industry by publishing papers and blog posts, delivering presentations and webinars, and hosting discussion boards, because they know that the entire community benefits when everyone shares their knowledge and insights.

Although giving with no expectation of a return is best, you will soon find that when you are generous, you attract generosity. You model the behavior, and others begin to follow your lead. The same is true of the opposite. When people are selfish and self-centered, those around them follow suit. Everyone becomes stingy with whatever they have, and the entire community suffers as a result.

Let Life Flow Through You

When you are born, you own nothing, you know very little, you have few marketable skills. Nothing is *yours*. In your childhood, you'd probably feel the same way if you didn't have people around you modeling selfishness. After all, kids learn to say "That's *mine*"; they aren't born with that mindset. But when they get a little older, most kids become fairly generous, readily sharing what they have with friends and even complete strangers. When they become adults, however, they often return to their toddler days of saying, "That's *mine!*" And the more they appear to have, the more possessive they become.

The fact is that nothing is really ours. We were born with nothing, and we cannot carry our possessions into the afterlife. In other words, everything we "own" during our lives is borrowed. In a way, everything we acquire during our lives, including our imagination, knowledge, skills, and expertise flows through us. When we block the flow by refusing to share, we tend to close ourselves off from the source that brought us so much. In short, we stop growing.

Let everything you have and everything you are flow through you to the world around you, and you will find the fullness of life gushing through you.

Take the Contributor's Challenge

Sometimes a challenge or a dare is all the motivation you need to make a positive change in your life. I can tell you again and again how fulfilling it is to contribute selflessly, but until you feel it yourself, you cannot imagine the feeling. And once you feel how rewarding it is, you will be hooked. Having a purpose outside yourself, your work, your family, and your friends will energize you. It will take you out of your head and bring you closer to your heart and soul. I encourage you to take the following contributor's challenge:

Write a one page (minimum) journal entry for each of the following two questions:

- **What is something so meaningful to me that it is worth fighting and dying for?** My spouse? My family? Freedom? Equality? Women's rights? Discuss why you feel so passionate about this cause.
- **What living legacy do I want to leave after I pass from this life?** What impact do I want to make on this planet or the people on it that will live long after I die? Describe the positive impact you will have had on the world. Discuss why you want to be remembered for having had this impact.

I also challenge you to contribute your time, talent, and money to a cause of your choice. After you choose one, I want you to make a cash donation to it, however large or small, within the next seven days. I also want you to state one way you will contribute your time and talent to furthering this cause.

Take this challenge again in three months to keep your why, your mission, your purpose, and your legacy in front of you at all times.

In summary, I urge you to avoid the common practice of thinking of giving as "giving up" something. Think of it instead as pouring light into a dark room. As soon as you give your light, everyone begins to shine. Think of it as giving wisdom to eliminate ignorance or giving love to purge hatred. Most of all, remember that when you give, you lose nothing—you meet a need, whether it's yours or someone else's. One thing I always say to the people I train all over the world is, "Make every transaction of your life and business about the mission, not the commission. Life is about contribution, not acquisition."

Part 3

PRINCIPLES AND PRACTICES

The 9 Guiding Principles

1

You are the key to your success.

2

Invest in yourself first and foremost.

3

Recognize your thoughts and feed the right ones.

4

Dedicate yourself to purposeful continuous learning.

5

Be certain in the face of uncertainty and adversity.

6

Dream + Desire = Direction + Drive

7

Forget the past. Act in the present. Prepare for the future.

8

Hold yourself accountable or find someone who will.

9

Be generous, expecting nothing in return.

28 Practical Techniques and Exercises for Success

Following is a list of twenty-eight techniques and exercises I have used throughout my career to achieve success. You may want to try only a select few that you find pertinent or helpful to you, or you may want to try all of them! Either way, do review this list often to determine if any of the exercises or techniques have become more relevant to where you are. For example, certain exercises may be better when you're feeling down, while others are better if you're lacking direction or need a confidence boost.

Negative: I can't work another day at this company.

Positive: *I will give my best every day until I can find a better opportunity.*

Negative: I can't stand another client complaining.

Positive: *I will do my best to help every client, no matter how the client feels.*

Negative: I can't sell this home.

Positive: *I will find a family who will buy this home and build a lifetime of memories here.*

Negative: I can't sell this car at this price.

Positive: *I will focus on the features and find someone to buy this car.*

Negative: I can't take another no.

Positive: *I understand that it takes five no's before I'll get a yes.*

Negative: I am not meeting my quota.

Positive: *I will meet my quota and visualize my 150% bonus check.*

Negative: I am not smart enough to pass this test.

Positive: *I will study harder to improve my personal development so that I am able to help my family and others in my life.*

Negative: I will never get the promotion because there are others in line who are more qualified.

Positive: *I will do more than anyone in the company and rise like a star.*

Negative: I can't lose weight.

Positive: *I will work hard to get optimal results so that I can improve my health and enjoy life more.*

Negative: I can't follow this diet.

Positive: *These foods are amazing because they will make me healthier.*

Negative: My spouse doesn't understand me and fights me on everything I do, and I can't seem to get the support I need.

Positive: *I will be present and listen to my spouse's needs and love him or her like never before.*

2. Set a learning goal in a specific area of your life (physical, financial, career, family, spiritual, or intellectual) that completes one of the following statements:

   - I would like to know . . .
   - I would like to know how to . . .
   - I would like to be able to . . .
   - I would like to become certified in . . .

   Write an educational plan for meeting your learning goal, along with a date when you will start and a date you will meet that goal.

3.　　Laser focus on your number-one priority:

- Describe your number-one priority right now—an objective or deadline you need to meet, a problem you need to solve, or an obstacle you need to remove.
- Write down three things you can do every day to address that priority.
- Every night, ask yourself what you did that day to address that priority, and write down the three things you will do tomorrow.

4.　　Find an accountability partner or a mentor for one area of life in which you're currently struggling or would like to improve—physical, financial, career, family, spiritual, or intellectual. Ask one person every day until you find someone who is perfect for that role and who will enthusiastically commit to your success in that area.

5.　　Practice the Triple Trizzo Carlito's Way Technique daily by answering the following questions:

- What three things am I most grateful for?
- What are three things I can do or say that align with my core values and goals before handling any good or unpleasant situation?
- What three things are a must for me today and will make me extremely happy once I accomplish them? These can be objectives or specific situations you need to deal with. (Visualization is powerful!)

6.　　Focus on your daily goals by answering the following questions every morning:

- What do I want to accomplish today?

- Why do I want to accomplish this? Will this bring me closer to my goal?
- What will I get for accomplishing this?
- How will I feel after accomplishing this?

7. When you experience adversity, ask yourself the following questions:
    - Is the universe trying to teach me something?
    - What else could this mean?
    - How can I maintain productivity and motivation during this adversity?
    - How would the best version of myself handle this matter?

8. Learn from others by asking them the following questions:
    - What do you do?
    - Why do you do what you do?
    - Are you happy with what you do? Why? or Why not?
    - How do you think you'll feel when you achieve your goal?
    - What mistakes would you avoid making in life or business?
    - If you could start over, what are three things you would do differently to succeed?
    - What are your secrets or rituals that have brought you success?
    - If you failed in your (career, business, marriage, etc.), what led to it?
    - How would you like to be remembered when you die?

9. Become a servant-leader:
    - Identify a person or cause you can selflessly and passionately serve with your time, talent, or treasure.
    - Describe three ways you can help this person or cause.

- Choose one person or cause to support and set a date to get started.

10. If your mind is engaged in negative thinking, it is probably because you're asking questions that elicit negative answers. Ask better questions, such as:
   - What is true, as opposed to my impression of it?
   - What is my purpose in life?
   - Who depends on my support?
   - Are my actions leading to my daily, weekly, monthly, and yearly goals?
   - What can I do today to achieve my goals?
   - What positive thoughts can I sow in the fields of my mind?
   - Whom can I call or surround myself with who has similar goals and values?

11. Make data-driven decisions. Guessing is wasteful and can be destructive, so make sure you're working with the facts before you decide, speak, or take action in your personal or professional life.

12. Make sure your words, actions, and decisions that involve other people are motivated by love and are in their best interests. Before acting or speaking, ask yourself, *Is what I'm about to say or do motivated by love for that person or by some other negative emotion (frustration, anger, fear)*. If it is not motivated by love, rethink what you're about to say, do, or decide.

13. When you're planning to scale your business, ask yourself and your team the following six key questions:

- What value can I add for my client that none of my competitors have to offer?
- Am I using a compelling tag line that communicates directly to my clients?
- Am I developing an extraordinary buyer's experience for my clients?
- Are my services convenient and easily accessible to my clients once they are ready to buy? (What might be getting in the way?)
- Am I offering something unique? Am I charging too much or too little?
- Is my offer providing a strategic price innovation that is irresistible to refuse?

14. Seek input from your clients or your competitors' clients, or hire an outside firm to study the buying habits of customers to figure out what is driving them to buy the products and services you sell, whether they are buying from you or a competitor. Don't try to guess.

15. Talk *to* people, not *about* them. If you have an issue with someone, deal directly with that person and try to find out what is motivating them to say or do what they're saying or doing. Resist the urge to form an opinion until you have all the facts and insight to form a wise opinion.

16. When you are dissatisfied with the outcomes of your efforts in your personal or professional life, ask yourself the following questions:
   - What are the wins in my life/career/business this week?
   - How can I make it better?

- What isn't working?
- How can I improve what's not working?
- Are there any areas in which I'm spending more time than is necessary?
- Are there any areas I'm not spending enough time on?
- Is there anything else I can do to add value to what I offer?

17. When someone advises you not to follow a certain path you're considering, ask yourself the following questions:
    - How does this person know that I won't be successful and happy doing this?
    - Who is this person? Is he or she an expert?
    - Is this person happy and successful in what he or she is doing?
    - Has this person ever helped others succeed?
    - What is this person's motivation for telling me this?
    - Has he or she ever mentored others to help them in this area?

18. Every so often, check whether you're on track to becoming healthy, wealthy, happy, and fulfilled by asking these three questions:
    - Am I happy?
    - Am I fulfilled?
    - Do I truly love my mind, body, and soul?
      This is the moment of truth—when you determine whether you're truly living life or the life that someone else convinced you was best for you, and if you have been living on autopilot, never realizing how unhappy you have become.

19. Love yourself. Close your eyes, imagine looking back at yourself as a baby, and say:
    - "I love me."
    - "I'm a love champion."
    - "I love myself so much, I'm tattooing my name on my chest, and I'm about to give myself a hug."

      Then, give yourself a big hug. You may think this is silly, but even if you do, it will make you laugh and feel better about yourself and others.

20. If you are in sales, follow these three rules:
    - **Rule 1:** Treat every customer the same. Give the same attention and focus to everyone with whom you interact. It doesn't matter what you sell: cars, real estate, cable television, software, whatever. Your first and last customer interaction of the day should be the same in peak performance and deliver results above and beyond the customer's expectations. That's how you acquire repeat business.
    - **Rule 2:** Never forget Rule 1.
    - **Rule 3:** Don't forget where you came from when you achieve success. Always treat others the way they want to be treated. Remember that you weren't successful in the beginning either. You had to learn and grow. That's what made you who you are today.

21. Learn from your mistakes by answering these three questions:
    - Why haven't I achieved what I want out of life?
    - What are three choices you wish you'd made differently in the past?
    - How have those choices shaped my life today?

If you're not where you want to be today, then pay special attention to the mistakes you have made. Be thankful, because you are now able to avoid making those same mistakes.

22. Sow the seeds of a healthy mindset with thoughts of love, happiness, action, courage, connection, contribution, and growth. Start by asking better questions, and make new choices that align with your core values. If you're not exactly sure what your core values are, then try answering the following questions:
    - What do you need most to achieve in life to feel fulfillment?
    - What matters the most for you to be happy?
    - Whom do you love the most? Why?
    - What do you truly want out of life?
    - What moral or ethical values do you possess?
    - What values do your friends, mentors, or family members have that they use to make decisions?
    - Do the values mentioned above align with your own?
    - What do you dislike doing or seeing happen?
    - Is there anyone you dislike? If so, what are his or her core values?
    - Have you ever tried to find something good in those you dislike? If so, what was it?
    - Have you ever tried to find the good in a bad situation? When?

23. Identify your desires—what you truly want out of life—by writing down your answers to the following questions:
    - What are your deepest desires?

- What does your dream home look like?
- What does your dream family look like?
- What is your dream career?
- What kind of business would you like to own?
- How is your best self going to show up every day?
- What kind of body do you visualize so you can be healthy long into your golden years?
- How much money do you want to have when you retire?
- How will you leave a lasting positive impact on the world?
- What do you want to be remembered for?
  Be as specific as possible when answering these questions. Type, print, and hang copies of your answers where you can see them every day. You need to eat, sleep, and breathe those desires.

24. Focus only on what you want, *not* on what you don't have. Create a vision board with photos of everything you want most in life, and hang it in a place in your home or office where you'll see it several times a day. Whenever you feel tired, lazy, unworthy, stuck, depressed, or sad, say this: "I am unstoppable and will focus relentlessly on achieving what I want until I win."

25. Visualize success by performing this magic wand exercise:
    - Close your eyes.
    - Imagine yourself waving a magic wand that makes your dream come true.
    - Imagine what's different about you. Are you happier or more loved or more motivated?
    - What actions would you take differently today now that you have all you want?

26.   Do something every day that leads to the achievement of your goals. If you don't work toward your dreams, you will be like most people in the world. You'll work hard to earn a limited income that the corporate world believes you deserve, and you'll be at the mercy of the promotion process if it exists in your workplace. That is a dead-end path that will not lead to fulfillment.

27.   Remind yourself that you are a warrior and that you deserve to have your dreams fulfilled. You won't settle for less. You will not be average. You will miss those parties on the weekends and turn off your mobile device if you have to in order to make your goals become realities.

28.   Whatever you do in life, remember that our most priceless memories will come from a place of contribution, not acquisition. Three hundred years from now, what would you love people to say about your future best self when you are no longer here? Whatever that is, journal and focus on doing something every day that will lead to more of those moments to evoke that future self. Even if the one you see in the mirror is far away from that, know that if you put in the miles, work strategically, and pay attention to all spheres of life, you will meet the best version of you. When you look at yourself in the mirror from now on, thank yourself and applaud yourself for pushing, for trying, for not giving up; for not allowing anyone, even your loved ones, to change your attitude, your behavior, or your emotions; and for not quitting on your dreams. At the beginning and end of every day, look at your future self in the mirror and promise to give it all you've got at all times until you win.

Conclusion

While my personal story of growing up poor on the streets of Brazil surrounded by violence and crime—and then forging a new life in America—may be far from your own, I hope you have witnessed through my journey why I titled this book, *Work Like an Immigrant*.

Yes, my strong work ethic may have started young from the examples of my parents, but I realized as I thought about writing this book that the immigrant spirit runs through me, and it's largely what drove me to enjoy the success and fulfillment I do today.

When a non-English speaker comes to the U.S., there inevitably are challenges: the language barrier, the cultural differences, the overwhelm of getting to know cities that are foreign to you and engaging with unfamiliar people. And there's also the sense that you have to strive extra hard to be accepted and taken seriously, even when people are kind to you. Not every American sees an immigrant this way, but when you've heard all your life about "The American Dream," and you finally get the chance to make that dream come true, I believe most of us will do just about anything not to squander that chance. And that includes giving your all to master the language, bring your A-game to whatever job you obtain no matter how menial it may seem, and being open to learning from everyone and every source available to you. As you improve yourself, so too can your job or career—and life—improve, as did mine.

I didn't come here for a handout; I came here for the opportunity to live up to my fullest potential. But I believe that all too often, people forget how blessed they are to have the opportunities they do. Even if they don't seem ideal, you can always shift your mindset and apply the skills you *do* have to make your situation better. For example, when I got my job at Boston Market, I didn't see it as a mediocre position at a chain restaurant; I saw an opportunity to make my customers and coworkers happy—and to earn respect and admiration from my boss—from the beginning to the end of each of my shifts. Yet, another person may embrace the attitude that "this job sucks," sulk around, and do only the minimum. What good does that do anyone? It may not be your dream job, but it's where you are *now*, and you can always make the best of any situation if you simply decide that's what you're going to do.

Sure, you may have a difficult boss, or a horrible commute, or an environment that doesn't suit you in your current job; it can be tough to power through when that's your situation. But while you're looking for a more favorable job—and if you're truly not aligned with your work, you should—you can still bring your best self to the job each day, make other people feel good, and in turn feel good about yourself.

Think about it: a difficult boss may be feeling pressure from higher-ups, and you can try to see things from his or her point of view—then ask what you can do to help. A horrible commute may give you time to listen to self-help recordings or podcasts you enjoy. An environment that doesn't resonate with you may benefit from some of your creative ideas for making it more pleasant. You simply never know unless you try.

I know a lot of people who would have hated going door to door selling cable TV, phone, and Internet services, but I saw it as a gold mine and made it become one for me. But I wasn't ready for that position when I first arrived; I needed to improve my English before I could talk to people as a salesperson. You, too, may be in a transitional place in your work, but think of everything you're learning as leading toward your next exciting prospect—even if it's not evident at the moment—and then put your best self into it.

The same is true in life itself. If something isn't going the way you want it to—a relationship, your role as a parent, where you're living—look at what you're giving to it and the mindset you have about it. What books could you read or experts could you learn from? How could you show up differently or be more thoughtful? What other areas might suit you better to live in? Don't expect all of these people or things to simply bow to your needs and wishes—*you* must strive to make them better.

When Angie was depleted from months on end of sleep deprivation with Isabella, I had to look inward and see where I wasn't supporting her in our marriage. Once I decided to make changes and dedicate myself to her well-being, our marriage—and Angie—came alive again.

What does that have to do with working like an immigrant, you may ask?

It all ties back to the spirit I talked about earlier, that determination to make a success of yourself no matter the challenges. It means showing up full out, holding none of your gifts back—even if that gift is simply making people smile at the drive-thru window, or taking the initiative to do the tasks other employees ignore, or being on time and having a positive attitude. When you hone those traits of positivity and ambition, they can take you anywhere—they took me to the top of my sales team, and later the founding of my own heart-centered business helping thousands achieve their dreams. They inspire my strong marriage and close relationship with my daughter. They motivate me to help my family back in Brazil, grateful I'm able to do so.

You don't have to be an immigrant to embrace what it means when I say to "work like one." In fact, I would say it's easier when you don't have all the challenges I faced when I arrived. This is not to say that plenty of Americans aren't faced with their own adversity: clearly everyone experiences varying levels of hardship—whether emotional, physical, financial, or spiritual—throughout their lives. But the underlying message of this book is the same no matter where you come from or what circumstances you're up against: nothing is impossible when you decide in your mind to bring your best self to every encounter, every job, every relationship, every partnership. It may not work out in the long term, but take what you learn, be respectful to all involved, and move upward to your next opportunity.

You must remind yourself daily why you're putting effort into the tasks you're doing toward creating your dream job, career, or business. If you're going to build something, make it count. Raise the standards with each brick you lay of your legacy, one day at time. Learn and implement a skill every day that will make you a master of your craft. Strive to do more for others than they are willing to do for themselves. Separate yourself from the transaction of what you do, and instead focus on the contributions and impact you're making on others' lives. If you ignite your best self and bring joy, love, presence, and vibrancy for being alive to each day and to each encounter, I promise you that your life will never be the same.

This is the core message I hope you take away from this book.

As I say from the stage, "We are one." Let's support each other in finding our voices, our callings, and building our own "American dream"—no matter what country you reside in. When you sincerely believe the universe has your back and wants you to succeed, *you* can believe it too. And when you show up with the intention of giving your all and making a positive difference, remarkable doors will open for you. I am living proof.

About Expert Advisor Alliance

We take business owners and serial entrepreneurs who feel stuck in growing their businesses and unlock their next opportunities to grow!

Over the last fifteen years, we've provided massive results for thousands of clients worldwide, which we then showcase on our site and throughout social media. Because we are obsessed about raising the standard in the mentoring, consulting, coaching, and speaking industry, we always tell our clients that they can't call themselves experts until 1) they provide consistent results for others, and 2) the market recognizes them as an expert. This is our goal for every client.

We also realize that if you're going to build something, you should strive to build a legacy that will create lasting impact for generations to come. With that in mind, we teach people how their level of focus, engagement, research, training, and mentoring is quite different when working on a legacy versus simply starting another business—in fact, when the competition builds "just another business" but you build a legacy, you may eventually receive a call from them! This is the power of our work at Expert Advisor Alliance.

If you are ready to receive support to make more sales, elevate your customer experience to higher levels of excellence, and generate more cash flow *fast*—potentially skyrocketing the financial power of your advice and growing a seven-figure coaching business as THE trusted advisor—all without having to work like an immigrant or spend over 18,000 hours and $5 million to figure it out, visit our site at:

www.ExpertAdvisorAlliance.net

* * *

Need some energy and inspiration at your next event?

If you're looking for an entertaining and inspiring speaker for your upcoming keynote, board meeting, mastermind, or team retreat, let's talk about how I can supercharge your results!

Some popular audience topics include:

- The Millionaire Mindset — Make the leap into your greatness and ignite your millionaire mindset today.
- Aligning with Your Why — Let your passion and purpose drive you toward greatness every single day.
- Being Disruptive as You Build Your Legacy — Get comfortable dealing with successful leaders to build and live your legacy.

I'd love to talk to you about your next event! Reach out to me at:
Carlos@ExpertAdvisorAlliance.net